THIS BOOK BELONGS TO

_____

❏ LONGTIME FAN LOOKING FOR THE AUTHORITATIVE GUIDE TO THE CLASSIC FIRST 50 EPISODES OF *FAMILY GUY*

❏ JOHNNY-COME-LATELY WHO'S TRYING TO BONE UP ON HIS *FAMILY GUY* TRIVIA SO HE'LL FIT IN DURING FIFTH PERIOD P.E.

❏ CONFUSED SIGNIFICANT OTHER TRYING TO FIGURE OUT WHAT HIS/HER MATE IS CONSTANTLY QUOTING TO ALL OF HIS/HER FRIENDS

❏ CONCERNED PARENT AND/OR FCC OFFICIAL LOOKING FOR EVIDENCE TO USE IN BUILDING A CASE AGAINST MORAL DECAY

❏ PARENT WHO IS TRYING TO ENDEAR THEMSELVES TO CHILD

❏ PARENT WHO ACTUALLY STILL IS A CHILD (AND FINDS THIS SHOW FUNNY)

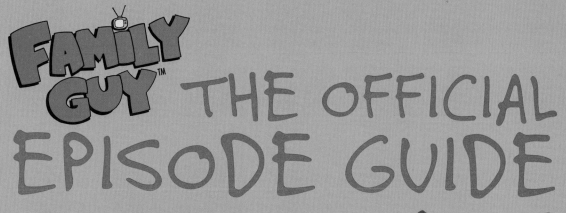

THE OFFICIAL EPISODE GUIDE

Seasons 1-3

Compiled and edited by
STEVE CALLAGHAN

Based on the series created by
SETH MACFARLANE

Harper
An Imprint of HarperCollinsPublishers

HarperCollins books may be purchased for educational, business, or sales promotional use. For information please write: Special Markets Department, HarperCollins Publishers, 10 East 53rd Street, New York, NY 10022.

FIRST EDITION

Designed by Timothy Shaner

Printed on acid-free paper

Library of Congress Cataloging-in-Publication Data

Callaghan, Steve.
   Family Guy: the official episode guide, season 1–3/compiled and edited by Steve Callaghan; based on the series created by Seth MacFarlane.
     p. cm.
   ISBN-10: 0-06-083305-X
   ISBN-13: 978-0-06-083305-3
    1. Family guy (Television program) I. MacFarlane, Seth. II. Title.

PN1992.77.F27C35 2005
791.45'72—dc22   2005050294

05 06 07 08 09 ❖ 10 9 8 7 6 5 4 3 2 1

Contents

Contents

An Introduction
FROM PETER GRIFFIN

Greetings Fellow Couch Potato,

What you hold in your probably sweaty hand is the final word, the end-all-be-all, the bottom-line, official guide to the fifty classic episodes of *Family Guy* that led to those dopes at Fox putting our freakin' sweet show back on the air. As a gigantic TV fan myself, I am in huge awe of the way you, the fans, made the thing happen, too. I mean, that was frickin' awesome how you made your voices heard and gave the man a piece of your mind. I seriously haven't seen something that cool since they brought back the McRib. Speaking of which, how in the hell *do* they get that thing to look like there's bones in there? 'Cause, I mean, there's no bones. I checked. Like four times. Freakin' amazing.

Anyway, Lois told me I should also tell you all thanks, 'cause without you buying all those DVDs and watching the shows on Cartoon Network, she'd still be a has-been housewife, trying to live off the past glory of bein' a poor man's Bonnie Franklin. Me, on the other hand, I kind of enjoyed the time off. I got to watch a lot of sports, and me and Lois "did it" a lot. I'm talking all the time. 'Cause face it, we weren't workin', and you can only watch so much *Texas Justice* before you wanna scarf down a sandwich and then go knock one out. So, for me, being back to work's not so great, 'cause it means I get way less nooky from my wife. So, thanks America, thanks a lot, you jackasses. But, yeah, Lois and Brian and Chris and all them say thanks a lot for bringing us all back.

So, I guess you can move on now to readin' about all the episodes you've probably seen like a hundred times or whatever. But, enjoy, and God save the queen, and good night, and have a pleasant tomorrow. I'm not sure how to end this thing. But that's probably mostly 'cause I'm drunk right now.

—Peter Griffin

Oh, one more thing. As a bonus for you know-it-all fans, we've added this little trivia quiz. Now no cheatin'—if your *Family Guy* IQ is as high as you say it is you'll get all this stuff right on your own. And if it's not, you can take a makeup test after you've actually read the book. Chris does that all the time.

Test Your Knowledge of the
Evil Monkey

A few easy questions to get you started . . .

1. Where does the evil monkey live?

2. What does the evil monkey do virtually every time we see him?

Now we're getting into it . . .

3. What made the evil monkey evil?

4. What is the evil monkey wearing the one time we see him in clothes?

Only for the most hard-core fans . . .

5. Who provides the voice of the evil monkey (on the one occasion in which he spoke)?

6. Which *Family Guy* writer first conceived of the notion of the evil monkey?

And one more to pique your interest . . .

7. Will we see the evil monkey in future seasons of *Family Guy*?

ANSWERS 1. Chris's closet. 2. Gives an evil point and stare. 3. Walking in on his wife cheating on him with another monkey. 4. A suit and tie, from the corporate job he once had. 5. *Family Guy* writer, Danny Smith. 6. Mike Barker. 7. You better believe it!

11

Season One

Episode
DEATH HAS A SHADOW

EPISODE NUMBER: 1ACX01

ORIGINAL AIRDATE: 1/31/99

WRITER: Seth MacFarlane

DIRECTOR: Peter Shin

EXECUTIVE PRODUCERS:
Seth MacFarlane,
David Zuckerman

SUMMARY

When Peter is invited to a stag party, Lois allows him to go, but only on the condition that he refrain from drinking while he's there. At the party, Peter breaks his promise and wakes up the next morning with a huge hangover, causing him to fall asleep at his job as a toy inspector at the Happy-Go-Lucky Toy Company.

Peter's negligence costs him his job, but he can't bring himself to tell Lois about having been fired. After hiding his unemployed status for a while, Peter realizes he'll need some source of income, so he decides to go on welfare. When he receives his first check, Brian points out that due to a clerical error Peter is receiving $150,000

per week from the government. Peter goes on a spending spree, telling Lois that he actually got a promotion at work. But when Lois catches wind of what's really going on, she's furious. Peter realizes he has to make things right, so he decides to return the money to Joe Taxpayer by dropping it from a blimp into the crowd at the Super Bowl, which only results in him being shot out of the sky and subsequently arrested by the police.

Peter goes on trial for welfare fraud and gives an impassioned speech in his own defense. But when the judge threatens to put both Peter and Lois away for a long time, Stewie (who grudgingly realizes his own dependence on his parents) uses his ray gun on the judge to get him to reconsider the sentence.

MEMORABLE MOMENTS

Origin of the Holocaust

LOIS: You know, most of the world's problems stem from poor self-image. *(Cutaway to a gym where a scrawny Adolf Hitler does curls. He hears tittering and sees a buff Rabbi laughing alongside two hot babes. Hitler scowls with jealousy.)*

And So It Begins

STEWIE: *(to Lois)* Damn you, vile woman! You've impeded my work since the day I escaped from your wretched womb!

STEWIE: Mark my words: when you least expect it... your uppance will come.

STEWIE: Blast you and your estrogenical treachery!

Man of the House

PETER: Now, Lois, I work hard all week to provide for this family. I am the man of the house and as the man I order you to give me permission to go to this party.

Peter Has an Irish Coffee before Seeing *Philadelphia*

(The family and audience watch weepy. Peter finally stares intently at the screen, then claps with recognition.)

PETER: I got it! That's the guy from *Big*. Tom Hanks. That's it! Aw, funny guy, Tom Hanks! Everything he says is a stitch!

(On the movie screen, we see Tom Hanks.)

TOM HANKS: I have AIDS.

PETER: Hahahahahahaha!

A Fun Game

QUAGMIRE: Hey, who wants to play "drink the beer"?

(Peter zips in, holding a beer can.)

PETER: Right here!

QUAGMIRE: Heh. You win!

PETER: All right! What do I win?

QUAGMIRE: Another beer!

PETER: Aw, I'm goin' for the high score!

Momentary Remorse

PETER: Heh. Y'know, I feel kinda bad, you guys. I promised my wife I wouldn't drink.

QUAGMIRE: Aw, don't feel bad, Peter.

PETER: Huh, gee, I never thought of it like that.

Marital Trap

LOIS: Peter, what did you promise me last night?

PETER: That I wouldn't drink at the stag party.

LOIS: And what did you do?

PETER: Drank at the stag party— Oh, I almost walked right into that one!

The Stockbrokers in Peter's Head

WALL STREET GUY #1: Dick, do you ever wonder what's outside those walls?

WALL STREET GUY #2: Say, now, that's dangerous thinking, Paul. You'd best stick to your work.

WALL STREET GUY #1: Okay.

Excuses, Excuses

MR. WEED: *(to Peter)* Are you sleeping on the job?

> Peter, I like you, but I need you to be more than just eye-candy around here.

Scene Stealers
JONATHAN WEED

OCCUPATION
Supervisor, Happy-Go-Lucky Toys

TURN-ONS
Promptness, efficiency, Peter's rugged physique

TURN-OFFS
People who send Christmas cards with only photos of their children

EXTRACURRICULAR ACTIVITIES
Coaches company softball team

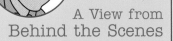

A View from Behind the Scenes

"The Family Guy *pilot was based on a student film I did called* Life with Larry. *One small difference between the two was that* Life with Larry *was shown primarily in my dorm room and* Family Guy *was shown after the Super Bowl."*

—SETH MACFARLANE, CREATOR AND EXECUTIVE PRODUCER

PETER: Oh, uh, no, there's, uh, a bug in my eye and I'm tryin' to suffocate him.

Not Quite Getting the Concept

MR. WEED: Peter, I am appalled. Your negligence has damaged this company's reputation. You're fired!

PETER: Aw, geez. For how long?

The New Family Order

PETER: Now, don't worry, kids, your father's still gonna put food on this table, just not as much, so it might get a little competitive.

A Horrible Poker Face

PETER: Now, not a word to your mom about me getting canned.

(Lois enters.)

LOIS: What's that, Peter?

PETER: Ah, ah, nothing. Ooh, the lost-my-job smells great.

LOIS: What?

PETER: Uh, uh, Meg, honey, can you pass the fired-my-ass-for-negligence?

LOIS: Peter, are you feeling okay?

PETER: Oh, I feel great! I haven't got a job in the world.

The Truth May Set You Free

BRIAN: Peter, I know it's a dangerous precedent, but, uh, you might want to just tell Lois the truth.

PETER: What, that I can't provide for my family? That she's always right? That I didn't really stand up to that tank in Tienanmen Square?

(Flashback to Tienanmen Square, where Peter stands next to an incredibly brave Chinese Student as a Red Chinese tank slowly bears down on them.)

PETER: Oh, screw this, I just came over to buy some fireworks.

(Peter sprints off.)

Brian Checks Up on Peter's Coming Clean to Lois

BRIAN: Hey. How'd she take it?

PETER: I told her she was fat.

(Brian smacks Peter's nose with the newspaper.)

BRIAN: *(firmly)* No. No.

Peter Goes on the Dole

PETER: Guys, our money problems are over! We're officially on welfare! C'mon, kids, help me scatter car parts on the front lawn.

Peter Shows Up with the Statue of David

LOIS: You bought this?

PETER: No, no, no, I just rented it. They're gonna be ticked, though. The penis broke off while I was loadin' it into the car.

(Peter holds up the stone penis and throws it out of the yard. It crashes through Mr. Weed's window.)

MR. WEED: *(to the penis)* I shall call you Eduardo.

Stewie Channels Forrest

STEWIE: You know, Mother, life is like a box of chocolates. You never know what you're going to get. Your life, however, is more like a box of ACTIVE GRENADES!!!

Peter on the Witness Stand

JUDGE: Mr. Griffin, don't you think you should have alerted the government of such a gross overpayment?

PETER: Well, uh, I was gonna call 'em, but um . . . my favorite episode of *Diff'rent Strokes* was on! You know the one where Arnold and Dudley get sexually molested by the guy who owns the bike shop?

(Cutaway to a bike shop, where the Bike Shop Owner stands bent over with his butt facing Arnold and Dudley.)

BIKE SHOP OWNER: All right, now, I want you boys to scream real loud at my ass.

The Crowd Reacts

JUDGE: Mr. Griffin . . . I'm sentencing you to twenty-four months in prison.

LOIS: Oh, no!

BRIAN: Oh, no!

CHRIS: Oh, no!

MEG: Oh, no!

(The giant, pitcher-shaped Kool-Aid Guy bursts through the wall of the courtroom.)

KOOL-AID GUY: Oh, yeah!

(Everyone turns and looks at him, nonplussed. He looks back—it's an awkward moment.)

STUFF THAT MIGHT HAVE SLIPPED BY

■ The transitional music in this episode is never heard again throughout the series.

■ The beginning of the opening credits are intentionally reminiscent of the *All in the Family* opening, with Peter and Lois sitting at the piano like Archie and Edith did.

■ The Providence, Rhode Island, skyline is visible behind the Griffins' house.

■ The name of the gym where Hitler is working out is called Das Gym.

■ The porno that Peter and the guys watch at the stag party is called, *Assablanca.*

■ The unsafe toys Peter lets slip through include a knife, a powerstrip, a can of gasoline, razor blades, and a porcupine.

■ The local newspaper is called the *Daily Informant.*

■ The sign in front of the Quahog Institute of Cosmetic Surgery reads "Because You're No Prize."

Episode
I NEVER MET THE DEAD MAN

EPISODE NUMBER: 1ACX02
ORIGINAL AIRDATE: 4/11/99
WRITER: Chris Sheridan
DIRECTOR:
Michael Dante DiMartino
EXECUTIVE PRODUCERS:
Seth MacFarlane,
David Zuckerman
GUEST VOICE: Erik Estrada
as Ponch

SUMMARY

Lois is annoyed that Peter spends more time watching TV than with the family. She suggests that instead of sitting in front of the boob tube all day, Peter should spend some time teaching Meg how to drive so that she'll pass her driver's test. Peter grudgingly agrees, but gives Meg lousy driving tips that she follows

during her road test, causing her to fail. On their way home from DMV, Peter gets distracted and crashes the car into a main cable TV transmitter for the town of Quahog, knocking out reception for the whole town. Meanwhile, Stewie devises a plan to get out of eating the broccoli that he so despises: he intends to build a weather-altering machine that will freeze broccoli crops everywhere.

Peter blames Meg for the town-wide cable outage and bribes her to go along with the lie by promising her a new car. Meanwhile, Peter suffers without his precious TV to comfort him. He finally decides to strap a TV cutout to himself so that his whole world appears to be a television show. When Meg can no longer deal with the public scorn, she rats Peter out as the one really responsible for Quahog's TV-less existence, causing the town to turn on him instead.

Lois saves Peter's neck by giving a compelling speech to the community about how TV keeps us all from enjoying one another and from other fulfilling pursuits, too. Having persuaded even Peter, he soon takes things to the other extreme, dragging the family on one activity after another. When the family can no longer keep up with him, Peter goes off with buddy William Shatner. Stewie's weather machine is now fully functional, causing a huge rainstorm. Peter and Shatner head home in the downpour just as Lois is taking Meg out to practice her driving. In the storm, Meg accidentally hits Shatner with the car, killing him. As Peter recovers at the hospital in a body cast, he is forced to watch TV, which transforms him back into the TV lover he used to be.

MEMORABLE MOMENTS

Stewie Plays with His *Sesame Street* Phone

STEWIE: *(on toy phone)* Put me through to the Pentagon!

ERNIE'S VOICE: Do you know what sound a cow makes?

STEWIE: Don't toy with me, Ernie! I've already dispatched with Mr. Hooper, I've got six armed men stationed outside Big Bird's nest, and as for Linda? . . . Well, it's rather difficult for a deaf woman to hear an assassin approach, now, isn't it?

Fatherly Priorities

PETER: Ah, sorry, Meg, Daddy loves ya, but Daddy also loves *Star Trek*, and in all fairness, *Star Trek* was here first.

Family Time

LOIS: For God's sake, Peter, you've been sitting in front of the TV since you got home from work. Why don't you spend some time with your family?

PETER: I will, I'm-I'm just gonna do it during the commercials. And if that's wrong, well, then, then maybe I'm missing the point of having commercials.

Stewie Plots Against Broccoli

STEWIE: Cold kills broccoli! It's so simple! All I need to do is build a machine to control the global environment. Forecast for tomorrow: a few sprinkles of genius, with a chance of DOOM!

Fighting Off the Angry Mob

(An angry man rolls up his sleeves and steps toward Peter.)

PETER: Oh, boy. Uh . . . um . . . hey, look! There's Bigfoot!

(The crowd looks over to where Peter points. Bigfoot is indeed there.)

BIGFOOT: Whoa, whoa, whoa, this isn't about me. This is about you.

(They turn back to Peter.)

"The Scooby-Doo Murder Files"

FRED: Gee whiz, gang, looks like the killer gutted the victim, strangled him with his own intestines, and then dumped the body in the river.

VELMA: Jinkies! What a mystery!

SCOOBY: *(grossed-out Scooby noise)*

FRED: You're right, Scoob. We are dealing with one sick son of a bitch.

Booze Hound

BRIAN: Hey, barkeep, whose leg do you have to hump to get a dry martini around here?

Aw, crap.

Scene Stealers
ENSIGN RICKY

DISTINGUISHING TRAIT
His red shirt

WHAT IT VIRTUALLY GUARANTEES FOR HIM
A quick and certain death

HIS MOMENT OF VINDICATION
Watching Shatner die before him

HIS ONE DREAM
Maybe a blue shirt. Or a yellow one. Pretty much anything but red.

Forecast for tomorrow: a few sprinkles of genius, with a chance of DOOM!

Lois Saves the Day <and Peter>

(The crowd murmurs as it starts to rush Peter. Lois steps between Peter and the crowd.)

LOIS: Stop! Stop! What is wrong with you people? O-okay, yes, my husband is responsible for knockin' out TV, but we should be thankin' him. He's broken television's hypnotic spell over us. Now we can see the world for what it is, a beautiful place full of wonderful things just waitin' to be experienced!

(The crowd is moved. Peter turns to Man #2.)

PETER: Aw, geez, another chick flick.

PRINCIPAL: She's right! All the hours we've wasted on that damn idiot box! I'm gonna paint my house.

PARACHUTIST: I'm gonna build a ship in a bottle.

OLD GUY: I'm gonna push a hoop with a stick down a dirt road.

Peter Discovers Alternatives to TV

PETER: What-what-what could you and me do together? *(Lois giggles.)*

PETER: Lois! You've got a sick mind.

LOIS: Peter, I'm talking about making love.

PETER: Ohhh. I thought you wanted us to murder the children and harvest their organs for beer money.

The Cable Comes Back On

TOM: . . . Well, Diane, that last report was so good, I think you deserve a spanking.

DIANE: Oh, Tom, I don't think your wife would appreciate that.

TOM: Diane, that frigid old cow lives in Quahog. She can't hear a word I'm saying.

STAGE MANAGER: Actually, we're back on the air in Quahog.

(Tom looks at the camera, unsure of what to do next.)

Active Peter

PETER: Come on, everyone. We're late for the Bavarian Folk Festival. Heh. You know those Germans. If you don't join the party, they'll come and get ya!

Meg Hits William Shatner with the Car

(Lois jumps out of the car and runs to Peter, who lies next to a dying William Shatner. Meg stands over Shatner, distraught.)

MEG: Ah, my God! I hit William Shatner!

(Shatner still gesticulates wildly as he speaks his final words.)

WILLIAM SHATNER: Light . . . growing dimmer. Can't breathe . . . Beam me up, God.

A View from Behind the Scenes

"This was the first episode we did after the pilot. All the writers who were there look back at that time like it was boot camp. We didn't have offices yet, so we were working out of one small office at King of the Hill. Twelve guys sitting eighteen hours a day for three months in a 10 x 12 room turned us all a little bit gay."

—CHRIS SHERIDAN, WRITER OF THE EPISODE

STUFF THAT MIGHT HAVE SLIPPED BY

■ When Meg runs the Amish guy off the road, his wagon explodes. Then his horse explodes.

■ Meg attends James Woods Regional High School, named after native Rhode Islander, James Woods.

■ The airbags in the Griffins' car deploy long after the impact of Peter and Meg's collision.

■ In this episode, we learn that Quagmire is an airline pilot.

■ **When Stewie is done converting his See-'n-Say to a weather-altering device, the animal designations have been replaced with: "Freezing Rain," "Blizzard," "Tornado," "Partly Cloudy," "Hurricane," "Apocalypse," "Sand Storm," and "Pestilence."**

Episode
CHITTY CHITTY DEATH BANG

EPISODE NUMBER: 1ACX04
ORIGINAL AIRDATE: 4/18/99
WRITER: Danny Smith
DIRECTOR: Dominic Polcino
EXECUTIVE PRODUCERS:
Seth MacFarlane,
David Zuckerman
GUEST VOICE: John O'Hurley as
the Cult Leader (a.k.a. "The
Man in White")

SUMMARY

Lois has booked Cheesie Charlie's for Stewie's upcoming first birthday party and sends Peter (along with Chris) to drop off the deposit check at the restaurant. However, once they arrive, Peter sports an attitude that causes the manager to give their reservation to someone else—a move Peter later realizes will infuriate Lois. Meanwhile, Stewie misinterprets the meaning of his birthday and assumes that the same mysterious "Man in White" who delivered him as an infant will be returning to force Stewie back into the womb from which he escaped just one year ago. Also, Meg, who has been having trouble fitting in at school, discovers a new friend named Jennifer.

Peter covers his ass by telling Lois that they don't need to have Stewie's party at Cheesie Charlie's because he's already planned an extravagant party at home. Meanwhile, Stewie makes it all the way to the airport before deciding that he should face "The Man in White" after all. Peter tries desperately, but ultimately unsuccessfully, to put together a party in time for Stewie's birthday. He finally reroutes a circus into the Griffins' backyard, saving the day—that is, until he reveals to Lois that he gave Meg permission to go to a party at her friend's house. Lois, who wanted the whole family together for Stewie's party, is upset with Peter for letting Meg go. What Peter and Lois don't realize is that Meg's "party" is actually a cult meeting where all the members are about to commit group suicide.

Peter goes to retrieve Meg from her "party," oblivious to the fact that he is sparing her life in the process. The Cult Leader chases after them (wearing his ceremonial white robe) and is mistaken by Stewie as "The Man in White." Stewie does away with him and, feeling victorious, joins the others to enjoy his party.

A View from Behind the Scenes

"This was the first of many times Seth used my voice for his shows. But he made me audition with everyone else. Jerk."

—RACHEL MACFARLANE, VOICE OF JENNIFER IN THIS EPISODE AND CREATOR SETH MACFARLANE'S SISTER

MEMORABLE MOMENTS

Stewie's Emancipation Day from the Womb

DOCTOR: Congratulations, Mrs. Griffin. It's a boy! Wait a minute, I don't think we're through here.

LOIS: Oh, my God, is it twins?

DOCTOR: No, it's a . . . a map of Europe?

Ah, Simple Pleasures

LOIS: I just confirmed everything with the birthday party planner down at Cheesie Charlie's.

PETER: Why Cheesie Charlie's?

CHRIS: Ahh, it's cool, Dad! They have this game where you put in a dollar and you win four quarters! I win every time!

Sound Fatherly Advice

MEG: I don't get it. The harder I try to make friends, the more people hate me.

PETER: Listen, Meg, you're a one-of-a-kind girl with a mind of her own. Now, see, that's what people hate.

MEG: Really?

PETER: I'm tellin' ya, just be the girl you think everyone else wants you to be.

Show Your Pride

PETER: Meg and I just had a little father/daughter talk.

LOIS: Well, it seems to have worked.

PETER: Hey, I wasn't just blowin' smoke when I bought this T-shirt.
(He raises his overshirt, revealing a T-shirt that says "#1 DAD!")

LOIS: Well, you're the number one husband, too.

PETER: I know, that's why I bought this T-shirt.
(He raises the T-shirt up, proudly revealing another T-shirt underneath that reads "NO FAT CHICKS." He looks, then quickly pulls his shirt down.)

PETER: Whoops.

Stewie Learns to Count in the Womb

STEWIE FETUS: Day one-seventy-one. I've sprouted another finger. Counting the one from yesterday . . . *(He glances down.)*

STEWIE FETUS: . . . I'm up to eleven.

Stewie Packs for Managua

STEWIE: I must prepare for my journey.
(He takes out his Winnie the Pooh backpack and begins packing.)

STEWIE: Let me see. . . grenades, mace, Baggie full of Cheerios . . .

Brian Reacts to Peter's Tall Tale

BRIAN: Bravo, Peter. You are the Spalding Gray of crap.

Peter Griffin, Lousy Fibber

BRIAN: Peter, face it. You're a terrible liar.
(Flashback to an elevator, where Peter stands with another Guy. The guy sniffs, reacts, then looks at Peter. Peter's eyes shift back and forth.)

PETER: Uh . . . it was you.

STUFF THAT MIGHT HAVE SLIPPED BY

■ Brian is sitting on the couch reading a magazine called *Doggy Style*.

■ When Jennifer goes to poison the punch, she adds cyanide, arsenic, rat poison, and Paul Reiser's book, *Couplehood*.

■ Stewie's full name is Stuart Gilligan Griffin.

If you're gonna pull a party out of your ass, you might want to stand up.

Eternal Pursuit

BRIAN: You know, clowns and petting zoos book months in advance. Ah, you're-you're . . . gonna have a tough time finding . . . Oh, hold on.
(A moment later, a tiny chuck wagon pulled by a team of tiny horses tears through the living room into the kitchen.)
CHUCK WAGON DRIVER: Yah! Yah!
(Brian tears after the chuck wagon into the kitchen, but it disappears through a cabinet door. Brian opens the cabinet and there's just a bag of dog food. Brian sighs.)
BRIAN: Someday.

Just Take the Compliment

JENNIFER: What a lovely house, Mrs. G. Meg, you didn't tell me your mother was just like Martha Stewart.
LOIS: Oh, no, once you get to know me I'm really very nice.

Booking the Entertainment

(Peter, looking very uncomfortable, stands across a counter from a sleazy-looking guy in a Spider-Man suit.)
PETER: I, uh, I-I don't think I'm in the right place. I'm looking for a guy to come entertain the kids at my son's birthday.
PERFORMANCE ARTIST: Oh, sure I can do that.
PETER: You-you do children's parties?
PERFORMANCE ARTIST: Oh, yeah, I can do, like, a handstand, or some somersaults, maybe. I . . . I can make pretend like the children are little bugs in my web . . .
(Peter smiles and backs away, then turns and bolts for the door.)

Time Runs Short

BRIAN: Well, Peter, you've only got a couple of hours left. If you're gonna pull a party out of your ass, you might want to stand up.

Party Supplies

PETER: Brian, Stewie's birthday is gonna suck. The only stuff I could get on such short notice was a cake and that big ass piñata.
(Peter points to a large, ass-shaped papier-mâché piñata.)
BRIAN: I sure hope candy comes out of that.

Peter's Grand Entrance

(Peter crashes through the backyard hedge, riding an elephant.)
PETER: Hey, Lois, look, the two symbols of the Republican Party! An elephant and a big fat white guy who's threatened by change!

Be Sure to Follow Instructions

CHRIS: Hey, birthday dude. You want some ice cream?
STEWIE: Yes, but no sprinkles. For every sprinkle I find, I shall kill you.

Hard to Get Attention

JENNIFER: Meg, you seem sad. Today's a happy day!

MEG: I know. It's just that . . . well, I really like that guy over there, but he doesn't even know I exist. He must think I'm a total dog.

JENNIFER: Oh, that's so not true!

MEG: Then what is it?

JENNIFER: He's a eunuch.

MEG: Really?

JENNIFER: Sure! All the guys here have been castrated. It's cool!
(We see two Cult Boys near the punch bowl, checking out girls.)

CULT KID #1: Hey, do you think that girl is hot?

CULT KID #2: No.

CULT KID #1: Me, neither! *(The two boys high-five.)*

Brian Keeps Busy at the Party

(A Clown with a seltzer bottle walks past Brian. He holds up his glass.)

BRIAN: Hey, you. Hit me.
(The Clown squirts some seltzer in his glass.)

BRIAN: Ah, there, now if I can find a midget with some gin I'll be in business.

The Bar Is Pretty Low

JENNIFER: *(to Cult Leader)* This is Meg, oh, wise one. Can she come with us?

CULT LEADER: Perhaps. Do you have a mind that seeks enlightenment and a heart that seeks purity?

MEG: Well . . . not really.

CULT LEADER: Okay, are you a confused adolescent desperately seeking acceptance from an undifferentiated ego mass that demands conformity?

MEG: Wow, that sort of sounds more like me . . .

CULT LEADER: Great! Well, then all you need is a dark blue jogging suit.

He Always Knows Just What to Say

MEG: Oh, Daddy, you must think I'm the worst daughter ever!

PETER: Aw, no, you're not, honey. What about that fat girl from the Judds?

Eww . . .

PETER: I cannot wait to taste this cake. The guy who sold it to me said it was delicious *and* erotic.

LOIS: Peter, there's a naked man on this cake.

PETER: Well, there were only two left, and-and trust me, you did not want the one of Al Roker with the Hershey Kiss nipples.

MORE . . .
STUFF THAT MIGHT HAVE SLIPPED BY

■ The map of Europe that comes out of Lois's uterus along with Stewie is marked with various Xs that say "Bomb Here."

■ Meg attends James Woods Regional High School, but the cheerleaders in this episode wear sweaters that have a Q on them (presumably for "Quahog").

■ At Cheesie Charlie's Chris plays a video game called "Virtual Indy 500," while Peter plays a video game called "Virtual Stuck Behind a Bus."

■ Stewie's *Soldier of Fortune* magazine features an article titled, "Top 10 Sexiest Chemical Explosives."

SCENE STEALERS
"THE MAN IN WHITE"

OCCUPATION
Nutjob cult leader

TURN-ONS
Poisoned punch, blue jogging suits, transcendence

TURN-OFF
Committing suicide alone

Ah, let's see what jogging suits we have in stock. What're you, about a nine?

Episode
MIND OVER MURDER

SUMMARY

Stewie is in terrible pain from teething and cannot find comfort anywhere. When Lois tells him that his pain will ultimately pass, it gives him the idea to build a machine that will move time forward to the point where his teething will have already stopped. Meanwhile, Peter drives Chris to his soccer game, where he gets into a fight with another parent. He punches the parent, who Peter then realizes is not a man, as he had assumed, but rather a pregnant woman.

Peter is put under house arrest for assault and soon finds that he misses his buddies. He decides to build a bar in his basement so that his friends can come to visit and hang out with him. It isn't long before the basement bar becomes a local hotspot. When Lois discovers this, she's upset, but then she gets a chance to sing on stage before an adoring crowd. As she savors the spotlight, Peter becomes increasingly uncomfortable with all the attention she's getting, especially from the male patrons.

Meanwhile, Stewie's time machine plans are discovered, causing him to panic about the breach of security. In a clear move to protect the plans, he uses the machine to go back in time before the plans were actually found. But he reverses time just as Peter is having an epiphany about how poorly he treats Lois and seconds before the basement bar goes up in flames. Stewie even manages to back time up to before Chris's soccer game, successfully avoiding the whole altercation between Peter and the pregnant soccer mom. But, unfortunately, his teething pain is still with him.

EPISODE NUMBER: 1ACX03

ORIGINAL AIRDATE: 4/25/99

WRITERS: Neil Goldman & Garrett Donovan

DIRECTOR: Roy Allen Smith

EXECUTIVE PRODUCERS: Seth MacFarlane, David Zuckerman

GUEST VOICES: Alex Rocco as the Soccer Parent, Leslie Uggams as herself

MEMORABLE MOMENTS

End the Suffering

LOIS: Oh, you're just teething, Stewie. It's a normal part of a baby's life.

STEWIE: Very well, then. I order you to kill me at once!

LOIS: Aw, honey. I know you're hurting, but Mommy has to clean up the house, all right?

STEWIE: No it's not all right. For the love of God, shake me! Shake me like a British nanny!

The Hazards of Diaper Changes

PETER: I just hope he doesn't need changin'. I'm a little gun-shy after what happened last time.

(Flashback to Stewie's room, where Stewie lays on his back, while Peter changes his diaper. Peter grabs the wrong bottle next to him.)

STEWIE: No, no, no, you imbecile, that's not talc, that's paprika!

(Peter sprinkles the paprika between Stewie's legs.)

STEWIE: Aaaah! Take that!

(Stewie shoots a stream into Peter's eye.)

Unappreciated Effort

LOIS: (singing) "Lullaby, and good night . . ."

STEWIE: Oh, enough! The only thing worse than the wretched pain in my mouth is the excrement spewing from yours!

Watch That Temper

BOY: (to Peter) Hey, you hit my mom!

PETER: No, I hit your dad.

(A crowd starts to gather.)

PARENT #1: Whoa, stand back. Give her some air.

PETER: You-you mean, give him some air.

PARENT #2: Call an ambulance! She's going into labor!

PETER: Y-you mean, he's going into labor.

(There is the sound of a newborn baby crying.)

PETER: Whoops.

The Perils of House Arrest

PETER: I'm so bored I can't even watch TV anymore. All the shows are starting to run together.

(On TV, title card reads: Homocide: Life on Sesame Street.)

ANNOUNCER: This show contains adult content, and is brought to you by the letter H.

(In a run-down New York apartment, a telephone rings. Bert from Sesame Street groans, rolls over, and answers the phone.)

BERT: (into phone) Hello . . . (sighs) Son of a bitch . . . I'm on my way.

(Bert pulls on a pair of dirty jeans.)

BERT: Some poor bastard got his head blown off, down at a place called "Hooper's."

(Bert takes a slug from a bottle and coughs. Ernie, also in bed, sits up and starts eating a cookie.)

ERNIE: Bert, I wish you wouldn't drink so much, Bert.

BERT: Well, Ernie, I wish you wouldn't eat cookies in the damn bed.

ERNIE: Bert, you're shouting again, Bert.

Stop Speaking Now

PETER: I know you can't understand what I'm goin' through, Lois. I mean, all this stuff that makes you happy, y'know, like cooking and cleaning, it's, it's right here in the house, just waiting for you. You are one lucky . . .

BRIAN: Ah, ah, stop now.

LOIS: Peter, I don't do those things because I enjoy them, I do them because I love my family.

PETER: Hehehehehe. (taunting) Lois loves her family. Lois loves her family . . . (singing) Lois and her family sitting in a tree. . . . See, now, Lois. The guys would've found that hilarious.

> Oh, look at the time. I promised Loretta I was gonna trim the hedges and be tender with her.

Scene Stealers
CLEVELAND BROWN

WHO HE IS
Peter's neighbor, dedicated family man, and slow talker

OCCUPATION
Deli owner (formerly an auctioneer, before a Sotheby's-related accident altered his speech)

WHY PETER LIKES HIM
Because of his even-keel nature, his sage advice, and his free day-old hoagies

A View from
Behind the Scenes

"Sure Peter's basement expands to unrealistic proportions over the course of the episode. But did you laugh? Then what are you complaining about?"

—SETH MACFARLANE, CREATOR AND EXECUTIVE PRODUCER

That's a Whole Different Thing

PETER: Hey, hey, you're the Pawtucket Patriot.

PATRIOT: Verily! Come hither and give heed!

PETER: Whoa, whoa, whoa, I don't swing that way, pal.

Home Improvement

LOIS: This is why you missed our dinner? To make a bar for your friends?

PETER: Yeah, isn't it great? Boy, I feel just like Tim Allen. I build stuff, and I have a criminal record!

The Kid Can't Hold His Liquor

STEWIE: *(drunk)* You see . . . Misty, my time manipulator employs axioms from the quantum theory of molecular propulsion . . .
(His pencil breaks.)

STEWIE: I've broken my pencil.

MISTY: I have a Barney pen in my purse, hmmmm.
(She hands it to Stewie. He leans in close to her.)

STEWIE: You . . . are spectacular!

Uncomfortable . . .

BRIAN: Something troubling you, Peter?

PETER: Aw, no, nothing. Just all my friends are eye-humpin' my wife.

Duh

LOIS: Aw, I bet your gums are still sore.

STEWIE: Oh, you're so observant, aren't you? Are you a detective?

Who's That MILF?

MAN: Wow, Lois Griffin! Hey, I love your act. Nice melons.
(Peter spins around, ready to clock the guy.)

PETER: Hey, listen, pal . . .

LOIS: Peter. I'm holding melons.
(Lois is, in fact, holding a couple of melons.)

PETER: Oh.
(Peter and Lois continue down the aisle.)

MAN: And her hooters ain't bad, either.

PETER: Now hang on a second there!

LOIS: Peter! I'm holding hooters.
(In addition to two melons, Lois is also holding two owls. One of the owls hoots.)

PETER: Oh. Sorry.

MAN: Huh, no problem. *(then)* Your wife's hot. *(The guy runs away.)*

PETER: All right, that's it!

Episode

A HERO SITS NEXT DOOR

EPISODE NUMBER: 1ACX05

ORIGINAL AIRDATE: 5/2/99

WRITERS: Mike Barker
& Matt Weitzman

DIRECTOR: Monte Young

EXECUTIVE PRODUCERS:
Seth MacFarlane,
David Zuckerman

GUEST VOICES: Patrick Warburton
as Joe Swanson, Jennifer Tilly
as Bonnie Swanson

SUMMARY

When Peter accidentally injures the star player on the Happy-Go-Lucky Toy Company's softball team, his boss, Mr. Weed, is furious. Mr. Weed demands that Peter find the team a new ringer. Meanwhile, the Griffins get some new neighbors, Joe and Bonnie Swanson. Peter resists pressure from Lois to get to know the new neighbors better until he learns that Joe used to be a star baseball player in college. Peter invites Joe to join his team, but is surprised when Joe shows up for the toy company's big game in a wheelchair.

Joe not only helps win the game for Peter's team, but he also invites everyone over to his house for a postgame luau, where he is the life of the party. Peter, upset at being upstaged by Joe, figures he can only win back the family's attention by becoming a hero, just like Joe is every day in his work as a police officer. So, when Peter hears about a bank robbery in progress, he rushes the family to the scene of the crime and does his best to thwart the robbery, but he only makes things worse. When Joe arrives and successfully talks the robbers out of their plan, Peter only gets more frustrated. But finally, Peter's family tells him that while Joe is *a* hero, he's not *their* hero.

MEMORABLE MOMENTS

Those Darn Seductive *Teletubbies*

(Stewie slams his book shut.)

STEWIE: Machiavelli, you've told me nothing I don't already know. *(picks up another book)* Ah. Sun Tzu's *The Art of War*.
(He opens it. Lois enters.)

LOIS: Stewie, those books aren't for babies. Here, watch the *Teletubbies*.
(She turns on the TV and exits.)

STEWIE: How dare you! That book may hold the key to my enslaving of all mankind— *(notices TV)* —Ooo, fuzzy . . .

Some Emotions Run Deep

PETER: Ah, man, I hate those guys. More than I hate spinach, traffic jams, and the last few years of *M*A*S*H*. You know, when Alan Alda took over behind the camera and the show got all dramatic and preachy. Ah, am I right? Who's with me?! Hah?

Close but No Cigar

(Peter and Chris watch Wheel of Fortune. *The puzzle reads, "G O _ U C K Y O U R S E L _ _ _".)*

CONTESTANT *(on TV):* Pat, I'd like to solve the puzzle. "Go tuck yourself in."

PAT SAJAK *(on TV):* You got it!

CHRIS: Well, you were close, Dad.

PETER: Yeah. And I still can't believe we missed the phrase "my hairy aunt."

Mixed Signals

(Brian sits in the empty bleachers. A woman walks by and he begins panting.)

WOMAN: *(offended)* Huh, pervert.

BRIAN: Oh, oh, don't flatter yourself, honey. I don't have any sweat glands.

It's All Fun and Games . . .

LOIS: Oh, Quahog can be pretty exciting, too. Last week, someone lost an eye at Bingo.

(Flashback to the VFW Hall, where a Bingo Announcer picks a ball out of the bingo drum and announces.)

BINGO ANNOUNCER: I-17.

(He drops the ball.)

BINGO ANNOUNCER: Oh, darn it.

(He leans down to get it and slams his eye on the table corner. He grabs it in pain.)

BINGO ANNOUNCER: Ahhhh!

Introductions

BONNIE: Joe, you have to meet our new neighbor, Lois Griffin.

JOE: It's a pleasure, Lois. Who's the little guy?

LOIS: This is Stewie. Honey, say "Hi" to Mr. Swanson.

STEWIE: You will bow to me.

Promises, Promises

(In a sushi bar, Peter sits at a table across from a Japanese Baseball Player and his Interpreter.)

Scene Stealers
JOE SWANSON

Eat up, everyone. Tonight, my wife won't be the only one enjoying a pig in a blanket.

OCCUPATION
Decorated Police Officer and Generally Congenial Next-Door Neighbor

FAMILY
Wife, Bonnie; son, Kevin; and unborn baby, many years in the gestating

HOW HE BECAME DISABLED
Battling the Grinch in the line of Duty

SPECIALTIES
Baseball, pumping up those around him, and other manly type stuff

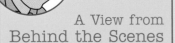

A View from Behind the Scenes

"It was with this episode that we abandoned the ill conceived notion of giving the episodes ominous, old fashioned-radio-play-like titles. Looking back over titles that all contained 'murder' and 'death,' it just became too confusing to try to remember what the episode was actually about. Well, you gotta give us credit for trying something, right?"

—SETH MACFARLANE, CREATOR AND EXECUTIVE PRODUCER

INTERPRETER: Hideo-san would be honored to play for your team, but he wishes to know what compensation you offer.

PETER: Uh . . . me, me love you long time?

Off on the Wrong Foot

JOE: This is a surprise. I kinda thought you didn't like me.

PETER: Oh, what, because of what I said this afternoon? Oh, no, no see, I-I have that disease where stuff just pops out of my mouth. Go to hell, go to hell! Whup, huh, see what I mean? Hehehehe.

Hope We Don't Get Sued

JOE: Sounds like fun.

PETER: Hey, so much fun it should be illegal. Like copyright infringement.
(Peter morphs into Mickey Mouse.)

PETER: *(Mickey Mouse voice)* Ha-ha! See ya at the game, Joe! Ha-ha!

All in Good Fun?

(Peter's team, the "Toy Boys," warms up. A Pawtucket Joke & Novelty "Merry Prankster" approaches a Toy Boy.)

MERRY PRANKSTER: Hey, you want a piece of gum?

TOY BOY: Oh, thanks.
(He takes the gum and chews it.)

MERRY PRANKSTER: Ha ha! That was joke gum.

TOY BOY: What do you mean?

MERRY PRANKSTER: Now you're addicted to heroin!
(They both laugh.)

TOY BOY: *(laugh trails off)* . . . I'm cold.

No Tolerance for Small Talk

BONNIE: The movers tracked grease all over my carpet. I tried every thing to get the stain out.

LOIS: What about lemon juice?

BONNIE: Oh, what about club soda?

STEWIE: What about shutting the hell up!

Good Times . . .

MEG: We want to hear more of Mr. Swanson's stories!

CHRIS: He's cool, Dad. He killed a guy.

JOE: Well, technically he was killed by the state, but funny story . . . he did curse my name just before the injection.

That's the Spot

PETER: *(annoyed)* Well, look who finally came home. Geez, I thought you were gonna spend all night over at Joe's.

BRIAN: Huh, I could've. That man has got magic fingers. He, he found this one spot behind my ear— I, forget about it, I thought my leg was never gonna stop.

PETER: I don't believe this. My whole family worships the ground that guy can't walk on.

Take That, Music Industry

(Peter turns the dial of a police scanner. Brian comes in.)

DISPATCHER: (from radio) We have a gang shooting on Third and Main. Three wounded, one dead.

BRIAN: Is it me, or is rap music just getting lazier?

Maybe I'll Stick with Answer Number One

MEG: Mom, what do you do when you like a boy, but he doesn't even notice you?

CHRIS: Meg loves Kevin!

MEG: Shut up, you big sack of dog vomit!

LOIS: Meg, you're a sweet, lovely girl. He'll come around.

MEG: Such a "Mom" answer.

LOIS: Well, have you tried showing off the goods? How's that for a "Mom" answer?

MEG: Creepy.

Way to Not Keep Your Mouth Shut

SHORT ROBBER: All right, if we want the cops to take us seriously we're gonna have to waste a hostage. But who?

PETER: Excuse me, but shouldn't that be "whom"?

SHORT ROBBER: Okay, you.

That's Reassuring, I Guess

BONNIE: Don't worry, Joe's an excellent negotiator. I was a virgin when we met; it took him three hours.

Lesson Learned

PETER: Huh. Y'know, I guess bein' a hero isn't always about savin' lives or catching bad guys. It's also about just bein' there for the people you love.

(A Frantic Old Woman runs up.)

FRANTIC OLD WOMAN: Help! Someone just stole my purse!

PETER: Who cares? I don't even know you.

STUFF THAT MIGHT HAVE SLIPPED BY

■ At the beginning of the episode, Stewie is reading Machiavelli's *The Prince* and Sun Tzu's *The Art of War*.

■ Joe is shown only from the waist up until it is revealed that he is in a wheelchair.

■ The sign in front of the orphanage where Joe confronts the Grinch reads, "Lucky's Orphange—No One Knows You're Here."

■ As Tom Tucker reports on the hostage situation at the bank, an erroneous graphic appears over his shoulder that reads "Pit Bull Attacks Single-Engine Cessna."

Episode

THE SON ALSO DRAWS

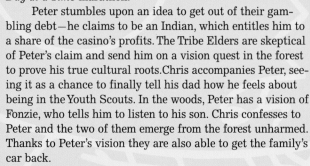

SUMMARY

Chris is not enjoying his experience in the Youth Scouts and wants to quit, but he's afraid to tell Peter. So, when Chris is finally kicked out of the scout troop, he is relieved . . . that is, until Peter finds out and decides to take the whole family to New York so he can complain to the Youth Scout head office directly.

Peter packs everyone but Brian into the car and heads off for New York, but on the way there, he has a bathroom emergency and has to hastily stop at an Indian casino in order to use the bathroom. In that time, Lois goes on a video poker spree and manages to lose the family's car to the casino. Meanwhile, Brian gets trapped watching a *One Day at a Time* marathon.

Peter stumbles upon an idea to get out of their gambling debt—he claims to be an Indian, which entitles him to a share of the casino's profits. The Tribe Elders are skeptical of Peter's claim and send him on a vision quest in the forest to prove his true cultural roots. Chris accompanies Peter, seeing it as a chance to finally tell his dad how he feels about being in the Youth Scouts. In the woods, Peter has a vision of Fonzie, who tells him to listen to his son. Chris confesses to Peter and the two of them emerge from the forest unharmed. Thanks to Peter's vision they are also able to get the family's car back.

EPISODE NUMBER: 1ACX06

ORIGINAL AIRDATE: 5/9/99

WRITER: Ricky Blitt

DIRECTOR: Neil Affleck

EXECUTIVE PRODUCERS:
Seth MacFarlane,
David Zuckerman

GUEST VOICE: Bobby Slayton as
Leonard "Lenny" Cornfeathers

MEMORABLE MOMENTS

Easily Amused

PETER: I gotta surprise for ya, Chris. *(He notices the TV.)* Oh, aw, geez, it'll have to wait. This is the one where the Fonz goes "aaaaay."

FONZIE: *(on TV)* Aaaaay.

PETER: *(laughs)* Take that, 1950's society!

Easily Amused, Part 2

CHRIS: Uh, Dad, w-what would you say if I told you I didn't want to be in the Scouts?

PETER: I'd say, "Come again?" And then, I'd laugh 'cause I said "come."

Chris's Competition at the Soapbox Derby, Speed Racer

POPS: Speed, I do not think you should be in this race, ha ha, the Mach Five is not ready, ha ha!

SPEED RACER: But Pops, I must be in this race, ha ha!

POPS: Very well, ha ha, but you know I am not really your father, ha ha!

SPEED RACER: Aaah!

Bad with Numbers

MITCH: All right! All right! You've got three days to earn a badge.

PETER: Three days? That's tomorrow!

No Appreciation

LOIS: Stewie, look what Mommy made for dessert.

STEWIE: Oooh, Jell-O! How exotic! Why, I feel like I'm on the deck of the QE2.

Peter Helps Chris with His Insect Study Merit Badge

PETER: Look, Chris, it's a whole family of WASPs.
(We see they're standing in a dining room watching a stoic, upper-crust Family eating dinner.)

WASP DAD: My, Margaret, what a subpar ham.

WASP MOM: Perhaps I can't bake a ham, but what I can cook up is a little grace and civility at the table.

WASP DAD: *(to daughter)* Patty, did you know that your mother is a whore?

Speed Racer Shows Up Again

PETER: Pack your bags, you guys, the Griffins are hitting the Big Apple!
(Speed Racer and Pops are outside the window.)

SPEED RACER: Ha ha, did you hear? The Griffins are going to New York, ha ha!

POPS: This does not affect us at all, ha ha!

SPEED RACER: Ha ha!

Loading Up for the Trip

(Lois starts to strap Stewie into his car seat.)

STEWIE: What the hell do you think you're doing?

LOIS: Strapping you in, honey. So you don't get hurt.

STEWIE: So I don't get hurt? That's the best you can come up with, you dull-witted termagant?

LOIS: I brought your Raffi tape.

STEWIE: *(grudgingly)* Play "Wheels on the Bus" and get the hell out of my sight.

STUFF THAT MIGHT HAVE SLIPPED BY

■ When the Griffins are leaving for New York, Brian is reading the Utne Reader.

■ While en route to New York with the family, Peter desperately has to go to the bathroom. Some of the signs he passes include a highway sign reading "Dump, Next Left," a mobile home with a sign reading "Wide Load," a furniture store with a sign in the window reading "All stools must go!," a car with a bumper sticker reading "I ♥ my Shih Tzu," and a billboard reading "Only 15 Miles to Bob's House of Feces."

■ The Indian Casino the Griffins stop at is called Geronimo's Palace.

■ Some of the employees of the casino are named Running Bear, Change for a Buck, Deals with his Wrist, and Sees You Coming.

■ The slot machines at the Indian casino include one called Gold Teepee.

■ Peter's comment at the end of the show, "Canada sucks," inspired angry mail from Canadian viewers.

A View from Behind the Scenes

"To those of you who wrote letters, the writer of this episode is also Canadian. So, as he would say, chill oot."

—SETH MACFARLANE, CREATOR AND EXECUTIVE PRODUCER

Brian Bails Out

PETER: Hey, aren't you coming?

BRIAN: Aw, thanks, but no thanks. I've been to New York. It's like Prague, sans the whimsy.

LOIS: Will you be okay by yourself?

(Brian sips his martini and just looks at her.)

BRIAN: Oh, I think I'll manage.

Car Games

LOIS: Okay, I'm thinking of a movie.

MEG: Is it an action movie?

LOIS: No.

CHRIS: Aw, is it a musical?

LOIS: No.

PETER: Aw, is it a good movie?

LOIS: Well, it has its moments.

PETER: *Cool Runnings*.

LOIS: Right!

It's Their Nature

LOIS: Peter, we're lost. Would you please find some place to ask for directions.

PETER: We are not lost. And even if we were, you-you know I can't ask another human being for directions.

LOIS: Why not?

PETER: 'Cause I'm a man. Geez, haven't you ever seen a stand-up comedian, Lois?

Lois Folds Like a House of Cards

LOIS: Thank you, but I really don't approve of . . . a-ha, you know, gambling.

SEES YOU COMING: Technically, it's not really gambling. It's just us trying to rebuild our shattered culture after you raped our land and defiled our women.

LOIS: Well, as long as you're not using it for firewater.

How to Get the Car Back

MEG: Nice going, Mom. I finally get my driver's license and you lose the car to a poker machine. How ironic.

PETER: Hey, hey, hey, don't talk about your mother that way. She is not an i-ron.

The Elders Consider Peter's Claim

ELDER #2: He's an Indian, all right.

LENNY: How do you know?

ELDER #2: I can tell.

LENNY: Oh, you think everyone's an Indian. He could just be another mook trying to get a cut of our profits.

ELDER #1: Maybe we can put him through some sort of test. You know, like a-a really impossible stunt to "prove" he's the real deal.

LENNY: Hey, way to think outside the box, Frank.

Peter Gets His Orders

LENNY: To prove you are truly a member of our tribe, you must go on a visionquest.

(Peter stares blankly.)

LENNY: Do you know what a vision quest is?

PETER: Why, of course, I do. I'm an Indian. Butta, why don't you explain it to my wife? She's a little slow in the head.

Peter Talks to the Trees

PETER: Oh, my God, I'm- I'm communicating with nature! Ah, ah, hey, ah, Tree, if, if one of you falls and there's no one around, do-do you make a noise?

TREE #1: Are you kidding? Scott fell last week, he hasn't shut up about it since.

(Angle on Scott, a nearby tree that has fallen over.)

SCOTT: Sure, stand there and bitch, but would any of you take the time to help me?

TREE #2: Ooo, ooo, I'm playing the world's smallest violin, Scott.

Peter Speaks to His Vision of Fonzie

PETER: Um, sure, w-whatever you say. Heh, um, Fonzie, there's something I always wanted to ask ya. You were with a lot of girls. D-did you ever get a sexual disease?

FONZIE: Herpes twice. And the clap. *(awkward pause)* Ayyy!

Peter Returns from the Forest

PETER: Oh, it was amazing! I spoke to the trees, and I saw the Fonz and . . .

LOIS: Really? What's the Fonz like? I bet he's stuck up.

Scene Stealers
LEONARD "LENNY" CORNFEATHERS

OCCUPATION
Indian Casino Manager

LIKES
Protected government tax status

DISLIKES
Fruit compote at the casino buffet

Get the hell outta here, you nut, and go have yourself a spiritual vision.

Episode
BRIAN: PORTRAIT OF A DOG

EPISODE NUMBER: 1ACX07
ORIGINAL AIRDATE: 5/16/99
WRITER: Gary Janetti
DIRECTOR:
Michael Dante DiMartino
EXECUTIVE PRODUCERS:
Seth MacFarlane,
David Zuckerman
GUEST VOICE: Dick Van Patten
as Tom Bradford

SUMMARY

Quahog is in the grip of an unusual heat wave and, not having air-conditioning, the Griffins are suffering. Peter learns about an upcoming dog show offering a top prize of $500, which he sees as the perfect way to buy the family an air conditioner. He persuades a reluctant Brian to participate, but when Peter wants Brian to perform a demeaning trick at the show, Brian refuses to do anything so degrading and exits in a huff.

On the way home, Peter and Brian argue until, finally, Brian angrily gets out of the car. The police give Brian a ticket for violating local leash laws, which Peter has to pay, only further widening their rift. Brian leaves the house, whereupon he is treated shabbily by the community, and ultimately forced to sleep in the bus station. By the time Peter decides to apologize to Brian, Brian has hit rock bottom, having actually attacked a man on the street and having been hauled off by the police.

At the pound, Brian is sentenced to lethal injection. But when he finally gets the chance to plead his case, it's Peter who actually steps in and delivers an emotional appeal on his behalf. The charges against Brian are finally waived and the town shows him new respect.

Excuse me, do I know you?

MEMORABLE MOMENTS

Stewie Trash-Talks to Brian

STEWIE: I'm on to you, oh, yes. Your pathetic attempts to hinder my work have not gone unnoticed. You prance about this house like the cock o' the walk, but will you be prancing . . . when . . . when . . . when there's nothing to prance about. Hmm? Will you be prancing then?

A Glimpse of Tom Tucker's Painful Home Life

DIANE: *(on TV)* Meanwhile, here at home, Quahog remains in the sweltering grip of a freak heat wave.

TOM: I don't think you should use the word "freak," Diane. Some people might find it offensive.

(Flashback to Tom's Kitchen earlier that day. Tom is sitting at the table with his son, Jake, who has an upside-down face.)

TOM: Finish your oatmeal, son.

JAKE: Why bother? I'm just a freak! A freak!

(Tom dies a little inside.)

Who Is an Idiot?

BRIAN: Can't you get the money some other way?

PETER: Believe me, I've been trying. That's why I went on that game show.

(Flashback to the set of Jeopardy!, *where Peter and two other Contestants listen to Alex Trebek read the answer.*

ALEX TREBEK: For eight hundred dollars, "This chemical dye is found in over ninety-five percent of all cosmetic products."

(Peter buzzes in.)

PETER: Diarrhea! *(Everyone laughs. Peter looks confused.)*

PETER: What? Oh, oh, oh, sorry, sorry. What is diarrhea?

Jagged Little Pill

LOIS: Peter, are you offering Brian drugs?

PETER: Not drugs, Lois. Just, just the little blue things celebrities take to help 'em perform.

LOIS: Well, those celebrities are wrong.

PETER: Lois, if Liza is wrong, then I don't want to know what right is.

(Cutaway to Liza's Dressing Room. There's a knock at the door.)

STAGE MANAGER: Two minutes to curtain, Miss Minnelli!

(A bleary, desperate-looking Liza Minnelli talks to someone off-screen.)

LIZA MINNELLI: Oh, c'mon, baby, Mama's gotta sparkle, it's time to make life a cabaret.

(Reveal she's talking to the Blue M&M Candy, who is up against the wall, terrified.)

Grrrrrrrrrrr.

Scene Stealers
THE PIT BULL

WHERE WE MEET HIM
He's Brian's cellmate
in the pound

WHAT LANDED HIM THERE
Probably attacking a
baby (I mean, isn't that
always the case?)

WHY HE KEEPS GOING ON
Periodic, "Midnight Express"-
like visits
from his girlfriend

BLUE M&M CANDY: Lady, for God's sake, I'm just a hard-shelled chocolate candy! Get help!

Peter Reacts to Brian's Exit from the Dog Show

PETER: Why, this was the one thing I ever asked you to do for this family. Well, you know, this and not, ah, do that thing when you drag your ass across the carpet.

The Cops Return Brian Home

OFFICER: The fine is ten dollars. *(to Brian)* You behave, little fella, y'hear me?
BRIAN: *(subservient)* Oh, lordy, lordy, I never roam again.
　　(The Officer smiles and leaves. Peter shuts the door.)
BRIAN: Jackass.

Watch Out for That Rolling Pin

MEG: Mmm, something smells good.
LOIS: Homemade cinnamon buns. Fresh from the tube.
　　(Lois reaches over and pokes the tiny Poppin' Fresh Pillsbury Doughboy.)
DOUGHBOY: *(giggles)* Nothing says lovin' like something from—
　　(Lois begins flattening him with a rolling pin.)
DOUGHBOY: What the hell are you doing, you crazy b—
　　(Lois flattens his head with a squish.)

Wishful Thinking

BRIAN: I can never go back to the way things were. Not after the way I was treated. Not after the things I've seen.
CHRIS: What did you see? W-was it breasts?

Please Pick Up After Yourself

(Brian walks up to the counter of a convenience store and puts a box of plastic Baggies on the counter.)
BRIAN: And a pack of El Dorados. Unfiltered.
　　(The Cashier just stares at him. Brian looks at him, then glances outside.)
BRIAN: What, oh, that, yeah.
　　(He taps the box of Baggies.)
BRIAN: I'll clean that up on my way out.

Rock Bottom

(In a bus station, Brian is huddled on a bench, trying to sleep. A Security Guard shakes him gently.)
SECURITY GUARD: Sorry, pooch, you gotta sleep outside. No dogs allowed in the bus station.
　　(Brian gestures toward the bathroom with his thumb.)
BRIAN: Oh, um . . . my-my-my blind guy's in the john.

The Pound Is No Place for the Weak

(Brian shares a cell with a Pit Bull.)

BRIAN: Hi, how's it goin'?

(The Pit Bull growls and advances a little toward Brian.)

BRIAN: Oh, God, aw, I-I know karate. Hoo-wah-he-yah, uuh.

(Brian does a couple of lame karate-style moves. The Pit Bull advances again. Brian points behind the Pit Bull.)

BRIAN: Oh, look, a tasty little baby.

(The Pit Bull quickly turns around to look. Brian grunts as he kicks the Pit Bull between his hind legs. The Pit Bull doesn't even flinch, he just growls more.)

BRIAN: Well, I see somebody's been neutered.

A View from Behind the Scenes

"This show was our first exploration of Brian as well as our first season finale. Little did we know what the Fox Scheduling Department had in store for us."

—SETH MACFARLANE, CREATOR AND EXECUTIVE PRODUCER

Brian's Sentencing

(Brian is led in to an Official standing with the Arresting Officer behind a desk. The Griffins are present.)

DOG POUND OFFICIAL: Oh-ho, he's cute. Aren't you precious? *(then)* Lethal injection. Next!

BRIAN: What?!

LOIS: Oh, no!

PETER: Oh, you can't do this!

STEWIE: Well, who's up for a little lunch, hmmm? Something festive. Did someone say "Tex-Mex"?

Peter's Clumsy Plea

PETER: Wait! Please, please, I-I gotta say something. Look, all Brian's ever wanted is the same respect he gives us. Well, you know, that and Snausages. He's mental for those Snausages. And, ah, sure, sometimes we have arguments, like when he's asleep on the bed, and Lois is in the ood-may but Brian won't am-scray . . .

Emotion Takes Over

CHRIS: *(weepy)* I stole ten dollars from Meg's room.

MEG: *(weepy)* I stole ten dollars from Mom's purse.

LOIS: *(weepy)* I've been making counterfeit ten-dollar bills for years.

Season Two

Episode

PETER, PETER, CAVIAR EATER

EPISODE NUMBER: 1ACX08
ORIGINAL AIRDATE: 9/23/99
WRITER: Chris Sheridan
DIRECTOR: Jeff Myers
EXECUTIVE PRODUCERS:
Seth MacFarlane,
David Zuckerman
GUEST VOICE: Robin Leach
as himself

SUMMARY

Peter is annoyed to learn that Lois's Aunt Margarite is coming to visit, but when she arrives, she literally drops dead on the Griffins' doorstep. Margarite's lawyer informs Peter and Lois that she left her opulent Newport mansion to Lois in her will, which, of course, thrills Peter. When the Griffins arrive at Margarite's old home (known as Cherrywood Manor) they are treated to a lavish musical welcome by the servants, who then inform the Griffins that the entire staff has been fired. Peter hires them all back, causing Lois to ask how they could ever afford such a thing. Peter sheepishly admits that he sold the Griffins' old house in Quahog.

The family convinces Lois to try living in Newport for a while, but it's not long before Peter is such an embarrassment that he gets thrown out of the Yacht Club. Feeling bad, Peter asks Brian to teach him how to act like a gentleman. At the Newport Historical Society Annual Auction, Peter arrives in a tuxedo and sporting a stilted, hoity-toity accent. And in an attempt to outdo the wealthy crowd, he foolishly bids one hundred million dollars for a vase.

When Peter continues to act like a pretentious boob, Lois declares that she's going to return to Quahog. Brian finally gets Peter to snap out of it, but by then, Mr. Brandywine from the Historical Society has arrived at the house to collect the money for the vase. Peter lamely tries to convince Mr. Brandywine that the house has some historical significance and, therefore, he should take the house in lieu of the debt. But when Mr. Brandywine is unconvinced, Peter is stuck. Peter confesses his failure to Lois, and just as they are about to return to Quahog, he finds some incriminating photos that solve all their financial problems.

A View from Behind the Scenes

"This was our season premiere in our new time slot. On Thursdays. Opposite Friends *and* Survivor. *Good thinking, Fox."*

—SETH MACFARLANE, CREATOR AND EXECUTIVE PRODUCER

MEMORABLE MOMENTS

Patience Is a Virtue, Just Not One Possessed by Stewie

STEWIE: I say, Mother, this hot dog has been on my plate for a full minute and it hasn't yet cut itself.

LOIS: Honey, I'll be right there.

STEWIE: Oh, by all means, take your time. Oh, and when you do finally get around to it, I'll be the one covered in flies with the belly that protrudes halfway to bloody Boston.

The Value of Swearing

PETER: Lois, sometimes it's appropriate to swear.

(Flashback to a Courtroom, where a Bailiff stands facing Peter as he takes an oath.)

BAILIFF: Do you swear to tell the truth, the whole truth, and nothing but the truth, so help you God?

PETER: I do . . . You bastard.

Sibling Fun

(Chris and Meg look upon Aunt Margarite's dead body.)

CHRIS: What if they bury her and she, like, wakes up because she wasn't really dead, she was only sleeping?

MEG: Yeah, that's what happened to our big brother, Jimmy. That's why Mom and Dad adopted you.

CHRIS: What?!

What Urban Legend?

COCO: Jonathan and I just returned from sailing our yacht around the world.

PETER: Oh, oh, funny sailing story. All right, this guy's on his boat in the middle of the ocean, right, and he sees a little black dog. And let me tell you, this dog's been swimmin' for days and he stinks like a dead otter, right?

LOIS: Peter, maybe this isn't the place for . . . uh, okay . . .

PETER: Hey, hey, hang on, Lois, hang on, so the guy takes the dog in to the vet and the freakin' vet tells him—get this—it's not a dog. It's a rat! A big stinkin' Mexican rat! True story.

Not Exactly Upper Crust

PETER: I can't believe they kicked me out of the Yacht Club. I barely had time to stuff Lois's salmon in my jacket.

You Gotta Start Somewhere

PETER: You gotta help me, Brian. Teach me how to be a gentleman.

BRIAN: Well, Peter, it's really not that hard. Ah, let's start with polite conversation. For example, "It's a pleasure to see you again. Lovely weather we're having." Now you try.

PETER: It's a pleasure to see you again. After *Hogan's Heroes*, Bob Crane got his skull crushed in by a friend who videotaped him having rough sex. *(proudly)* How's that?

You Have to Know How to Deal with the Help

STEWIE: Cut my egg.

(The Butler, Carlson, does.)

CARLSON: Your eggs are cut, Sir.

STEWIE: Cut my milk.

CARLSON: I can't, sir, it's liquid.

STEWIE: Imbecile. Freeze it, then cut it, and if you question me again, I'll put you on diaper detail, and I promise I won't make it easy for you.

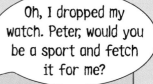

Oh, I dropped my watch. Peter, would you be a sport and fetch it for me?

Scene Stealers
CARTER AND BABS PEWTERSCHMIDT

WHO THEY ARE
Lois's parents

WHERE THEY LIVE
In the exclusive enclave of Newport, Rhode Island

WHAT THEY'RE ALL ABOUT
Money. Money. And more money.

WHAT THEY DO FOR AMUSEMENT
Day trade, set their son-in-law on fire

STUFF THAT MIGHT HAVE SLIPPED BY

■ The front door knobs of Cherrywood Manor are two huge Ps for "Pewterschmidt.

■ Stewie has the muzzle of a gun concealed under Rupert's head.

■ Stewie's encounter with the two creepy twins in the hallway of Cherrywood Manor is a parody of *The Shining*.

■ In the scene of Brian at the Academy Awards, he is seated next to Jack Nicholson.

■ At the Newport Historical Society Auction, the transformed Peter is introduced as "Lord Peter Lowenbrau Griffin, the first."

■ When Peter is trying to fool Mr. Brandywine about the historical significance of Cherrywood Manor, he shows him a mantel where presumably Peter has carved "Jesus was here, 2/15/57 B.C."

■ The photos that Peter discovers to get the Griffins out of their predicament include a photo of Abe Lincoln, standing with a prostitute, wearing nothing but boots and his stovepipe hat over his crotch.

■ After Peter sells the photos to a tabloid, the accompanying headline reads "Lincoln Liked the Whores."

Miracles . . .

SEBASTIAN: Master Brian, do you really believe you can pass him off as a gentleman at the auction?

BRIAN: Well, we've got a long road ahead, but hey, I've worked miracles before.
(Flashback to the Academy Awards, where an Oscar Presenter is on stage, opening an envelope.)

OSCAR PRESENTER: And the Oscar goes to Marisa Tomei.
(Marisa Tomei kisses Brian and walks to the stage. Brian applauds and smiles knowingly at the camera.)

Just Trying to Fit In

SOCIALITE #1: It's a fabulous vase, Peter darling. Do you collect objets d'art?

PETER: Well, if that's French for *Star Wars* collector's glasses, then si.

Faking It

MR. BRANDYWINE: So, you're saying that Jesus carved his name into this mantel fifty-one years before he was born?

PETER: Yeah. He's Jesus. He can do anything. And look over here . . .
(Peter points to a huge hole in the wall. There's plaster on the floor around it.)

PETER: That's where the stock market crashed.

Spoiled Rotten

CHRIS: If I ever go back to Quahog, it'll be just so I can poke poor people with a stick.

Home Sweet Home

LOIS: Peter, you're back! Oh, let's go home.

PETER: We can't. I sold our home. Our beautiful home with the stolen cable and the little man with the penis for the light switch.

Episode
HOLY CRAP

SUMMARY

After Peter's father, Francis, retires from his job at the mill, Peter invites him to come and stay with the family, seeing this as a chance to connect with his dad in a way that he was never able to when he was young. Francis intimidates much of the family with his fiercely religious ways, but Peter persists in his efforts to bond with him. He even tries taking Francis to a baseball game, but midway through Francis takes off to break into the old mill where he used to work.

Peter decides that since his dad loves work so much, the only real way to bond with him may be for them to work together, so he gets his dad a job at the toy factory. However, Francis is immediately promoted above Peter, and when Peter spouts his true feelings to Francis, Francis fires Peter.

Desperate, Peter sees the Pope's visit to the local area as his last chance to connect with his dad. He kidnaps the Pope and brings him to his father, thinking this will finally win his dad over. Instead, Francis insults the Pope. Ultimately, Peter and his dad realize that even though deep down they truly love each other, they just don't really *like* each other that much. But that's okay with them.

A View from Behind the Scenes

"Yeah, you know that whole 'let's move Family Guy *to Thursdays' thing? Not so much."*

—FOX EXECUTIVE

MEMORABLE MOMENTS

Watch Your Tongue

PETER: Hey, listen up, everybody. Your Grandpa Griffin is finally retiring!

MEG: Grandpa Griffin?

CHRIS: Is he that guy who smells like firewood and has those big, gray pussy willows in his ears?

LOIS: Chris, that's a terrible word. Pussy willows.

Is That a Compliment?

FRANCIS: You're a good woman, Lois. Perhaps you won't burn in hell after all. Maybe you'll just go to purgatory, with all the unbaptized babies.

PETER: Hey, there you go, Lois. You love kids.

Scene Stealers
FRANCIS GRIFFIN

OCCUPATION
Retired mill worker, Peter's father, and fervently religious grouch

TURN-OFFS
Indecency, slacking off, and the (mistaken) notion that his grandson is pleasuring himself in the bathroom twice a day

TURN-ONS
Leviticus

WHAT THIS EPISODE TEACHES HIM
Even though you love your kids, it doesn't necessarily mean you will like them

Break up the sewing circle and get back to work!

Rise and Shine . . . and Pray
LOIS: *(stifling a yawn)* That was a lovely service, Francis.
MEG: Super. And only three more hours 'til school.
CHRIS: I didn't even know there was a five A.M. Mass. I didn't even know there was a five A.M. *(to Lois)* What else haven't you told me?

Stewie Finds His Favorite Author
STEWIE: You know, I—I rather like this God fellow. Eh, very theatrical, you know. A pestilence here and a plague there. Omnipotence! Gotta get me some of that, hmm?

Bad Liar
FRANCIS: What's your favorite book of the Bible?
PETER: Uh . . . Uh, uh, the one when Jesus swallows the puzzle piece and the Man in the Big Yellow Hat has to take him to the hospital?

Mixed Signals
MEG: Grandpa, we were just holding hands.
FRANCIS: Well, it'll be easy for him to take your hand when God strikes your sinful heart with leprosy! He can take it right home with him! *(then)* Lord, it's great to see you kids.

Francis Vanishes
LOIS: He just left without saying anything? Where would he go?
PETER: I don't know. I just asked him to buy me some peanuts and crackerjacks.
BRIAN: I don't care if he ever gets back. I wasn't being cute. I really hope he's dead.

Poor Choice of Words
DIANE: Well, Tom, the city of Boston is examining its conscience tonight in preparation for a visit from the Pope.
TOM: That's right, Diane. And I'll tell you what else will be examined: his cock.
(Tom reaches below his desk and produces a Rooster.)

TOM: Yes, the Rhode Island Cock Society will be sponsoring free check-ups for this year's Cock Awareness Week. I don't know why they went with such a suggestive name. They could've just as easily gone with "rooster." Diane?

Peter Shows Off His Workplace

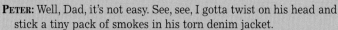

PETER: And this is the nerve center of the whole factory—my station. I assemble our new action figure, Zeke the Moody Drifter.

FRANCIS: You mean to tell me you stand here all day playin' with dolls?

PETER: Well, Dad, it's not easy. See, see, I gotta twist on his head and stick a tiny pack of smokes in his torn denim jacket.

(Peter pushes a button on the Zeke doll. The doll shakes as he takes a drag on his tiny cigarette.)

ZEKE THE MOODY DRIFTER DOLL: Any of you kids want to see a dead body?

Come Again?

FRANCIS: Y'know, something's wrong with your shower. The water's not cold enough. I like me showers colder than a well-digger's curflaughin.

Peter Imagines Himself in Hell

PETER: Wow. Adolf Hitler. Al Capone, John Wilkes Booth! Hey, what are you doin' here?

SUPERMAN: I killed a hooker. She made a crack about me being faster than a speeding bullet, so I ripped her in half like a phone book.

Nice, Real Nice

LOIS: Honey, you're a wonderful husband, a loving father, and, for some reason I'll never understand, a very devoted son.

PETER: That's a nice thought, Lois, but sadly, it means nothing coming from you.

Now That's a Lucky Break

(Peter topples out of the trash chute at the feet of a Priest.)

PRIEST: My heavens, son, are you okay?

PETER: Yeah. I just got bounced by the Pope's road crew.

PRIEST: Well, good thing you missed me. I'm set to drive the Pope Mobile, and any slight bump on the head knocks me unconscious for a few hours. I always wake up feeling fine, but it's just so darned inconvenient to be knocked out that easily. Even by the slightest tap. Like this.

(The Priest raps his knuckles on the side of his head, demonstrating. He smiles, then collapses.)

Get Ready for This . . .

PETER: Hey, guys, remember when we brought in that stripper for Lombardi's birthday, and it turned out to be his son? Well, I think this is gonna top it.

STUFF THAT MIGHT HAVE SLIPPED BY

■ In the flashback to Peter's wedding, Francis has adjusted the signage on the back of their car so that it now reads "Just Married . . . to a Protestant Whore."

■ The sign outside the Quahog Mariner's Banquet Hall reads "Now Free of that Urine Smell."

■ **After Francis is hired at the toy factory, he names Jesus Employee of the Week.**

■ On the golf course, Jesus wears a baseball cap with a cross on it.

■ When the Pope arrives at Logan Airport, he is traveling via Blessed Virgin Airways.

■ Among the crowd waiting to greet the Pope are several nuns holding handmade signs that read "We ♥ U, Pope!"

■ The marquee outside the Pope's hotel reads "Hourly Rates. Welcome Pope."

■ The Pope's "roadies" wear jackets that read "Pope-apalooza."

Episode
DA BOOM

EPISODE NUMBER: 2ACX06

ORIGINAL AIRDATE: 12/26/99

WRITERS: Neil Goldman
& Garrett Donovan

DIRECTOR: Bob Jaques

EXECUTIVE PRODUCERS:
Seth MacFarlane,
David Zuckerman

GUEST VOICES: Victoria Principal
as Pam Ewing, Patrick Duffy
as Bobby Ewing

SUMMARY

On New Year's Eve of the new millennium, Peter receives a dire warning from a man in a chicken suit about the Y2K computer bug and the havoc it will wreak at the stroke of midnight. Terrified, Peter dresses the family in radiation suits and corrals them into the basement for the ringing in of the new year. They are all disgruntled about missing their big plans, but when midnight finally arrives, so does Armageddon.

One week later, the world has only barely begun to recover. Quagmire and Cleveland have been fused together, Joe has melted into his driveway, and the entire town of Quahog is virtually uninhabitable. The Griffins set off in search of food, led by Peter's notion that the Twinkie factory in nearby Natick is the most logical destination. When they finally arrive, they find that the Twinkies have, in fact, survived the nuclear devastation, but just as they are beginning to feel hopeful again, Stewie steps in a puddle of nuclear waste causing his hands to turn into tentacles.

One year later, the town of New Quahog has been established with Peter as its permanent mayor. Of course, Peter has made all the wrong choices, insisting that everyone in town own a gun. Meanwhile, Stewie has become even more octopuslike and is multiplying, laying a large number of eggs everywhere. After Stewie's offspring overrun the town, the Griffins are driven out of New Quahog. And in the show's final minutes, Bobby Ewing reveals that the entire episode was just a dream and that Quahog and the rest of the world were not really destroyed by the Y2K bug after all.

A View from Behind the Scenes

"The title, 'Da Boom,' came from a cheesy FOX promotional campaign that was going on at the time. In Jamaican slang, "da boom" means "the best."

—GARRETT DONOVAN, ONE OF THE WRITERS OF THE EPISODE

MEMORABLE MOMENTS

Why So Gloom and Doom?

CHICKEN MAN: There won't be any other time. The world is gonna end at midnight tonight! Y2K!

PETER: "Y2K?" What are you selling, chicken or sex jelly?

Crying Wolf?

PETER: Ah, forget the party, the world's gonna end. Y2K! I heard it from a chicken man!

CLEVELAND: Oh, Peter, you are the height of just-too-muchery.

PETER: Well, laugh all you want. But when you die, you'll have to go to heaven, and you know what? You know what? I bet you'll run into those two dead bailiff ladies from *Night Court*. And you're not gonna know which one is which, and it's—and it's gonna be really awkward. So bite me.

Come Clean

LOIS: Aren't you a little overdressed?

BRIAN: Oh, well, I, actually, I'm just stopping off at Quagmire's. There's a benefit gala at the Boston Pops tonight, and, well, I'm-I'm trying to nail the flautist.

Wish Lists

PETER: Okay, okay. Hey, uh, you guys, you know that one Christmas present you really wanted but didn't get?

MEG: A phone?

CHRIS: A pony?

BRIAN: A humidor?

STEWIE: A dead Lois?

Just Checking

PETER: Honey, are you pregnant?

LOIS: No. *(Peter shoves her through the basement doorway and down the stairs.)*

LOIS: Aahh!

That's a Little Creepy

BRIAN: Thanks a lot, Peter. Right now I could be in Boston pretending I give a rat's ass about Vivaldi.

MEG: Yeah, and I could be getting felt up by Kevin.

LOIS: Now, Meg, don't you give it all away up front. Make him work for it.

Stop Rubbing It In

PETER: Good morning, family. Hey, Lois, you remember when I was the third Hardy Boy?

LOIS: Peter, there was no third Hardy Boy.

PETER: Oh, really? Just like there was no apocalypse? He shoots he scores!

You Gotta Do What You Gotta Do

TOM: What do you think, Diane? Can I cook, or what?

DIANE: Delicious, Tom. I guess we should be eating her with chopsticks.

BRIAN: Oh, my God! They're eating Asian reporter Tricia Takanawa!

PETER: That's crazy! They're just gonna be hungry again in an hour!

Hard Choices

(Chris struggles to fit a large potted tree into the backseat of the car.)

CHRIS: *(to tree)* Come on, Woody. We're gonna search for food.

PETER: Sorry, Chris, the plant can't come.

LOIS: *(to Peter)* It's his best friend.

PETER: Lois, it'll just be another mouth to feed. *(to Chris)* I'll take care of Woody, son.

(Peter takes the potted tree around the corner of the house. There is a single gunshot.)

Scene Stealers
THE GIANT CHICKEN

OCCUPATION
Peter's periodic nemesis

SOURCE OF THEIR LONG-STANDING FEUD
Once gave Peter an expired coupon

SPECIAL SKILLS
Judo, hand-to-hand combat, laying eggs

A View from
Behind the Scenes

"This episode aired as a holiday special around Christmas at a time when the show had not really been on the schedule. Well, at least with this episode, viewers who hadn't seen the show in a while got a chance to catch a very ordinary and typical Family Guy *episode—one where we destroy the entire town of Quahog. And, oh yeah, the planet, too."*

—SETH MACFARLANE, CREATOR AND EXECUTIVE PRODUCER

CHRIS: What was that?

PETER: Nothing. Let's go.

Obstacles on the Way to Food

HIGHWAY MAN: I am Jorad. I and my band of highway warriors control this territory. Do you have any food?

PETER: Uh, no, that's why we're on the road.

HIGHWAY MAN: Then you may not pass until you answer the following question. Name something you take on a picnic.

GRIFFINS: Chicken! / A blanket! / Merlot. / Potato salad. / A dead Lois.

Probably Not the Best System of Government

BRIAN: Uh, excuse me, Mr. Mayor. We have an "outsider" who wishes to join our community.

PETER: Welcome to my fair city. If you want to become a citizen, you have to get a job.

MAN: Well, before the disaster I was a physician.

CLEVELAND: That's terrific! We need a doctor!

PETER: We sure do. Let's hope you get it. *He pulls out a hat with pieces of paper in it.*

PETER: Now pick a job out of the hat.

(The man picks out a slip of paper and hands it to Peter.)

PETER: Aaah! Village idiot! That's a good one. On Tuesdays, you get to wave your penis at traffic! Congratulations!

You Have to Adapt

LOIS: Honey! Mommy's making you some new feety pajamas.

(She holds up a child's pair of pajamas with eight pairs of feet. She unsnaps a panel in back.)

LOIS: And look! It has a little trapdoor for when you gotta make "inky."

Fire Your Speechwriter

PETER: Attention, New Quahogians. Today, my vision for our future comes true: "A chicken in every pot, and a cap in every ass!"

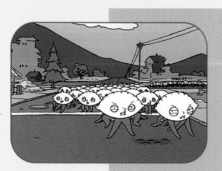

Family Guy Goes Live-Action to Save the World

(Pam Ewing is asleep in bed. She wakes up and notices the sound of the shower. Puzzled, she gets out of bed and tentatively walks toward a bathroom. As she opens the bathroom door, we see Bobby Ewing.)

PAM: Bobby?

BOBBY: Good morning. *(Bobby steps out of the shower.)*

PAM: Oh, Bobby. I just had the weirdest dream. I dreamt I saw the strangest episode of *Family Guy*. And there was a giant chicken . . . and Stewie was an octopus—

BOBBY: Shhh . . . Hey, hey, hey, hey, c'mon now. It's all right. It's going to be okay. *(then)* What's *Family Guy*?

Episode

BRIAN IN LOVE

SUMMARY

When the latest in a string of pee stains appears on the carpet, Peter and Lois suspect that Stewie is to blame and assume he may be ready for potty training. While Peter does some research on the subject and even tries to give Stewie a lesson in using the toilet, Brian tries to cover up the fact that *he* is actually the one who has been having accidents around the house. The family soon learns about Brian's secret, though, when he urinates in the grocery store, forcing him to finally seek help.

When Brian goes to a therapist to get to the root of the problem, the therapist suggests that perhaps Brian is having a midlife crisis. At the therapist's prompting, Brian pursues several exciting, life-affirming activities, which appear to cure him of his troubles. But when Stewie frames Brian for another peeing incident, Brian thinks he's backsliding. He returns to therapy where he ultimately reveals his long-suppressed, romantic feelings toward Lois.

Brian, with all this baggage brought to mind, is now uncomfortable around Lois. Of course, Stewie picks up on this and goes out of his way to get under Brian's skin about it, causing an outburst from Brian, which quickly clues Lois in. Brian and Lois dance around the issue, but ultimately agree that, despite the fondness they feel for each other, their relationship is best left as is.

EPISODE NUMBER: 2ACX01
ORIGINAL AIRDATE: 3/7/00
WRITER: Gary Janetti
DIRECTOR: Jack Dyer
EXECUTIVE PRODUCERS:
Seth MacFarlane,
David Zuckerman
GUEST VOICE: Sam Waterston
as Dr. Kaplan

A View from Behind the Scenes

"This was, technically, our third season premiere, simply because FOX had pulled the show off the air and moved it around so much. The only upside—and I do mean only—to all that time-slot shuffling is that we kept having a premiere party each time the show would come back on the air."

—SETH MACFARLANE, CREATOR
AND EXECUTIVE PRODUCER

MEMORABLE MOMENTS

Super Kinky Phone Sex

CHRIS: So, uh, what are you wearing? Wow, I bet you could see right through that.
LOIS: Chris, who are you talking to?
CHRIS: Grandma.

Registering His Complaint

(Stewie enters carrying Rupert and holding up half a sandwich.)
STEWIE: There you are! What the hell is this?
LOIS: Sweetie, that's tuna salad.
STEWIE: Oh, is that what it is, really? Because I could've sworn it was mayonnaise and cat food.
(He throws the sandwich at her, then fishes in his pocket for two coins.)
STEWIE: Here's fifty cents. Do me a favor, sweetheart, the next time you're out shopping why don't you splurge on a tin of solid white albacore.

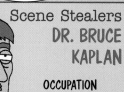

I'd like to pet you. Would that be okay?

Scene Stealers
DR. BRUCE KAPLAN

OCCUPATION
Brian's therapist

SPECIAL TRAINING
Knowledge of canine issues, dealing with upside-down-faced adolescents

HIS OWN SHAMEFUL SECRET
He gouges patients with his exorbitant hourly rate

This next one you can blame on the dog.

Someone Buy That Man a Parenting Book

LOIS: No, it's Stewie. He peed on the carpet.

PETER: *(unsure)* Do I— do I hit him?

The Indignity!

STEWIE: Well! The outrages I have suffered today will not be soon forgotten. I will not be forgetting . . . those outrages, no, no. No they won't be forgotten. Not the out—

BRIAN: Outrages, yeah, I think we got it.

So, That's What Happened

LOIS: Maybe it's time for Stewie to start potty training.

PETER: Geez, isn't he a little young for that? You know what happened to the Lindbergh baby.

(Flashback to the Lindbergh bathroom, where Charles and Anne Lindbergh watch as their very young baby Son is awkwardly perched on a 1920's style toilet.)

ANNE: Charles, he's only six months old.

CHARLES: Honey, would you relax? God, I flew across the Atlantic by myself, I'm a national treasure for God's sake, I think I know how to—

(The baby reaches up and pulls the flush cord. He is immediately sucked down the toilet with a whoosh of water.)

CHARLES: Ahhh! Oh, God! Oh, God!

(He straightens up, collecting himself.)

CHARLES: All right. He was kidnapped. You call the police, I'll write the ransom note.

ANNE: *(whispering)* What about Amelia? She saw everything.

(Reveal Amelia Earhart, standing in her aviator outfit, hand over her mouth, horrified.)

CHARLES: *(darkly)* You leave her to me.

A Bit Defensive?

MEG: Mom! Stewie peed on the rug again!

BRIAN: *(shocked)* No.

(Lois enters.)

LOIS: Oh, this has gotta stop.

MEG: Oh, God, it smells gross!

BRIAN: Well, Princess, I don't see anyone dabbing yours behind their ears.

A Book for All Occasions

(A Bookshop Owner is helping Peter find a book.)

PETER: Yeah, uh, I'm looking for toilet training books.

BOOKSHOP OWNER: Oh, yes. We can help

you there. Uh, *Everybody Poops* is still the standard, of course. Ah, we've also got the less popular *Nobody Poops but You.*

PETER: Huh. Well, see, we're Catholic, so ah . . .

BOOKSHOP OWNER: Oh, then you want *You're a Naughty Child and That's Concentrated Evil Coming Out the Back of You.*

PETER: Perfect!

Potty Training Lesson

PETER: Huh, maybe you don't have to pee. Hey, I oughta just give you some beer, goes right through ya.

STEWIE: Wonderful, and while we're at it we can light up a doobie and watch porn.

Whatever Turns You On

TOM TUCKER: And now part two of our very own Asian correspondent Tricia Takanawa's special report on sex.

(Cut to a middle-class bedroom, where Tricia Takanawa stands with a microphone next to a bed with two people sitting at the foot of it.)

TRICIA TAKANAWA: Tom, I'm standing in the bedroom of Judy and Glenn Isaacs, ten years married and still in love. What's their secret? Judy has an inoperable brain tumor the size of my fist, and that just happens to be Glenn's fetish.

A Glimpse behind the Curtain

(Tom Tucker is in the therapist's waiting room with his upside-down-faced son, Jake, who sits with his arms crossed, looking petulant.)

TOM: Look, I know Stacey isn't your mother, but upside-down face or not, you have to respect her.

Impatient for a Cure

PETER: So what the hell, Brian, you cured yet? 'Cause, you know, I don't wanna have to live in a house with plastic on the furniture, like some Italian family.

Tricia's Report Continues

TRICIA TAKANAWA: Thank you, Diane. Sex. Some people have it anonymously. "What kind of person would do that?" you might ask. Well, I'm about to find out.

(She begins taking off her clothes.)

TRICIA TAKANAWA: I just picked up a complete stranger in a hotel bar and he's in the bathroom right now, possibly doing drugs. Watch as I have sex with this potentially dangerous man as we take you in depth and undercover.

(She gets into bed. Quagmire exits the bathroom in his boxers.)

QUAGMIRE: I've never had a Spanish chick before. Oh . . . lay! end up with some idiot. Serves her right.

STUFF THAT MIGHT HAVE SLIPPED BY

■ At various times during the episode, Brian can be seen reading *Into Thin Air, Memoirs of a Geisha,* and *The Perfect Storm.*

■ One of the candy bars that Peter wants Lois to buy him is called a Middlefingers.

■ At the archaeological dig, Brian digs up a bone, brushes it off, then reburies it.

■ Lois is seen reading *Martha Stewart Living.*

Episode
LOVE THY TROPHY

SUMMARY

When Peter's theme is chosen for the Annual Quahog Harvest Festival Parade, he successfully unites the neighborhood in a float-building effort. But after the gang from Spooner Street ends up winning an award for their float, everyone feels personally entitled to the trophy, causing bitterness all around. Meanwhile, Meg wants to earn money for a new, chic purse and realizes she can get hired at a local pancake restaurant by pretending that she is an unwed teenage mother and that Stewie is her son.

The neighbors agree to build an arch in the middle of Spooner Street where they will display the trophy, but when the trophy goes missing, suspicions run wild. Before long, all the neighbors are at one another's throats. Meanwhile, Meg continues playing up her hard-luck story at work, even embellishing it by claiming

that Stewie is addicted to crack (when, in fact, Stewie has since become addicted to pancakes). An employee of Child Services overhears Meg's tales and comes to the Griffins' house to take Stewie away.

Stewie, now jonesing for pancakes, is placed with a foster family that cares for an ethnically diverse array of children. The neighbors realize how petty they've all been and decide to come together to get Stewie back for the Griffins. As a group, they infiltrate the foster home, but fail in their plan. Ultimately, Meg's Prada purse proves instrumental in securing Stewie's safe return. In the end, we learn that it was actually Brian who stole the trophy, his canine instinct driving him to bury any shiny object he finds.

EPISODE NUMBER: 1ACX13

ORIGINAL AIRDATE: 3/14/00

WRITERS: Mike Barker
& Matt Weitzman

DIRECTOR: Jack Dyer

EXECUTIVE PRODUCERS:
Seth MacFarlane,
David Zuckerman

MEMORABLE MOMENTS

Stop the Presses

DIANE: Good evening, I'm Diane Simmons. A stunning development tonight as O. J. Simpson is proven innocent. We have the identity of the real killer, but first . . .

TOM: It's Fall! The time of year when leaves turn that pretty purply orange and Quahog prepares for its annual Harvest Festival Parade.

Stewie Watches Peter's Clumsy Dancing

STEWIE: Ugh! Clumsy oaf! Michael Flatley must be turning over in his grave. Wait a minute, he's not dead. Yet. *(writing on a pad)* Michael Flatley.

Time to Fire Those Guys

LOIS: Peter, it's great they picked your theme, but isn't it a little esoteric?

PETER: Esoteric?

(Zoom into Peter's brain, where several Executives sit around a large table, looking at the word "esoteric" on a screen.)

EXECUTIVE #1: Could it mean "sexy"?

EXECUTIVE #2: I think it's a science term.

EXECUTIVE #3: Fellas, fellas, esoteric means "delicious."

(Cut back to the Griffins' living room.)

PETER: Lois, *Who's the Boss?* is not a food.

BRIAN: Swing and a miss.

Paternal Instincts

MEG: I have no friends and it's all because of this stupid purse!

(Peter picks up the purse and shakes it violently.)

PETER: What did you do to my daughter?!

(Peter slams the purse up against the wall.)

PETER: Swear to God, if you touched her . . . !

That's Nasty . . .

JOE: Peter, your theme is a dud.

CLEVELAND: Yeah, I've never even seen *Who's the Boss?*

QUAGMIRE: Tuesdays in the eighties? I was always in bed by eight. And home by eleven. Oh!

Now, That's Teamwork

BRIAN: Amazing, Peter. You've inspired the whole neighborhood to work together.

PETER: You know what's really amazing, Brian? I haven't brushed my teeth in three days and no one has said a thing.

Does He Think Before He Speaks?

DIANE: Welcome to the Eighty-third Annual Quahog Harvest Festival Parade! Are you as excited as I am, Tom?

TOM: Are you kidding, Diane? I've got wood.

(Tom pulls out a clipboard.)

TOM: And clipped onto this piece of wood is a list of this year's float entries.

Meg Works It

(An Elderly Couple gets up from their table and the man starts to leave a tip.)

ELDERLY WOMAN: *(to Meg)* What a precious little boy.

MEG: Oh, that's my—son.

ELDERLY WOMAN: Your son? But you're just a baby yourself. *(to husband)* Henry, give the little skank a nice tip.

Scene Stealers
FLAPPY JACK

OCCUPATION
Owner of Flappy Jack's
Pancake House

MOST UNLIKABLE FEATURE
His crusty exterior

MOST LIKABLE FEATURE
His soft interior

HOW HE UNKNOWINGLY SPARES HIS OWN LIFE
Feeds Stewie pancakes, causing Stewie to decide not to kill him

Aw, nuts. I can't send an unwed teenage mother out on the street without a job.

A View from Behind the Scenes

"Prior to this episode, Quagmire had mostly been a guy who spoke in 1950's catchphrases, but in Quagmire's scene with the social worker, writer Danny Smith pitched the exchange of: 'Glenn, honey, I have a question for you. What do you do for a living?' To which Quagmire replies, 'Hey, I have a question for you, too. Why are you still here?' And from that moment forward, we all knew precisely what the character of Quagmire was going to be all about."

—Seth MacFarlane, Creator and Executive Producer

Ironic, No?

Joe: Clear the way! I'm a cop!
(Joe's gun fires. A man groans.)
Joe: Oh! Oh, my God! I thought the safety was on! I'm so sorry.
(Reveal Charlton Heston, holding his chest. A big red stain appears through his fingers.)
Charlton Heston: *(struggling)* That's okay, son. It's your right as an American citizen.
(Heston groans, then falls over, dead, banging his head on the car on the way down.)

Watch Your Mouth

Quagmire: What's all the noise, boys? I was just jerk *(sees the ladies)* —ed out of a sound sleep.

J'Accuse!

Joe: Wait a second! What about Peter? He's the one who wanted the trophy all along.
(They turn on Peter.)
Peter: I couldn't've stolen it. Last night I was stealing Joe's ladder so I could steal the trophy tonight.
Lois: Peter.
Peter: What? It's a ladder. He can't use it. It's like takin' a watch off a dead guy.

A Little ADD, Perhaps?

Lois: And to think they used to be our best friends.
Peter: Well, that was then. And this is now. And this is a chair. And that's a lamp. And you have boobies. And I'm gonna find that trophy!

Quite a Song and Dance

Meg: . . . Being a single mother is hard, but the real challenge is having a baby that's addicted to crack. Right, Stewie?
Stewie: What's that? Oh, yes, yes, I love crack. I'm absolutely cuckoo for crack.

Stewie Is Hooked

Stewie: No, no, I won't. Get that puree of loathsomeness away from me!
Lois: But you love mashed turkey and peas.
Stewie: I'm sorry, what was that? I'm sorry, I didn't quite catch that. Did you just tell me what I love? Hmm? Write this down, you toad-faced frump! I love pancakes!

What About the Stork?

(The family sits in the Child Services waiting room.)

CHRIS: So this is where babies come from?

BRIAN: Yes, Chris. This is where babies come from.

(Chris turns to Lois and points at her accusingly.)

CHRIS: You told me I came out of your vagina!

Stewie Rifles Through His Foster Family's Cabinets

STEWIE: Oh, dammit. I want pancakes! God, do you people understand every language except English? *Yo quiero pancakes! Donnez-moi pancakes! Click click bloody click pancakes!*

Doesn't Play Nice

CHINESE GIRL: Come complete our rainbow!

STEWIE: I've got a better idea. Let's go play "swallow the stuff under the sink."

Turning Them Against One Another

HAJI: Stewie, would you like to learn how to wrap a turban?

STEWIE: Well, why don't you teach it to the Chinese girl? Or perhaps she can learn after her people invade your country.

HAJI: Li, would your people really do this?

STEWIE: Oh, try and stop them. And try and stop Pablo's people from using drug money to buy arms from Li's countrymen, who will in turn sell them to Yuri's people, so that they can ethnically cleanse the rest of this nauseatingly diverse grab bag of genetic party favors you call a family. So now you understand, yes? You all hate each other.

Distraction Completed

CLEVELAND: Hey, where's Quagmire?

LOIS: Yeah, if it wasn't for him we never would've found out where Stewie's foster family lived.

PETER: I think he said he was going to distract that social worker.

(Cut to Quagmire's bedroom, where Quagmire enters in a kimono, holding a martini and the Social Worker is in his big heart-shaped bed.)

SOCIAL WORKER: Glenn, honey, I have a question for you. What do you do for a living?

QUAGMIRE: Hey, I have a question for you, too. Why are you still here?

STUFF THAT MIGHT HAVE SLIPPED BY

■ **In a reference to *The Shining*, the blocks Stewie is playing with spell out "RED RUM."**

■ Brian is reading a magazine called *Bone*.

■ During the Spooner Street construction effort, Quagmire is seen rubbing the giant breasts of the float.

■ A black and white Rod Serling is featured as a reference to the famous *Twilight Zone* episode titled "The Monsters Are Due on Maple Street."

■ When Peter is searching Quagmire's closet, the inside of the closet door is covered with photos of Lois.

■ The sign in front of Child Services reads "Taking Your Children Away for over 50 Years."

■ When the women are spying on the foster home from Cleveland's van, Lois mistakenly calls Bonnie "Debbie."

■ The final gag of the show features Stewie hallucinating an image of himself on the ceiling à la the movie *Trainspotting*.

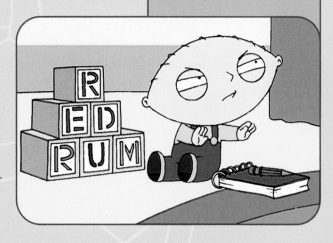

Episode

DEATH IS A BITCH

SUMMARY

During an intimate moment between Peter and Lois, Lois discovers that Peter has a lump in his breast. He goes to the doctor to have some tests done, and in the interim, he prepares for what he assumes will be certain death. Fortunately, Peter is given a clean bill of health, but he is saddled with a huge medical bill. On his insurance forms, Peter writes down that he is deceased, thinking this will get him out of having to pay his bill. But instead, Death himself arrives on the Griffins' doorstep to take Peter away.

Death insists that he has to take Peter with him, but when Peter tries to outrun him, Death sprains his ankle. With Death laid up on the Griffins' couch, it occurs to Lois that as long as Death is incapacitated, he can't kill Peter. Peter revels in his new immunity from death, but when word gets out that the rules of death no longer apply, Death angrily commands Peter to take over for him to show the world otherwise.

Death, convinced that Peter must perform a grand gesture to get the public's attention, orders Peter to kill the entire cast of *Dawson's Creek*. Peter boards a plane carrying all the kids from the show, but can't bring himself to go through with the plan. As Peter tries to save all the passengers, he accidentally kills the pilots, causing Karen Black to save the day by landing the plane. In the end, Death is content with the final body count; the pilots' demise assures the world once again that the rules of death still apply.

EPISODE NUMBER: 1ACX14

ORIGINAL AIRDATE: 3/21/00

WRITER: Ricky Blitt

DIRECTOR:
Michael Dante DiMartino

EXECUTIVE PRODUCERS:
Seth MacFarlane,
David Zuckerman

GUEST VOICE: Norm
MacDonald as Death

MEMORABLE MOMENTS

Anger, Then Denial

LOIS: The important thing is to stay calm. It's probably nothing, honey.
PETER: That's easy for you to say. You get to keep both your cans.
LOIS: Peter, don't talk like that. You'll see a doctor tomorrow and—
PETER: Oh, no, no, I'm not gonna see a doctor, Lois. The healthiest thing we can do is just ignore this and pretend it doesn't exist. Just like we do with the squid.
(Reveal a giant Squid in a corner of the kitchen, who uses one of its tendrils to knock everything off the table. Peter and Lois search for an explanation.)
LOIS: Earthquake?
PETER: Yeah, yeah. Truck going by.

...and Acceptance

LOIS: I'm so worried about your father.
CHRIS: You mean 'cause he's a borderline alcoholic?
LOIS: No, Mommy's made peace with that.

Fantasy Support

MEG: Mom, Debbie Miller's dad had a lump on his breast and he turned out okay.

LOIS: Really? Who's Debbie Miller?

MEG: A girl I just made up.

Parting Is Such Sweet Sorrow

PETER: Oh, look, there they are. My family. You know, guys, I don't say this often enough, but, uh . . . I'm gonna die.

LOIS: Oh, my God!

(Stewie stretches out his palm.)

STEWIE: High five! Anyone? Anyone?

CHRIS: You can't die! Who's gonna take me to the Father-Son Dance?

Peter's Shameful Secret

(Peter lays in a casket.)

PETER: I'll take this one. But I won't pay a cent over sixty bucks.

SALESMAN: Sir, that casket costs a thousand dollars!

PETER: Okay, seventy bucks.

SALESMAN: What?

PETER: Two thousand bucks.

SALESMAN: That's twice what it costs.

PETER: Forty bucks.

SALESMAN: What?!

BRIAN: *(to Salesman)* He—he doesn't know how to haggle.

(The Salesman nods in sad understanding.)

Memories . . .

LOIS: Peter, what's goin' on?

PETER: I'm sellin' all my worldly goods. So you'll have some cash when I'm dead. Yeah, lot of memories here. Look, my first bike. Boy, I had so much fun playing with that.

(Flashback to Peter's childhood backyard, where a young Peter sits on the lawn across from his bike. He pours tea into a teacup.)

YOUNG PETER: More tea, Mr. Bike?

Wrong in More Ways Than One

DOCTOR: As it turns out the lump on your chest was just a fatty corpuscle.

PETER: Fatty corpuscle? Wait a minute. How the hell can a dead comedian from the silent movie era be lodged in my left bosom?

DOCTOR: Mr. Griffin, I'm saying you're fine.

Hey, how old is that TV? You could probably get the DuMont Network on that thing.

Scene Stealers

DEATH

SKILLS
Scaring the crap out of people, scythe work, passive-aggressiveness

MOST OFTEN MISTAKEN FOR
Calista Flockhart

LEAST-KNOWN FACT ABOUT HIM
Still keeps in touch with Stewie via e-mail

PETER: I'm "fine"? What are you, comin' on to me now?

LOIS: Peter, he's not coming on to you. He's trying to tell you that you're healthy.

DOCTOR: Can't it be both?

Way to Spoil the Moment

LOIS: Peter, who cares how much the bill is? You just got the most important bill of all. A clean bill of health.

PETER: Aw, geez, Lois, how long have you been waiting to crack out that gem?

The Paper Trail Resurfaces

PETER: Look, Death, you made a mistake. I'm not really supposed to be dead.

DEATH: I made a mistake, huh? Then what do you call this?

(Death shows them a copy of Peter's insurance form where he wrote "deceased.")

LOIS: Peter, is that your handwriting?

PETER: Hehehe. *(to Death)* Uh, how-how'd you get that?

DEATH: It was e-mailed to me by your HMO.

PETER: Look, I know my doctor was hitting on me, but you don't have to call him names.

Big Fan

LOIS: I don't care what that says, you can't take my husband!

STEWIE: Mother, where are your manners? Don't argue with our guest. Won't you join us for dinner, Death?

That's Pretty Dry

DEATH: Oh, do you mind?

STEWIE: Mind? Of course she wouldn't mind! It would be an honor, no, no, no, no, no, a privilege! I'd . . . That's, oh, dear, listen to me prattling on like a schoolgirl. Come! Come!

(Stewie leads Death to the dining room. He calls over his shoulder to Lois, snapping at her.)

STEWIE: You! Heat up some gravy for our guest. My last helping of white meat was drier than Oscar Wilde.

Didn't Need to Know That

(Death lifts a huge turkey leg and swallows it whole.)

MEG: Oooh, how did you do that?

DEATH: Oh, well, uh, let's just say when I was younger I ah, did some films I'm not . . . particularly proud of.

I Guess This Is Good-bye

PETER: I guess this is good-bye. *(to Meg)* Meg, you're the man of the family now. Be strong.

MEG: Oh, Daddy . . .

(She hugs Peter and starts to cry. Peter kneels down to talk to Stewie.)

PETER: Stewie, I guess I'm not gonna be here to see you become a man.

STEWIE: Yes, I think we all know what that's going to be like.

(Flashforward to a study, where an adult Stewie sits at a desk, paying bills.)

STEWIE: A twenty-minute call to Larchmont? Who do we know in Larchmont?

WOMAN'S VOICE: My sister-in-law.

STEWIE: Oh, right, right, Carol, yes, that's right. *(calling off)* How is Carol?

Ungrateful Patient

LOIS: Here's a couple of Tylenol.

DEATH: Oh, great, Tylenol. Yeah, I asked for Advil but, you know, Tylenol, whatever, that's good.

MEG: I got a B-plus in health. Is there anything I can do?

DEATH: Yeah, why don't you boil some water and rip up some sheets there, Einstein. It's a sprained ankle! I just have to stay off it for a few days.

Silly Skeptics

PETER: I'm gonna jump off this building.

CLEVELAND: Could you repeat that please, Peter? I believe I had something crazy in my ear.

QUAGMIRE: Wait. Hold the phone. You took me away from a Swedish girlie girl and her paralyzed, but trusting, cousin for this?

Hide It, Quick!

STEWIE: Yes, mothers can be quite the botheration, can't they? That's why we've got to get you well!

(Stewie massages Death's foot with more gusto. A piece of Death's foot bone snaps off in his hand.)

DEATH: What was that?

STEWIE: Nothing!

(He quickly hides it behind his back.)

Everyone's Got Problems

LOIS: Stewie, leave Death alone.

DEATH: He's okay. Y'know, he reminds me a lot of me at that age. I just hope his teen years go better than mine. Boy, talk about awkward.

(Flashback to Lover's Lane, where an old car is parked near a lake. It rocks and squeaks as a girl moans.)

DEATH: Oh, Sandy! Oh, Sandy! Oh—

(The girl groans. The car stops rocking.)

STUFF THAT MIGHT HAVE SLIPPED BY

■ On Peter's way to the doctor to have the lump in his breast examined, he encounters a black cat, then a black vulture, then a black man.

■ The cereal on the Griffins' breakfast table is called "Generic Puffs."

■ Lois and Death ironically pass the time by playing the board game Life.

■ Asian Reporter Tricia Takanawa shoots Peter in the head with the Channel Five Pistol.

■ When Death gives Peter his robe to wear, Death is seen wearing a borrowed Providence College sweatshirt.

■ In the credits of the *Hitler* talk show, Hitler is seen with a raccoon on his head, doing a cooking segment, and mugging with a doll of himself.

■ The phone number given at the end of the *Hitler* talk show for tickets is 213–DU WERDEST EINE KRANKENSCHWESTER BRAUCHEN (which translates as "you will need a nurse").

DEATH: Sandy? Oh, not again! I'm gonna be a virgin forever. *(then, slyly)* Or am I?
(The car starts rocking and squeaking again.)

Brainstorming Session

DEATH: You're gonna have to do something that will get everyone's attention. Something huge.

CHRIS: How about if you blow up the Earth?

DEATH: Too huge, but you're thinking. I like that.

MEG: You could kill all the girls who are prettier than me.

DEATH: Well, that would just leave England.

Discovering His Powers

(Peter looks at the plant on the lap of the passenger beside him.)

PETER: Hey, nice plant.

(Peter touches the plant. It wilts immediately and dies.)

PETER: Note to self. Do not go to the bathroom.

Probably Could've Kept That to Yourself

PILOT: *(over P.A.)* We now begin our final approach into Los Angeles International. If you look out the window to your right, you'll see the San Fernando Valley, where my brother Gary makes a very nice living directing porn. We'll be on the ground in ten minutes.

Older Reference, Lost on Younger Viewers . . .

PETER: Hey, hey, I was just trying to save your lives. But now you're all gonna die. There's no one who can land this plane.

(Karen Black steps forward.)

KAREN BLACK: I can!

PETER: Thank God! It's Karen Black!

(The Dawson's Creek *kids just stare blankly.)*

PETER: She landed the busted plane in *Airport 1975!*

(Karen gives Peter a modest wave. The Dawson's Creek *kids just stare blankly.)*

PETER: It was a movie! In the seventies!

(The Dawson's Creek *kids just stare blankly.)*

PETER: Aw, you damn kids, with your music . . .

News Recap

TOM: Both pilots were killed, but fortunately for the other passengers, actress Karen Black, star of such films as *Nashville* and *Five Easy Pieces* was on board.

DIANE: Our hats are off to Ms. Black for proving once again that, given the opportunity, actresses over fifty can land large aircraft.

TOM: Karen Black. What an obscure reference.

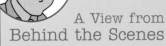

A View from Behind the Scenes

"This episode was originally intended to air as a Halloween episode, but after our air schedule got thrown into chaos, that plan obviously went out the window. The nice thing about that was we realized that the character of Death worked even outside the context of a Halloween show and so we decided to bring him back in future episodes."

—SETH MACFARLANE, CREATOR AND EXECUTIVE PRODUCER

Episode
THE KING IS DEAD

SUMMARY

After the artistic director of the local theater company dies, Lois is asked to take over the position. At the same time, Peter gives his pitch at work for a new toy called Mr. Zucchini Head, but his presentation fails miserably. Battered from having his creative instincts questioned, Peter is encouraged by the family to find another creative outlet, but to Lois's surprise, Peter chooses to do so by auditioning for the very same theater production of *The King and I* that she's directing.

Lois doesn't cast Peter in the play out of fear that he'll ruin it. When he seems hurt by this, she placates him by telling him that he can be the "producer." Peter runs with this new title and quickly begins implementing changes to the sets, dialogue, and even the cast of the show. Finally, Lois has had enough and she resigns.

Meanwhile, Peter begins to alienate the cast with his increasingly ridiculous ideas, even pushing the lead actress, Diane, to quit, too. When he decides to take over the role himself, he ends up contorting the story into something totally unrecognizable. Nevertheless, the audience loves what Peter has created and Peter ultimately redeems himself with Lois, thanking her for the opportunity she gave him to flex his creative muscles.

EPISODE NUMBER: 1ACX15
ORIGINAL AIRDATE: 3/28/00
WRITER: Craig Hoffman
DIRECTOR: Monte Young
EXECUTIVE PRODUCERS:
Seth MacFarlane,
David Zuckerman

MEMORABLE MOMENTS

Life ... So Fleeting

TOM: It was a moving scene today at Hatch Pond as six members of the Pawtucket fire department struggled valiantly to save the life of a fish trapped under the frozen ice. Rescue workers managed to get the fish out of the water, but unfortunately it died shortly after.

A Little Sucking Up Never Hurt

LOIS: All those years of paying my dues as musical director under that old hack have finally paid off.

BRIAN: Oh, Lois, congratulations! Our little theater group finally has a committed visionary at its helm, and such an attractive one—

LOIS: Brian, you'll have to audition just like everyone else.

BRIAN: Oh, God, of course! I-I— Oh, you didn't think I— You thought I was— Aaah! Lois!

CHRIS: I can paint scenery!

MEG: Can I be in the show, Mom?

A View from Behind the Scenes

"This was one of the first times we did a really big fart joke in the series. So, we decided to go all the way with it. The script even describes it as 'the longest fart in television history.' But that's me, I always like to give one hundred ten percent."

—SETH MACFARLANE, CREATOR AND EXECUTIVE PRODUCER

STEWIE: Yes, you can be the dumpy teenager who stays backstage and cries because nobody finds her attractive.

Intellectual Thief

PETER: Eh, ya shoulda heard 'em laughing at me, Lois. I got great ideas, but they look at me and all they see is a loser. Well, except for the guy with the lazy eye. He sees a loser and the snack machine.

LOIS: Peter, a lot of creative people had mindless jobs. Michelangelo worked in a marble quarry. Herman Melville was a customs agent. Albert Einstein worked for the patent office.

(Flashback to a Patent Office, where Albert Einstein is behind a desk, bored, and talking to an Inventor.)

ALBERT EINSTEIN: And what is it you want to patent, Herr Smith?

(The man pulls out a stack of papers.)

MAN: I call it "Smith's Theory of Relativity."

(Einstein looks through the papers, then looks around. He points to something on the papers.)

ALBERT EINSTEIN: Hey, look at this.

MAN: What?

(Einstein reaches up and slams the teller's window down hard on the inventor's head. The man goes limp. Einstein slams the window down a couple more times for good measure, then grabs the papers and runs.)

Okay, Enough with the Brownnosing

LOIS: Brian, that was beautiful! Thank you!

BRIAN: No, no, no, thank you. And-and that note you gave me— "louder?" Huh, I was, I was thinking that and then you said it. You are so intuitive. I, it is, a pleas— it's—

LOIS: Okay, okay, all right, next!

Star Sighting?

(Loretta checks out the cast list.)

LORETTA: Anna? Oh, baby, baby! I'm a star!

(She runs to Cleveland and hugs him.)

CLEVELAND: Wow, I've never hugged a celebrity before. Except for Pearl Bailey at a book signing once. But then we later found out that it wasn't actually her.

Casting Bed

(Peter stares at the list, puzzled.)

PETER: Uh, Lois, I think you made a mistake. I'm not the King. I'm not "I." I'm not anybody. So what, I had sex with you for nothing?

Creative Changes

LOIS: Peter, Chris says you told him to build a set for the North Pole?

PETER: Yeah, that's where Anna goes to talk with her best friend. A penguin.

LOIS: There is no talking penguin in *The King and I*.

PETER: There is in *Peter Griffin Presents "The King and I."*

LOIS: What?!

PETER: Now we just gotta think of some wicked funny stuff for him to say.

Mistaken Identity

(Peter knocks on Diane's door. Diane opens it.)

PETER: Oh, wow, Diane Simmons!

DIANE: You don't look anything like the ad. You better be huge.

Oh, Just Do It Already

DIANE: Our top story tonight: I will be playing the role of Anna in the Quahog Players' production of *The King and I*. Tom?

TOM: Thanks, Diane. In other news, I won't be going to the play because I'm sure it will be lousy.

Was That Really Called For?

PETER: I thought you wanted to do a good show. If you want to do a bad show, why don't we just do *Rent*?

Stands to Reason That Someone Out There Would Defend Him

LOIS: Good morning, Peter, I made your favorite breakfast.
(She drops a plate of burnt toast topped with olives, sardines, and a raw egg.)

PETER: What the hell is this?

LOIS: French toast. I just made a few creative changes to the recipe. I think it's a lot better now.

PETER: Lois, if this is your idea of a joke, you must write for Leno.

STEWIE: Oh, oh, you know, it— it's so fashionable to take a shot at Jay Leno. Look, look, the fact is, the man is out there every bloody night with fresh material and he's charming!

A Glimpse into the Writers' Room?

PETER: Oh, art, schmart. Put enough monkeys in a room with a typewriter, they'll produce Shakespeare.
(Cutaway to a room, where a horde of Monkeys sits around a computer as one Monkey types.)

MONKEY #1: Uh, let's see, a something by any other name . . . Hmm . . .

MONKEY #3: Carnation . . . peony . . .

MONKEY #2: No, they did that in last week's *Marlowe*.

MONKEY #1: Oh.

MONKEY #3: What about—a daisy?

MONKEY #2: Chrysanthemums!

Tom, I'm getting late word that you're a petty, jealous closet-case.

Scene Stealers
TOM TUCKER and DIANE SIMMONS

OCCUPATIONS
Channel 5 News anchors

WHICH OF THEM IS MORE SELF-ABSORBED
That's a photo finish

DOES DIANE HAVE A SECRET CRUSH ON TOM?
Perhaps

DOES TOM HAVE A SECRET CRUSH ON HIS OWN MUSTACHE?
Absolutely

Bit of breaking news . . . We now go live to Diane being a bitch. Diane?

MONKEY #3: Iris? Rose? What about rose?
MONKEY #1: Ro— Did you say "rose"?
MONKEY #3: Yeah, rose.
MONKEY #2: Oh, rose is good.
MONKEY #1: A rose by any other name . . . yeah, that, that works.
MONKEYS: Oh, I like that a lot. / All right! Rose!
MONKEY #1: All right, moving on, moving on!
MONKEY #2: Hey, what about tulip?
MONKEY #1: Rose is fine. Moving on.

Well Put

PETER: Hey, hey, I have more creativity in my whole body than most people do before nine A.M.
LOIS: The only thing you create before nine A.M. is exactly what you've turned my show into.
PETER: I think my work will speak for itself.
  (Peter exits. After a moment, he comes back in.)
PETER: Oh, ha-ha, I just got that. A poop joke? That's real creative, Lois.

Schaden-what Now?

MEG: I don't get it, Mom. If you're so mad at Dad for wrecking your show, why did you come to opening night?
LOIS: I came because I love the theater. I mean, if I just came here to enjoy watching your father be humiliated when this asinine spectacle of his is ridiculed by everyone in town, what kind of person would I be?
CHRIS: A bitch?

Episode

I AM PETER, HEAR ME ROAR

SUMMARY

Peter is excited to receive an offer in the mail for a free boat, even if it means he has to sit through a timeshare presentation to get it. But when he's given the choice between the boat or the contents of a mystery box, he falls for the mystery box scam and ends up with tickets to a comedy club. Upset that he was the only one from Spooner Street to come home from the timeshare presentation without a boat, Peter decides to drown his sorrows at the show. He ends up drunkenly taking the stage and getting laughs from the audience . . . but only because they mistakenly believe he peed his pants. Emboldened by his experience at the club, Peter tells an off-color joke at work, which causes one of his female coworkers to sue him for sexual harassment.

In order to keep his job, Peter is ordered to participate in a workplace sensitivity training class. But when

his case of sexism is even worse than expected, feminist lawyer Gloria Ironbachs requires Peter to attend a women's retreat. Peter doesn't fit in at first, but after his lip is pulled back over his head during a trust exercise in which he experiences a pain similar to that of childbirth, Peter becomes a changed man. When he returns home at the end of the retreat, his demeanor is totally different and very much female.

Peter begins expressing his feminine side, which Lois enjoys for a while. But after his behavior starts to annoy Lois, she asks Cleveland and Quagmire to help turn him back into a man. Their attempts fail, until Peter brings Lois to a charity dinner where Lois and Gloria Ironbachs end up sparring with each other, both verbally and physically. The catfight turns so sexy that Peter snaps out of his feminist trance. Turned on, he drags Lois home where the two of them discover that Peter is clearly back to his normal self.

EPISODE NUMBER: 2ACX02

ORIGINAL AIRDATE: 3/28/00

WRITER: Chris Sheridan

DIRECTOR: Monte Young

EXECUTIVE PRODUCERS:
Seth MacFarlane,
David Zuckerman

GUEST VOICES: Candice Bergen
as Gloria Ironbachs, Faith
Ford as Miss Watson

MEMORABLE MOMENTS

Everyone's Getting a Boat

PETER: Well, at least I'll be the fattest guy on Spooner Street to get a boat.
(*A little bit up the street, Fat Albert holds up a letter in front of his house.*)

FAT ALBERT: Hey, hey, hey. I'm gettin' a boat!

PETER: Aw, man, even Della Reese is gettin' a boat.

Hoodwinked

SALESMAN: Hold on, you have a choice. You can have the boat . . . or the mystery box!
(*He indicates a shoe-box-sized box.*)

LOIS: What, are you crazy? We'll take the boat.

PETER: Not so fast, Lois. A boat's a boat, but the mystery box could be anything! It could even be a boat! You know how much we've wanted one of those.

LOIS: Then let's just—

PETER: We'll take the box.

A Long Tradition

BRIAN: What are you so upset about? I never even knew you liked boats.

PETER: Hey, hey. Boating is in my blood. Ever since my great-grandfather Huck Griffin rafted down the mighty Mississippi.

(Flashback to the Mississippi River, where Huck Finn Griffin and an agitated Jim float down the river on their raft.)

JIM: What did you just call me?

HUCK FINN GRIFFIN: Uh, I-I thought that was your name.

JIM: That is our word! You've got no right usin' it.

HUCK FINN GRIFFIN: Hey, hey, hey, I'm cool. I'm cool. No problem. *(There's an awkward silence.)*

HUCK FINN GRIFFIN: Could you pass me the oar, N-word Jim?

JIM: Thank you.

They Say Comedy Runs in the Family

PETER: Hey, hey, Lois, what do you call a woman who takes forever to cook breakfast?

LOIS: I swear to God, Peter—

PETER: You call her 'Lois.' Hehehehehe.

(Lois rolls her eyes. Stewie laughs.)

STEWIE: Well, the fat man made a funny. I rather enjoyed that. *(then, to Lois)* Yes, yes, yes, you cook very slowly. As a matter of fact, if you were any slower at cooking, you . . . Well, you wouldn't be cooking very fast at all, now, would you? *(to himself)* That one wasn't very good.

Take Another Shot at It

STEWIE: Okay, okay, I've got it, I've got it. If you cooked any more slowly, you wouldn't need an egg timer, you'd need an egg calendar. Oh, that's right. I went there.

You Wouldn't Think You'd Need to Explain It

GLORIA IRONBACHS: Mr. Griffin, I'm Gloria Ironbachs. I represent one of your coworkers, Sarah Bennet. She's suing you and the company for sexual harassment.

PETER: *(trying to place her)* Sarah . . . Sarah . . . I . . . Oh, is she the one we videotaped taking a dump? *(then)* Why, what happened?

> Camille Paglia and I are gonna whip it out and see whose is bigger.

Scene Stealers
GLORIA IRONBACHS

OCCUPATION

Feminist attorney and all-around tight-ass

HOBBIES

Consciousness-raising, studying world "her-story," snowboarding

MOST PRIZED POSSESSION

Charred remains of her 1973 Cross-Your-Heart bra

A View from Behind the Scenes

"You may notice that the original airdate of this episode is the same as the original airdate of 'The King Is Dead,' something network executives call 'double pumping' a show, meaning to air two new episodes in a row. The truth is, 'double pumping' is just a nice way of saying, 'This show is all but cancelled, so we might as well air all these episodes we paid for and, while we're at it, let's blow through them as quickly as we can so we can rush Temptation Island 8 *onto the air.' So, needless to say, we all kinda thought we were in trouble at this point. And we were pretty much right."*

—SETH MACFARLANE, CREATOR AND EXECUTIVE PRODUCER

See, This Is Just What I'm Talking About . . .

GLORIA IRONBACHS: Sexual harassment is a very serious charge, Mr. Griffin.

PETER: Well, look. First of all, if I can speak in my own defense, all I did was tell a little joke. Second of all, women are not people. They are devices built by the Lord Jesus Christ for our entertainment.

Time to Update the Materials

MR. WEED: Ms. Ironbachs, I assure you this company in no way condones Peter's conduct. In fact, a film on employee relations has been a mandatory part of our personnel training for fifty years.

(Cut to a scratchy, black-and-white film of a 1950's office. A title card reads "Women in the Workplace." In a 1950's office, a row of Women are typing as a Narrator strolls into frame.)

NARRATOR: Irrational and emotionally fragile by nature, female coworkers are a peculiar animal. They are very insecure about their appearance. Be sure to tell them how good they look every day. Even if they're homely and unkempt.

(He turns to a homely, unkempt woman.)

NARRATOR: You're doing a great job, Muriel, and you're prettier than Mamie Van Doren.

(She smiles.)

NARRATOR: And remember, nothing says "good job" like a firm, open-palm slap on the behind.

(The Narrator walks past Another Gal and slaps her behind. She smiles and puts her hand to her mouth, blushing with pride.)

It's a Step in the Right Direction

MISS WATSON: Hello, ladies, I'm Miss Watson, director of the Retreat. I'd like to welcome Peter Griffin who's here to get in touch with his feminine side.

(The women applaud politely.)

MISS WATSON: This world would be a far better place if there were more men like him.

(The women murmur in agreement.)

PETER: Okay, okay, so here's what I'm thinkin'. I'll be Charlie and you can all be my angels.

(He turns to an Unattractive Woman.)

PETER: Except you. You be Bosley.

Almost There . . .

MISS WATSON: Lizzie, I know you feel alone and unattractive since your husband left you, but you are a beautiful person, and I am here for you. *(to class)* Notice I'm making physical contact with her in order to establish a connection.

PETER: I think you'd make even more of a connection if you hugged her, too.

MISS WATSON: Very good, Peter, that's true.
(Miss Watson hugs Lizzie.)
PETER: That's it. Now rub her back.
(Miss Watson rubs Lizzie's back.)
PETER: Okay, that's good. Yeah, yeah, comfort her. *(getting into it)* Yeah, oh-oh, you like that, don't you? Yeah, no it's-it's okay, it's okay to like it. It's very natural. Okay, good, good, now smell her a little.

Peter's a Chick

(Quagmire answers his phone.)
QUAGMIRE: Yello?
(Peter's on the other end, in a bubble bath, twirling his hair as he talks on a cordless phone.)
PETER: Hey, Quagmire.
QUAGMIRE: Hey, Peter, what's up?
PETER: Not much. *(There is silence.)*
QUAGMIRE: Well, whattya want?
PETER: Nothing. I'm just callin' to talk. Watcha thinkin' about?
QUAGMIRE: Whattya mean, "What am I thinkin' about?" You called me.
PETER: I just wanted to say "Hi." So what're you—
(Quagmire hangs up.)

Someone Needs a Biology Lesson

PETER: Lois, what— what day is it?
LOIS: Thursday.
PETER: Oh, my God. Oh, my God! I'm late!
LOIS: If you spent less time fixing your hair—
PETER: No, Lois. I'm late late. Do we still have that pregnancy test?
(He starts rifling through the medicine cabinet.)
LOIS: Are you insane? You can't have a baby.
PETER: Well, I don't have a lot of options. I'm Catholic. God, I thought you'd be happy.

Guessing Games

STEWIE: Oh, Mother, I come bearing a gift. I'll give you a hint. It's in my diaper and it's not a toaster.

Locked and Loaded

LOIS: Well, as you may have noticed, Peter's been acting a little . . . different lately. It was refreshing at first, but now—well, he doesn't even treat me like a woman anymore.
QUAGMIRE: Ah-hah! I know where this is going, Lois. And I'm already semi-there. Oh!

Episode
IF I'M DYIN', I'M LYIN'

SUMMARY

After Chris brings home a less-than-impressive report card, Lois forbids him to watch TV. Peter, who cannot go a week without seeing his and Chris's favorite TV show, *Gumbel 2 Gumbel*, lies to Lois, telling her that he's helped Chris with all his homework so they should be able to watch their program together. But when Peter and Chris finally tune in, they discover that the show's been cancelled. Peter takes Chris to the local TV station to complain, but gets nowhere. That's when Peter gets the idea to tell The Grant-A-Dream Foundation that Chris is dying so they'll intervene and get the show back on the air.

The Grant-A-Dream Foundation makes Chris's dream come true, but when word gets out about his "disease," a candlelight vigil forms outside the Griffins' house. Peter, wanting to avoid trouble with The Grant-A-Dream Foundation, lies yet again, saying that Chris is all better now because he cured Chris with his divine powers. But just when Peter thinks he's cleared away all his problems, a group of worshippers arrives at the house in awe of Peter's powers.

Peter is nervous at first about all the new followers who have showed up on his doorstep, but he quickly realizes that he can put them to use doing chores around the house. He soon becomes so caught up in having a doting group of disciples that he begins ignoring Chris and, ultimately, committing various acts of sacrilege. The family is then afflicted with a variety of plagues by an apparently upset God. When Chris is nearly struck down by all the chaos, Peter finally confesses to his followers that he is a fraud.

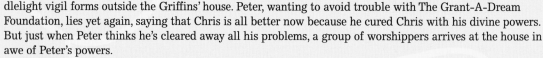

EPISODE NUMBER: 1ACX12

ORIGINAL AIRDATE: 4/4/00

WRITER: Chris Sheridan

DIRECTOR: Swinton Scott III

EXECUTIVE PRODUCERS:
Seth MacFarlane,
David Zuckerman

GUEST VOICE: Martin Mull
as Mr. Harris

MEMORABLE MOMENTS

Gone, but Not Forgotten

PETER: Don't worry, I'll talk to her. After I get a little bit of courage from my old friend, Mr. Jack Daniels.
(*Peter reaches past a bottle of Jack Daniels to the phone. He dials it.*)

PETER: (*into phone*) Mrs. Daniels? Mrs. Daniels? Is Jack in? (*then*) Oh, my God, when? (*then*) Ah, I am so sorry.
(*Peter hangs up the phone.*)

PETER: Poor old Jack. He was a wise man, but he just loved playing with that wheat thresher.

Bath Time

PETER: Hey, Stewie, I see your bum!

STEWIE: Oh, take a good look, fat man. And while you're at it, take a picture so I'll have something to bring to court, you wretched, filthy pervert.

You May Have Said Too Much

PETER: Hey, Lois, give Chris a break. I mean, no TV? So he failed a class. It's not like he felt up his cousin in the garage that Thanksgiving when I was nineteen.

Wouldn't Put It Past Them

LOIS: Peter, I want you to help Chris. Kids do better when parents take an interest in their schoolwork. I saw that on a two-part report on *Dateline Tuesday* and *Dateline Katilsday*.
PETER: What the hell is Katilsday?
LOIS: Oh, NBC invented a new day so they could add another Dateline.

Peter, the Sensitive One

PETER: But the Gumbel show is sacred to us. Bryant and Greg have the kind of father-son relationship I want me and Chris to have someday.
LOIS: Peter, Bryant and Greg Gumbel are brothers.
PETER: Oh, nice, Lois. So just 'cause they're black, we can't learn anything from them?

Cancelled

DIANE: Tom has dared me to do the news topless. I've got the goods, but have I got the guts? Find out at eleven.
TOM: And if you're settling in to watch *Gumbel 2 Gumbel*, you're out of luck. That show has been cancelled. The full story, and maybe Diane's boobs, tonight at eleven.

A Likely Story . . .

PETER: I'm tellin' ya, Chris is dying ten times worse than those other kids. He's got a very rare disease called, duh, duh, Tumor-syphillis . . . itis . . . o-osis.
MR. HARRIS: Mmm. Sounds sexy. What are the symptoms?
PETER: What are the symptoms? Take a look.
(Peter reaches over and lifts up Chris's shirt, revealing a dozen pepperoni slices scattered about Chris's chest.)
PETER: He's growing nipples all over his body.
MR. HARRIS: They look like pepperonis.
PETER: Who do you think you are? My son happens to be very sensitive about his extra nipples.
(Peter reaches over and grabs one of the "nipples.")
PETER: See, look, they're coming right off.
(Peter eats it and reaches for another.)
PETER: Nipples shouldn't just come off like that.

> I just came by to see if your son has taken a media-friendly turn for the worse.

Scene Stealers
MR. HARRIS

OCCUPATION
Chairman of The Grant-A-Dream Foundation

WHAT HE'S LOOKING FOR
Sick children with showy last wishes (telegenic children only, please)

SIGNS OF HIS WELL CONNECTEDNESS
He has the President of Television on speed-dial

I say, Mother. You have your work cut out for you now, don't you?

Now You Might Be Pushing It

MR. HARRIS: Mr. Griffin, I'm sorry we had to meet under these circumstances.

PETER: Are you kidding? I may see you again. I got two more kids at home and I've always wanted to see some new episodes of *Star Trek*.

Stewie Hates Bath Time

(Peter is washing the car. Stewie, stark naked, runs out of the house with Lois in hot pursuit.)

LOIS: Stewie, it's bath time. You're filthy again!

STEWIE: I'll show you filthy!

(He dives in the dirt.)

STEWIE: Mmm, yes, look at me, I'm a dirty, foul little boy. I'm a nasty, squalid little hobo!

(He stands up, covered in mud.)

STEWIE: I say, Mother. You have your work cut out for you now, don't you?

LOIS: Okay, you want to be dirty? Be dirty.

(She reenters the house.)

STEWIE: Where do you think you're going! I've defiled myself! I need to be cleaned! Ahh!

(Peter sprays Stewie with the garden hose.)

PETER: There you go, kiddo. All clean.

STEWIE: Blast! I'm frozen! I'm hypothermic. *(he looks down)* Bloody hell, I'm a woman!

Peter Takes Charge

PETER: I'll handle it, Lois. I read a book about this sort of thing once.

BRIAN: Are you sure it was a book? Are you sure it wasn't . . . nothing?

Would You Like Fries with the Sacrilege?

LOIS: Peter, these people are worshipping you. Don't you think there's someone who might resent that? A being who's all-knowing and all-powerful?

PETER: Well, someone's got a pretty high opinion of herself.

LOIS: Not me, Peter. God. The real God.

PETER: What's the big deal? So I told a little fib and now people think I'm God. I mean, when did God ever say He didn't want someone else being worshipped like Him?

LOIS: It's one of the Ten Commandments.

PETER: Oh, come on, Lois. Those were written like, two hundred years ago.

That's Nature for You

LOIS: Meg, what's wrong!

MEG: I was giving Stewie a bath and . . . and . . .

PETER: Trust me, Meg, at his age it's strictly involuntary.

A View from Behind the Scenes

"Many people have asked where the idea for Gumbel 2 Gumbel *came from. The truth is that was the show I pitched to FOX before I pitched them* Family Guy. *Thank God they were all drunk through that first meeting and have no recollection of it."*

—SETH MACFARLANE, CREATOR AND EXECUTIVE PRODUCER

■ Peter's note about Craig T. Nelson is altered by the Wite-Out he spills on it such that it changes from reading "If you don't put *Coach* back on the air I'll be really upset. The skillful acting of Craig T. Nelson will be missed a lot. Signed, Peter Griffin" to "If you don't put *Coach* back on the air, I'll kill Craig T. Nelson. Signed, Peter Griffin."

■ The Channel 5 station manager shares a name with *Family Guy* writer Steve Callaghan.

■ The celebrities in *Hollywood Squares* include LL Cool J, Suzanne Somers, Charlie Sheen, Scott Bakula, Whoopi Goldberg, Dennis Rodman, Betty White, and Fran Drescher.

■ The sign outside the NBC studios reads "We used to have *Seinfeld*, remember?"

■ The TV executive beats the other TV executive with a *Just Shoot Me* poster.

Peter Gives Up

PETER: Stop it, stop it! Stop worshipping me! I'm just a big fake! Like, like the moon landing! And Marky Mark's hog in *Boogie Nights*! And Tom Cruise and Nicole Kidman! Oh, I don't mean that completely untrue gay rumor, they're just both really phony!

As Chris Lies Dying . . .

CHRIS: Hey, Dad, you think they got *Gumbel 2 Gumbel* in Heaven?

PETER: Yes, son. And there's no reruns or commercials, and Kirstie Alley is still hot, and all those scrambled channels come in clear as a bell!

The Old One Got Promoted

(God sits behind his desk. An Angel, in a suit with wings, enters.)

ANGEL: Sir, we think the Griffin guy gets it.

GOD: Good, good. *(pushes button on his intercom)* Peggy, turn off the plagues please.

PEGGY: Yes, sir, Mr. Patterson.

GOD: *(to Angel)* She's-she's new.

Episode
RUNNING MATES

EPISODE NUMBER: 1ACX09
ORIGINAL AIRDATE: 4/11/00
WRITERS: Garrett Donovan
& Neil Goldman
DIRECTOR: John Holmquist
EXECUTIVE PRODUCERS:
Seth MacFarlane,
David Zuckerman
GUEST VOICE: Lee Majors
as himself

SUMMARY

Lois's campaign for school board president is interrupted by a call from Chris's principal—apparently Chris was caught peeking into the girls' locker room. While Peter and Lois are at the school talking to the principal, Peter runs into his favorite teacher from the past, Mr. Fargus, who has

been reduced from his former peppy (almost loony) self to a catatonic old man due to pills he has been required to take by the school board. Peter tells Mr. Fargus to stop taking the pills, which quickly causes Mr. Fargus to go off the edge and subsequently get fired. Furious about all of this, Peter decides to run for school board president, too, so that he can reinstate Mr. Fargus to his old position.

Peter mounts a campaign against Lois that shows some promise, but at a debate between them, Lois trounces Peter. Desperate to win, Peter airs a political ad, using a sexy picture of Lois (which Lois gave to Peter for their anniversary) to discredit her. Lois is horrified.

She's especially furious when Peter actually wins the school board presidency and then doesn't seem to take his new position very seriously. To calm her down, Peter tells Lois he's going to show her all the great changes he has in store, but, of course, all of his proposed "improvements" are ridiculous. During a TV interview it's revealed that the kids at Peter's school are reading pornography and, even worse, that Peter supplied it. This causes a huge scandal for Peter, who is advised to pin the whole thing on Lois. In the end, he can't bring himself to do that. In fact, he finds himself apologizing to her for his horrible behavior.

A View from Behind the Scenes

"This episode introduced Asian reporter Tricia Takanawa . . . and we all know what happened next."

—SETH MACFARLANE, CREATOR AND EXECUTIVE PRODUCER

MEMORABLE MOMENTS

After All, He's Still a Baby

STEWIE: I say, Rupert. These crumpets you've prepared look positively divine.
(Stewie grabs a clump of dirt and puts it in his mouth.)
STEWIE: Mmm-mmm. Excellent texture, provocative sapor. Mm, try another, you say? Well, aren't I the wicked one?

Not So Active Listening

PETER: Hey, Lois, what's with the sign?
LOIS: Peter, we discussed this, I'm running for school board. You never listen to me.
PETER: Oh, yeah, I remember. Hey, Cleveland, hey Quagmire. *(then)* Hey, Lois, what's with the sign?

Now, That's Not Helping

LOIS: We'll continue this discussion tonight, young man. A woman is not an object.

PETER: Your mother's right, son. Listen to what it says.

Now, That's Not Helping, Part 2

LOIS: I'm sorry, but I do have a mind of my own, and I happen to agree with the school board's decision.

PETER: Yeah, yeah, I know, you're a feminist, and I think that's adorable, but this is grown-up time, and I'm the man.

A Little Canine Advice

BRIAN: Peter, are you sure running against Lois is such a good idea? You know how competitive you get.

PETER: Hey, hey, I can be just as noncompetitive as anybody. Matter of fact, I'm the most noncompetitive! So I win.

That's Gonna Be Hard to Top

(Brian reads the paper. Stewie enters.)

STEWIE: Look where my hand is. It's in a very naughty place.

(Brian lowers his paper to see Stewie smiling before him, picking his nose with one hand and waving with the other.)

STEWIE: Does this not disgust you?

BRIAN: Kid, you're talkin' to a guy who uses his tongue for toilet paper.

Hitting a Little Close to Home?

BRIAN: What's the matter, miss your mommy?

STEWIE: Oh, yes, yes, that's it. Yes, yes, yes, that's quite good. Yes, I miss my mummy. Yes, yes, I also miss colic and rectal thermometry.

Think Fast

TOM TUCKER: Mr. Griffin, your opening statement, please?

PETER: Uh, okay. Uh, I'm Peter Griffin. Vote for me.

(There is an awkward pause. The crowd looks at him expectantly.)

TOM TUCKER: Is that it?

PETER: Uh, no. Uh, this is it. This is life, the one you get, so go and have a ball. Because the world don't move to the beat of just one drum, what might be right for you may not be right for some. You take the good, you take the bad, you take 'em both and there you have . . . my opening statement. Sit, Ubu, sit. Good dog.

Busted

DIANE: Mr. Griffin, your response? Maybe something about education?

PETER: Well, I-I have always cared deeply about young people. As a rich college-bound student, I once joined some underprivileged youths in saving a community center from being converted into a shopping mall.

(The crowd cheers.)

Well, no wonder this clown died. His lungs are filled with . . . candy!

Scene Stealers
RANDALL FARGUS

OCCUPATION
Borderline-insane middle school science teacher

WHY PETER LOVES HIM
Because he found a way to make dissecting a clown fun

THE INFLUENCE OF PETER'S ACTIONS ON HIM
Gets fired, ultimately reinstated, then shot with lasers by a menacing, robotic Hall Monitor

TONIGHT:
GRIFFIN DEBATE

TOMORROW:
PROCRASTINATORS' CONVENTION
POSTPONED

STUFF THAT MIGHT HAVE SLIPPED BY

■ Mr. Fargus's medication has a label that reads "Take One Bottle Daily."

■ In *The Six Million Dollar Man* cutaway, Peter has a metal trash can for one leg and a plunger for the other. One of his arms is a rake, and he has a magnifying glass taped in front of one eye.

■ When Stewie tries to get Brian's attention by writing "profanity" on the wall, he has actually written the word "poppycock."

■ During Peter's campaign, his car is decked out with signage that reads "Vote for Peter—Together We Can Beat My Wife."

■ During Stewie's song, he fondly looks at pictures from his baby album that include Stewie suspended from a cord as he aims a rifle at Lois, Stewie pouring a vial of something into Lois's drink as she turns away to reach for the mashed potatoes, Stewie poised over a sleeping Lois with a pillow near her face, and Lois showering as Stewie's silhouette approaches with a comically large knife.

■ The graphic over Tom Tucker's shoulder as he reports on Lois's seductive photo reads "Erection Day."

■ After being elected school board president, Peter changes the name of Chris's school from Buddy Cianci Junior High School to Peter Griffin Junior High School.

LOIS: Peter, that wasn't you, that was Adolpho Shabba-doo in *Breakin' 2: Electric Boogaloo*. You watched it last night.

Media Frenzy

TOM TUCKER: "Lewd," "obscene," and "a little blurry." Just some of the words used to describe Lois Griffin's prurient pic.

Now, That's Not Helping, Part 3

PETER: Hey, Lois. I gotta joke for you. How many losers does it take to make me breakfast? Just one: you. Hehehe. I'm, I'm just, I'm kidding, but french toast, please.

Peter Shows Off His Changes to the Schools

PETER: And, I've restocked our school library with books of some of our greatest movies and TV shows. Because if we don't teach our kids to read, how will they ever know what's on?

A Calming Force

CLEVELAND: Oh, there's quite a crowd outside. I haven't witnessed pandemonium like this since "Ridiculous Day" down at the deli. When prices were so low they were ridiculous.

You Find Something You Love . . .

PETER: Lois, I could lose my presidency.
LOIS: Too bad, I've already lost more than that.
PETER: Not my rainbow socks with the individual toes?
LOIS: No. I've lost my respect for you.
PETER: Oh. 'Cause I need those socks.

You Never Know

CHRIS: Are you and Dad gonna get a divorce?
LOIS: *(laughs)* Oh, honey. *(then)* Maybe.

They Always Know Just How to Wrap Things Up

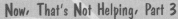

DIANE: And so ends a dark and shameful chapter in the history of Quahog, Rhode Island. One which leaves this reporter asking how much moral bankruptcy and perversion must we, the people, endure?
TOM: Next up, stay tuned for our special investigative report on the clitoris, nature's Rubik's Cube.

Episode

A PICTURE'S WORTH A THOUSAND BUCKS

SUMMARY

The gang from the neighborhood gathers at Bob's Funland and Putt-Putt Golf for a surprise birthday party for Peter. When Peter realizes that the owner of the place, Bob Funland, is an old high school classmate

EPISODE NUMBER: 2ACX07

ORIGINAL AIRDATE: 4/18/00

WRITER: Craig Hoffman

DIRECTOR: Gavin Dell

EXECUTIVE PRODUCERS: Seth MacFarlane, David Zuckerman

GUEST VOICES: Candice Bergen as Murphy Brown, Faith Ford as Corky, Charles Kimbrough as Jim, and Joe Regalbuto as Frank

of his, Peter can't help but make comparisons and soon becomes depressed about the lack of a legacy he has achieved up to this point in his life. Chris's birthday gift to Peter is a beautiful painting he created, but Peter fails to recognize Chris's talent and uses it to cover a broken window on his car. When a famous New York art dealer, Antonio Monatti, sees the painting, he offers to bring the Griffins to New York in order to help develop Chris's talent as an artist. Peter is excited by the chance to finally have a legacy, even if it means living vicariously through his son.

The Griffins arrive in New York and Peter quickly shows his boorish side to Antonio Monatti. Meanwhile, Antonio begins to completely make over Chris's image, with a new haircut and even a new name: Christobel. When Antonio tells Chris that his only hope of succeeding as an artist is to separate himself from his family (especially his father), Chris reluctantly goes along with the plan. Peter is upset by the fact that Chris has cut ties with him, but is only bothered long enough to stumble upon the idea that perhaps he can carve out a legacy for himself by tapping into Meg's potential skills.

Peter searches for any sign of talent in Meg and only comes up with her ability to do bird calls. When this proves insufficient, Lois tricks Peter into attending Chris's big art exhibit, where it is revealed that (against the wishes of Antonio) Chris has patterned all of his work in the likeness of Peter. Antonio is upset, but Peter is moved and realizes that even though he doesn't have his name on an amusement park and that he may never be famous, he's got three wonderful children and a wife who love him.

MEMORABLE MOMENTS

Phoning It In

(Stewie looks at a cheap stuffed Clown, hanging with the other prizes at a shooting gallery.)

STEWIE: How deliciously evil-looking. It's like something out of Stephen King.

(Cutaway to a book editor's office, where Stephen King sits opposite his Editor.)

STEPHEN KING: Okay, for my three hundred and seventh book, ah, this couple is attacked by a . . . a . . .

(He looks around and grabs the lamp off the desk and waves it around, making a scary face.)

STEPHEN KING: A lampmonster! Ooooooooh!

EDITOR: You're not even trying anymore, are you? *(then)* When can I have it?

Résumé Inflation

PETER: Wow, uh, you own this whole place?

BOB FUNLAND: That's right. This place is my legacy. So what have you done with your life, you jerk?

PETER: Umm, uh, uh, I'm Neptune, God of the Sea! I sink ships and conjure up storms.

(Neptune, carrying a trident, steps over to Peter.)

NEPTUNE: No, you're not. I am. And you know nothing of my work.

(Peter stands there uncomfortably.)

Now You're Just Grasping

PETER: Look at this, Lois. See, right here. I was voted "Most Likely to Succeed."

LOIS: Peter, that's not you. That's not even a yearbook. That's a *People* magazine.

PETER: Oh. Well, I wondered why they had the wrong picture and name.

I Believe That's a Felony

LOIS: Can't we just enjoy the rest of your birthday?

(She opens a card.)

LOIS: Look, it says "Happy Birthday, Daddy. Love, Stewie."

STEWIE: Let, let, let me see that! Did you forge my name? Oh, is that backward S supposed to be cute? Oh, I'm going to crap double for you tonight!

Eye of the Beholder

CHRIS: Don't be depressed, Dad. Here, I made you a present!

(Peter unwraps it. It's a very modern, expressionistic painting.)

BRIAN: My God. It's . . . good. Really good.

CHRIS: It's partly an expression of my teenage angst, but mostly it's a moo-cow.

So, That's Where They All End Up

PETER: I'd sell my soul to be famous.

(Cutaway to the fiery bowels of Hell, where Satan sits at a desk. An Assistant Devil is at a computer. Lost Souls are working in the fire pits.)

SATAN: Ohh, I got a live one! Peter Griffin.

(The Assistant checks the computer.)

ASSISTANT DEVIL: Oooh, sorry, chief. Seems he already sold his soul in 1976 for Bee Gees tickets. Oh, and again in 1981 for half a Mallomar.

SATAN: Aw, heck! Where's a lawyer when I need one?

(Everyone in the pit drops his pitchfork and raises his hand.)

Not a Nice Man

PETER: Lois, our son has been blessed with a great gift. I'm going to do everything I can to nurture that talent and help him succeed. And then I'm gonna use him to live out all my frustrated hopes and dreams. Because that's good parenting. Right, Bing Crosby?

(Bing Crosby enters.)

BING CROSBY: That's right, Peter. And if your kids give you any lip, you can beat them with a sack of sweet Valencia oranges. They won't leave a bruise and they'll let 'em know who's boss. There's noooo doubt about it.

The Griffins Arrive in the Big Apple

(The Griffins ride in a cab. A voice comes over the car's speaker.)

VOICE ON CAR SPEAKER: Hi, this is David Leisure. You probably remember me as the neighbor from TV's *Empty Nest.* No? Well, how about those car commercials when I was Joe Isuzu. The-the guy who lied? Oh, c'mon, those were really popular. Look, they ran all the time. Geez, all right, just buckle up. *(then)* Can I get my check now?

LOIS: Oh, kids, look at that man over there, grabbing his own crotch. Ah, so alive, this city!

The Usual, Sir?

BELLMAN: Welcome to the Big Apple, fella.

(Stewie palms a five-dollar bill and hands it to him.)

STEWIE: Well, just make sure there's a copy of *The Wall Street Journal* next to the changing table. And send a masseuse up. *(pointedly)* Legitimate.

Everyone Has to Start Somewhere

BRIAN: Mapplethorpe? I thought he just did photography.

CURATOR: Oh, no, early on he did caricatures.

(Cutaway to a beach boardwalk, where Robert Mapplethorpe sits at an easel drawing a guy named Tim who sits on a stool, posing for a caricature.)

MAPPLETHORPE: Uh, okay, Tim, uh, who's your favorite sports star?

TIM: Uh, Reggie Jackson.

MAPPLETHORPE: Okay, well, I'm gonna draw him pooping on your chest. What number is he?

> Now, if you'll excuse me, I have to go oil up and start squeezing into my leather pants.

Scene Stealers
ANTONIO MONATTI

OCCUPATION
Art dealer and bohemian snob

WHAT HE LOVES ABOUT LIVING IN NEW YORK
The art scene; the nightlife; the perfect blend of disposable income and a yearning to "out-chic" the Joneses that allows him to sell artwork of marginal quality at outrageous prices

FAVORITE STYLES OF ART
Whatever is selling that day

Everyone Has to Start Somewhere, Part 2

BRIAN: Peter, creating art takes a lot of training and technique. All the great artists I knew took classes.

PETER: Even Walt Disney?

(Cutaway to an art class, where a young Walt Disney is at an easel, drawing Minnie Mouse. On a nearby stool, Minnie Mouse poses. Tearfully, she starts to lower her top, then stops.)

MINNIE MOUSE: Do I— do-do I have to?

WALT DISNEY: You want to be a star, don'tcha? Then take it off!

(Minnie nods while she sobs and lowers her polka-dotted dress. Walt grins evilly and begins sketching furiously.)

WALT DISNEY: Yeah. Yeah, yeah, that's nice.

You Found the Level of the Room

ANTONIO MONATTI: I promise you, if you leave him in my hands, the name Griffin will be as well known as Kandinsky.

PETER: Who?

ANTONIO MONATTI: Rembrandt?

PETER: Who?

ANTONIO MONATTI: da Vinci?

PETER: Who?

ANTONIO MONATTI: Bazooka Joe?

PETER: There ya go.

She's *That* Thin

ANTONIO MONATTI: Mr. Griffin, he's going to be a great artist. He now belongs to the public.

CHRIS: And apparently I'm dating Kate Moss. Oh, and um, don't say anything bad about her. 'Cause she might be here right now.

A View from Behind the Scenes

"The opening of this show—where the role of 'Brian' is temporarily filled by an actor named Carter Banks—was probably the most blatant way in which we ever broke the fourth wall. And I'm sure if we're lucky enough to run this long, by season twelve we'll find a fifth wall and break that thing, too."

—SETH MACFARLANE, CREATOR AND EXECUTIVE PRODUCER

Might Want to Have a Word with R&D

PETER: Wait a minute! You can't just push me aside! I made you! And I can destroy you!

(He takes out a little device with a red button and pushes it. Nothing happens.)

PETER: Aw, damn. They musta put it in the wrong baby.

(Cutaway to a playground, where a teenage Girl is on the swing, coyly talking to a boy.)

GIRL: Oh, Bobby Williams. I'd love to go out with you. You're always—

(She explodes.)

That's a Serious Birdcall

MEG: Oh, oh, those are just my birdcalls.

PETER: Do it again! Do it again!

(Meg whistles softly again. A bird flies over to them. Then another. Big Bird walks over to them.)

BIG BIRD: Yeah. Well, what'd you want?

MEG: Uh . . .

BIG BIRD: You called me, right?

MEG: Oh, no, I wasn't calling you.

BIG BIRD: Oh, oh, oh, this is funny to you. You know what a pain in the ass it is to get across town this time of day?! Huh?

PETER: Listen, Big Bird, we don't want no trouble here.

(Big Bird pushes Meg hard onto the ground.)

BIG BIRD: I don't fly, you know. I take the subway like everybody else. Oh, and people don't stare. You make me puke.

(He spits on her shoes and walks away, shaking his head.)

BIG BIRD: *(muttering)* Bitch.

Peter Pushes Too Hard

PETER: Hey, it's show business, baby. You gotta start somewhere.

MEG: No, I don't. I quit!

(Meg stomps off. Peter follows her.)

PETER: Now wait just a minute, young lady! Don't you walk away from me!

(Peter stares after Meg.)

PETER: Hey, hey, don't you start running! *(then)* Wait, wait— Meg, Meg, get off that bus! *(then)* Don't you— Don't you go to LaGuardia! *(then)* Meg, Meg, you listen to me, don't you dare get on that plane! *(then)* Don't you shell out five bucks for head- phones for *Magnolia*. Okay, now I'm pissed.

Just Take the Compliment

CALVIN KLEIN: This child is beautiful! I must have him!

PETER: You mean like "Gina Gershon beautiful" or "beautiful, beautiful?"

STUFF THAT MIGHT HAVE SLIPPED BY

■ Peter's car has a bumper sticker on it that reads "I Lost My Self Respect At Wes' Rib House."

■ When the Griffins first arrive in New York, they pass a bus with a sign that reads "CBS: Why watch what everyone else is watching?"

■ Chris and Antonio Monatti eat at a trendy restaurant called FÜD.

■ **The Calvin Klein billboard that Stewie appears in has a slogan that reads "Stewie Griffin says: I can go anywhere in my Calvin Klein diaper."**

Episode

FIFTEEN MINUTES OF SHAME

SUMMARY

At Quahog's Annual Clam Day, Peter has the honor of playing the Magic Clam, an important figure in the founding of Quahog. However, when a giant wave pulls off Peter's swim trunks in front of the whole town, Meg is humiliated by her father yet again. In fact, at Meg's slumber party that evening, the entire family ends up embarrassing her. Tired of always feeling this way, Meg takes the family on a local TV talk show, *Diane!*, where she plans to confront them about their perpetually embarrassing behavior.

Although the taping of the *Diane!* episode is a disaster, it causes the family to be noticed by an ambitious TV executive named Trevor, who offers Peter the chance to make the Griffins the subject of their own *Real World*–type reality show. When the family's embarrassing (and now nationally televised) antics become too much for Meg to handle, she quits the show, assuming that will force its early end. However, the producers decide to continue the show by simply replacing Meg with a young, sexy actress.

Meg goes to live with the neighbors as the rest of her family fulfills their contract by carrying on with the show. While Chris develops a huge crush on his "sister," Peter soon feels upstaged by the new, hot "Meg." At the same time, Lois truly misses the real Meg and realizes they made a big mistake. The Griffins demand that Trevor bring Meg back to the show, but he responds instead by recasting all of the remaining Griffin family members with actors such as Tom Arnold and Fran Drescher. Finally, the family is reunited but they have to stay cooped up in a motel room for several months while the show finishes filming in their house.

EPISODE NUMBER: 2ACX08

ORIGINAL AIRDATE: 4/25/00

WRITER: Steve Callaghan

DIRECTOR: Scott Wood

EXECUTIVE PRODUCERS:
Seth MacFarlane,
David Zuckerman

GUEST VOICES: Adam West as Mayor West, Jay Mohr as Trevor, Will Ferrell as Fisherman

MEMORABLE MOMENTS

Good Clean Fun

(Quahog's Annual Clam Day is under way. The Griffins stand behind Chris, who holds a baseball at a dunk tank booth. The sign reads "Dunk the Fisherman in the Shark Tank.")

FISHERMAN: Ha! Boy, you throw like a fishwife! C'mon, ya herring lubbin' frigate rod!

PETER: Chris, are you gonna take that from a fisherman?

CHRIS: No way!

(Chris hits the bull's-eye. The Fisherman falls into the water. Shark teeth gnash and the Fisherman screams as the water turns red.)

FISHERMAN: For the love of Pete!

CHRIS: I'm good.

LOIS: Aah, how fun. And it's for a good cause. All the money goes to the families of fishermen who've been eaten by sharks.

It Could Be Worse

Lois: It's such an honor to play the magic clam. Aren't you proud of your dad, kids?

Meg: Are you kidding? God, this is worse than having Ronald McDonald for a father.

(Cutaway to Ronald McDonald's House, where Ronald McDonald sits reading a newspaper. His teenage daughter, Lisa, runs downstairs, dressed a little on the trashy side.)

Lisa: Bye, Dad, don't wait up!

Ronald McDonald: Whoa, whoa, whoa, wait a minute, wait a minute, Lisa. Come back here. You're not going out with all that makeup on.

Lisa: But Dad—!

Ronald McDonald: Upstairs. You're a McDonald. Not a whore.

Stewie's Take on Slumber Parties

Meg: How could you embarrass me like that? Nobody better pull this kinda crap at my slumber party tonight.

Lois: Don't worry, honey, you and your friends are gonna have a great time.

Stewie: Yes, yes, how delightful it will be. A pubescent herd of gabby-ratchets prattling on about boys and music and jelly beans and stickers.

Okay, That Is Weird

(Meg and Five Girlfriends, including Collete and Beth, are in sleeping bags, eating junk food.)

Collette: Okay, I'd put Brad Pitt's face on Brendan Fraser's body, with Ben Affleck's butt.

(The girls all squeal. Lois enters wearing a nightgown.)

Lois: My turn, my turn! I'd take James Brolin's face, Mark Spitz's body, and Milton Berle's legendary genitals.

(She sighs, dreamily. The rest of the girls look at her, stunned.)

Meg: Mom, what are you doing?

Lois: I love slumber parties! Okay, Truth or Dare. Who here has gone all the way? Hmmm?

(Lois shoots her own hand up. The girls look away uneasily.)

Stewie's Take on Slumber Parties, Part 2

(Stewie sits with the girls in a circle, drinking hot cocoa.)

Stewie: Well, Beth, what do you think? Does Mark find you attractive?

Beth: I don't know . . .

Stewie: Well, have you asked him?

Beth: Not exactly . . .

Stewie: All right, look, let's try some role playing. I'll be Mark and you ask me out to the-the box social or whatever the devil it is you children are doing these days.

Scene Stealers
TREVOR

OCCUPATION
TV executive and B.S. artist

TURN-ONS
Romantic evenings, walks on the beach, high ratings

HOW HE FIRMS UP HIS DEAL WITH PETER
They "shake" on it at the men's room urinals

Our research shows that Meg is the least popular character on the show.

Meltdown on the Set of *Diane!*

DIANE: Peter, do you think there might be any validity to what Meg is feeling?

PETER: Who are you callin' Uncle Tom?!

DIANE: What?

(Peter picks up a chair and starts to throw it at Diane.)

CHRIS: Okay, time-out. This kind of acrimony isn't gonna resolve our differences. May—

PETER: Just shut up and throw a chair!

CHRIS: Okay!

(He picks up the chair Lois is sitting in and hurls it across the room with her still in it.)

How Peter Amuses Himself in the Bathroom

(Peter stands in front of a urinal.)

PETER: Uh oh. Fire! Fire! City Hall is burning. Don't worry! I'll put it out! Aaaah!

(Peter giggles. Trevor enters and goes to the urinal next to Peter.)

TREVOR: Hey, great show out there!

PETER: Look, if you want an autograph right now, you either gotta give me a pen or get me some snow.

Now, Was That Called For?

STEWIE: You, cameraman! Make sure you use that Cybill Shepherd filter. If they can make her look half-human, they should be able to take six months off my face.

Breakfast Outrage and the First Hint of the Future Stewie

STEWIE: What the hell is this?! I said egg whites only! Are you trying to give me a bloody heart attack?

(He hurls his plate against a wall.)

STEWIE: Make it again!

(Cutaway to Stewie's room, where, later, Stewie sits casually in a chair, doing a "confessional" to the Camera.)

STEWIE: Ah, the breakfast thing. Yes. I-it wasn't even about the eggs, really. Frankly, I like the yolks. I-I-I do. I have no problem, It's just—

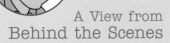

THE REAL LIVE GRIFFINS

There's always been a lot of tension between Lois and me. And, it's not so much that I want to kill her. It's just I want her not to be alive anymore. Ah, I-I sometimes wonder if, if all women are this difficult. And then I think to myself, my God, wouldn't it be marvelous if I turned out to be a homosexual.

A View from Behind the Scenes

"This episode establishes the character of Mayor West, the mayor of Quahog, thereby giving Adam West an outlet for his bizarre comedic genius and a place to steal snacks from when he comes in for his weekly recording sessions."

—SETH MACFARLANE, CREATOR AND EXECUTIVE PRODUCER

The Griffins Go M*A*S*H

MEG: So you're just gonna let them recast me?

PETER: Hey, it could've been worse. They could've gone with plan B.
*(Cutaway to the M*A*S*H Operating Room, where Peter, Lois, and Chris, dressed as the M*A*S*H surgical team, stand around the operating table as Brian, dressed as Radar, walks in, carrying a telegram.)*

PETER: Brian, put a mask on.

BRIAN: I have an announcement. *(reads telegram, with great despair)* Meg Griffin's plane was shot down over the Sea of Japan. It spun in. There were no survivors.
(After a long pause, Stewie enters, wearing a dress, hat, dangling earrings, and a feather boa like Klinger.)

STEWIE: Who do I see about a section eight?

Not the Brightest Bulb in the Pack

PETER: She'll be okay. C'mon, we gotta get back. The cameramen think we're taking Chris to soccer practice.
(Cut to the Griffins' car, which is parked in the driveway. Chris sits in the back seat. Raggedy Ann and Raggedy Andy dolls sit in the front seat.)

CHRIS: We're gonna be late! *(then)* Why won't you talk to me?!

Hot for Sister

NEW "MEG": Hi, Chris.

CHRIS: You know my name?

NEW "MEG": Of course I do, silly. I'm your sister, Meg.

CHRIS: Oh. Uh, I don't know if Mom and Dad told you, but we usually have breakfast naked and I'm allowed to videotape it.

Not Sure That's Working

NEW "MEG": I had the worst day! First I didn't make cheerleader because I'm so plain. And I still don't have a date for Friday night. As usual. I'm going upstairs and write in my journal about how I'll never grow big full breasts like these.

They Want Their Daughter Back

LOIS: To hell with the cameras. How could we ever let them replace our little girl? Oh, I miss her, Peter.

PETER: Me, too. She's like that dorky Baldwin brother who isn't as good-looking or successful and never answers my letters, but he's still a Baldwin, dammit. And so is Meg. Let's go get her back!

Episode
ROAD TO RHODE ISLAND

SUMMARY

Brian is going through a rough patch as his therapist helps him deal with the issue of having been abandoned by his mother as a puppy. All this emotional baggage causes him to drink even more than usual. As a way to clear his head, he offers to fly to Palm Springs to pick up Stewie, who's been visiting with the Pewterschmidts. But while Brian and Stewie are at the airport waiting for the flight back to Rhode Island, they lose their bags and their plane tickets. Meanwhile, Lois buys a relationship video that she hopes will help her and Peter communicate better as a couple.

Brian and Stewie crash at a local motel until their credit card is declined, forcing them to make a hasty getaway. Brian calls Lois to explain that they'll be home in a few days as they are taking the train instead of flying. Then he and Stewie hitch a ride in the back of a fruit truck. As they are passing Austin, Texas—the location of the puppy mill where he was born—Brian decides to take a detour. Optimistic that he will reconnect with his mother and put his emotional issues to bed, Brian arrives (with Stewie in tow) at the puppy mill, where he's informed that not only is his mother dead, but she's also been stuffed and is currently functioning as an end table in the home of the mill's owner. Meanwhile, Peter and Lois's relationship tape turns out to be little more than a scam to get horny husbands to keep buying more tapes.

Brian and Stewie make off with Brian's mom so that they can give her a proper burial, albeit in a nearby park. And Brian finally comes to peace with the fact that his mother only gave him up so that he could have a better life. After laying Brian's mom to rest, Brian and Stewie hop on a train for the last leg of their trip home. And Lois discovers what the relationship tapes are actually all about, then uses them in a unique way to cultivate intimacy between her and Peter.

EPISODE NUMBER: 2ACX12

ORIGINAL AIRDATE: 5/30/00

WRITER: Gary Janetti

DIRECTOR: Dan Povenmire

EXECUTIVE PRODUCERS:
Seth MacFarlane,
David Zuckerman

GUEST VOICE: Victoria Principal
as Amanda Rebecca

MEMORABLE MOMENTS

Just Mixing Things Up

BABS: Give Nana a big hug, sweetheart.
(As Stewie hugs Babs, he unhooks her diamond necklace. As they break the embrace, he surreptitiously slips it into the maid's pocket as she crosses away.)
STEWIE: Well, that should guarantee some after-dinner entertainment.

Exhibit A

LOIS: Peter, guess what I just got?! A relationship video! The infomercial said this tape will help us communicate better as a couple.
PETER: Lois, when have we ever had trouble communicating?
(Flashback to a mountaintop, where Peter and Lois stand together gazing at a gorgeous sunset.)
LOIS: Oh, Peter. I love you.
PETER: Ah, about a quarter past five.

You Don't Know Who You're Dealing With

BRIAN: Wait here at the gate. I gotta run a quick errand.

(Brian exits. Stewie takes a seat. A Traveler approaches him.)

TRAVELER: Aren't you a little young to be traveling alone?

STEWIE: Aren't you a little old to be wearing braces?

Not Your Best Wooing

(A drunken Brian sits on a stool at the bar flirting with the woman next to him.)

WOMAN: I think you've had about enough.

BRIAN: Well, I th— I think you're wrong, you . . . increasingly attractive-looking woman. Y'know, you're, you're really pretty.

WOMAN: Oh, stop.

BRIAN: No, I'm-I'm serious, you could— You could be in magazines. You could! And not just like *Juggs*, or, or *Creamsicle* . . .

(The Woman leaves in a huff.)

BRIAN: Call me? *(to Bartender)* She won't call.

Bad Liar

STEWIE: Oh, here's a pleasant sight—Cirrhosis the Wonder Dog.

BRIAN: *(slurring)* I-I'm not drunk, all right? I just have a speech impediment. *(He vomits.)*

BRIAN: And a stomach virus. *(He falls off his stool.)*

BRIAN: And an inner ear infection.

A Bit of Projection?

BRIAN: Where're the bags?

STEWIE: What the deuce do you mean, they're right—

(He sees that the seat where he left the bags is now empty except for Rupert.)

STEWIE: Rupert! I told you to watch the bags! But you were watching the boys again, weren't you? It's that steward, isn't it? That one who looks like Tab Hunter.

These Newfangled Phones These Days

STEWIE: Hello, Operator? Hello? Oh, God, that's right, you have to punch in the numbers nowadays.

(He stares at the phone pad and thinks for a moment.)

STEWIE: I should know this. Oh, yes: eight–six–seven–five–three–oh–nine. That's it. No, wait, that's not it. Damn you, Tommy Tutone! *(sighs)* Only one thing to do.

(He quickly punches numbers.)

STEWIE: One–one–one–one–one–one–one. Lois? Damn!

(He hits the hook and punches some more numbers.)

STEWIE: One–one–one–one–one–one–two. Lois? Damn!

(He hits the hook and punches some more numbers.)

STEWIE: One–one–one–one–one–one–three—

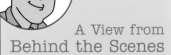

A View from Behind the Scenes

"This was our first episode back on the air after the network pulled us off for Sweeps, as well as the episode that got the series nominated for an Emmy. But, don't worry, the irony of that was totally lost on the network."

—SETH MACFARLANE, CREATOR AND EXECUTIVE PRODUCER

Car Selection

(Stewie and Brian tumble out of the window and run across the parking lot.)

STEWIE: All right, we need some wheels.

(Brian tries the handle of a car.)

BRIAN: This one's unlocked.

STEWIE: An SUV? Look, we're trying to elude someone, we're not driving to soccer practice. *(points to another car)* Let's take this one.

BRIAN: You-you like that color?

STEWIE: What's wrong with the color?

BRIAN: I-I don't know, it's just, it's so dark, it . . .

STEWIE: Well, yes, but it doesn't show dirt.

BRIAN: What?

STEWIE: It doesn't show dirt.

BRIAN: I-I guess, it ah, it . . .

STEWIE: You know, this really is the first place we've gone to. Perhaps we should try another lot.

(They see the Desk Clerk coming out of the motel.)

BRIAN: Sold.

Use Your Head

STEWIE: Yes, yes, you've got lots to think about, haven't you? Public drunkenness, grand theft auto . . .

BRIAN: You left out the part where I made you smash your head on the windshield.

STEWIE: *(confused)* Well, I-I don't recall—

(Brian slams on the brakes. The car screeches to a halt as Stewie slams his head into the windshield, then falls back into his seat.)

STEWIE: Yes, well, I suppose I walked right into that one.

One-Track Peter

LOIS: Stewie and Brian are taking a train home.

PETER: Geez, can we not talk about curtains for two seconds? I got another one of those relationship tapes.

LOIS: Forty-nine ninety-five?! That's three times as much as the first one.

PETER: Lois, our relationship cannot be measured in nipples and dimes. I-I mean nickels and boobs. Money.

A Very Twisted Family Tree

(Brian and Stewie approach a barn, where an Old Farmer is talking to a dusty-looking Pilot.)

OLD FARMER: I don't trust you. You put your seed in my daughter's belly. You're fired!

PILOT: But, Pa, you can't fire me!

OLD FARMER: You're lucky you're my brother, too, or I'd kill you!

Say What?

(Brian and Stewie are huddled with a couple dozen Latino Farmworkers in the back of a fruit truck. Brian turns to the man next to him.)

BRIAN: *Hola. Ah, me, me llamo es Brian. Ah, ah, let's see . . . ah . . . nosotros . . . queremos ir con ustedes.*

LATINO FARMER: *(with no accent)* That was pretty good. But actually when you said "Me llamo es Brian," you don't need the "es." Just "Me llamo Brian."

BRIAN: Oh, you speak English.

LATINO FARMER: No, just that first speech and this one explaining it.

BRIAN: You— You're kidding, right?

LATINO FARMER: *¿Que?*

There's No Accounting for Taste

(Stewie glances at pictures and knickknacks on the wall of Luke and Betty's house.)

STEWIE: Look at Jesus, hanging up there all by himself. You'd think those bulldogs would invite him to their card game.

A Bit of Brainstorming

BRIAN: You deserve better than this, Mom.

(Brian starts clearing items off of his stuffed mother.)

STEWIE: You know, this is actually a rather elegant solution for my problem of what to do with Lois.

For Posterity

BRIAN: Wait here. I'm gonna get directions to the nearest park so we can give my mother a proper burial.

(Brian exits. Stewie stares at Brian's mom.)

STEWIE: Come on, darling, stiff upper lip.

(Stewie laughs hard at his joke.)

STEWIE: I'm writing that one down.

(He reaches into his pocket, produces a little pad and pencil, and quickly jots it down.)

Rest in Peace, Biscuit

(Brian carries his mother and places her gently into a freshly dug grave. He is overcome with emotion.)

BRIAN: Say something.

STEWIE: What?

BRIAN: Ju-just say something! Please!

STEWIE: Oh, for God's sake. Um . . . Uh, yea, and God said to Abraham,

---

Scene Stealers
BISCUIT

WHO SHE IS
Brian's mother, who gave up Brian in a puppy mill near Austin, Texas

WHY SHE'S SO STILL
Because she's dead and stuffed

WHY BRIAN WAS SO SPECIAL TO HER
Because you never forget your 937th child

"You will kill your son Isaac." And Abraham said, "I can't hear you, you'll have to speak into the microphone." And God said, "Oh, I'm sorry. Is this better? Check, check, check. Jerry, pull the high end out, I'm still getting some hiss back here—"

BRIAN: Say something about my mother!

STEWIE: Oh, yes, I'm sorry. Um, ah . . .. I never knew Biscuit as a dog. But I did know her as a table. She was sturdy, all four legs the same length—

BRIAN: Thanks, thanks. That's enough.

STEWIE: Yes, yes, ah, *requiem interra pax* and so forth. Amen.

He Speaks the Truth

AMANDA REBECCA: We're going to add—
   (The picture cuts off. Amanda is gone. Suddenly Lois appears on the TV.)

LOIS: *(on TV)* Peter!

PETER: Ahhhh!

LOIS: *(on TV)* I know what you've been doing here and I'm very upset with you.

PETER: Wow. Usually beautiful women don't turn back into you until after I'm finished.

Almost a Genuine Moment

BRIAN: Listen, kid, there's-there's something I've been meaning to tell you. It's not easy for me to say . . .

STEWIE: Oh, God, you're not coming out of the closet, are you? Uh. Why does everyone always come out to me?

Not Where I Thought You Were Going

BRIAN: Hey, uh, kid, listen, uh, thanks for not ratting me out. Is there anything I can do to pay you back?

STEWIE: Oh, yes, you remember that episode of *The Brady Bunch* where Bobby saved Greg's life and Greg became his slave?

BRIAN: Yeah.

STEWIE: It's on this afternoon. You can tape it for me. And put a nice label on it.

STUFF THAT MIGHT HAVE SLIPPED BY

■ In the video store, the two videos Peter is torn between choosing are *Ernest Goes to the Beach* and *Ernest Doesn't Go to the Beach.*

■ The sign in front of Stewie and Brian's motel reads "Prostitutes: Ask about Our Continental Breakfast."

Episode
LET'S GO TO THE HOP

SUMMARY

Lois and Peter become concerned when a toad-licking problem arises in school. After finding a toad in Chris's pocket they suspect him, but then they discover that Meg was holding the toad for one of the popular kids in the hope that doing so would secure her a date to the Winter Snow Ball. Peter talks about his nervousness when he first asked his high school crush, Phoebe Diamond, to the prom. Later, Lois and Peter decide they need to do something to protect their kids from this drug problem. So, Peter talks with Meg's principal about it and arrives at school the next day as "Lando Griffin," an undercover student.

Before long, Peter (as Lando) actually succeeds in convincing the kids at James Woods High that it's not cool to lick toad. Meg, seeing an opportunity, tells the cool kids that Lando has asked her to the Winter Snow

Ball, which immediately increases her popularity. Meanwhile, Peter seems to be enjoying his "high school" experience and persona a little too much. In fact, when Meg shows up at school on the day of the big dance, she is stunned to learn that "Lando" is, in fact, going to the Winter Snow Ball with Connie, a member of the popular clique.

Lois can't believe Peter's preposterous behavior until Brian explains that Peter has transferred his feelings for his old crush, Phoebe, onto Connie. Against Lois's wishes, Peter sneaks out to go to the dance. Lois encourages Meg to go to the dance by herself. When Peter (as Lando) and Connie are crowned king and queen of the Winter Snow Ball, Peter uses the opportunity to tell the crowd that Meg was really his first choice as a date for the dance, which gets Meg lots of the attention she was seeking. "Lando" then drives recklessly off into the night, never to be heard from again.

EPISODE NUMBER: 2ACX04

ORIGINAL AIRDATE: 6/6/00

WRITERS: Mike Barker
& Matt Weitzman

DIRECTOR: Glen Hill

EXECUTIVE PRODUCERS:
Seth MacFarlane,
David Zuckerman

GUEST VOICE: Gregg Allman
as himself

MEMORABLE MOMENTS

Way to Just Say No

DIANE: In local news, a new drug craze may have Quahog students licked. It's called "Toad."

TOM: The Colombian Spotted Toad to be precise, Diane. When licked, these toads trigger an intense psychedelic euphoria that's—that's just great.

He's Just Trying to Be Friendly

CHRIS: Hello, little sea monkeys!

(Inside Chris's aquarium, a Sea Monkey Family eats dinner. Behind the glass, Chris's enormous face peers in at them.)

SEA MONKEY GIRL: He's back.

SEA MONKEY DAD: Don't look at him, honey. Eat your potatoes.

(Chris starts tapping the glass. The Sea Monkey Mom closes her eyes, frustrated.)

SEA MONKEY MOM: Steve, do something.

SEA MONKEY DAD: Brenda, we've been over this. Let's just pick up our plates and go eat in the hollow castle.

(They sadly pick up their plates and walk to the castle.)

Memory Erasure

CHRIS: Hey, maybe it's Meg's toad.

LOIS: Whoa, now don't you try to pawn this off on your sister. She's a good girl.

CHRIS: Oh, yeah? What about the time she strangled our other sister?

(Lois and Peter look at each other nervously.)

LOIS: Now, Chris, we told you, that was just a very bad dream.

CHRIS: But I remember it so—

PETER AND LOIS: It was a dream!

Just Another Night Talking About Responsible Parenthood

(Lois and Peter are getting ready for bed. Lois lights a few candles.)

LOIS: How could this happen? I thought we lived in such a nice small town.

PETER: Ah, there's no such thing anymore, Lois. Things are a lot different than when we were kids.

(Lois unlocks a dresser drawer and routinely hands Peter some leather chaps. He puts them on as she pulls on some black silk stockings and hooks them to something under her robe.)

LOIS: Well, it just makes me sad.

PETER: Hey, it makes me sad, too. But, ah, you know . . .

(Peter puts on a spiked dog collar and harness. Lois takes off her robe, revealing she's wearing a leather teddy and garter belt. Peter puts on two spiked wrist cuffs. Lois puts on fingerless gloves.)

LOIS: I mean, if Meg's at risk, then so is Chris. And Stewie'll be in preschool before we know it.

PETER: Well, we just have to trust our kids to stay off drugs is all.

LOIS: I do trust our kids. It's the other kids I don't trust.

(Peter pulls an unzipped leather hood on as Lois zips up some thigh-high leather boots.)

I guess Miss "Wears a Hat All the Time" is gonna narc on us, aren't you?

Scene Stealers
CONNIE D'AMICO

OCCUPATION
High school student and Queen Bee of the Popular Clique

HOBBIES
Shopping, ditching school, conforming

WHAT SHE'LL PROBABLY BE DOING TWENTY YEARS FROM NOW
Constantly reminiscing about her high school days, back when she had her looks and was popular (or at least that's what Meg hopes . . .)

PETER: Yeah, yeah, well, you know, I guess it's up to us as parents to be part of the solution. I'll go talk to the principal tomorrow.
LOIS: Thanks, honey.
    (She kisses him, then zips up his hood.)
LOIS: The safety word is "banana."
    (Peter's hooded head nods. He unzips his mouth.)
PETER: I love you.
    (Lois roughly shoves his face, knocking him back on the bed.)

You Need to Be a Little More Explicit
PETER: And that's my plan, Principal Shepard. So you with me?
PRINCIPAL SHEPARD: But you didn't tell me anything. You just sat down and said, "And that's my plan."
PETER: Oh. Oh, right.

Ah, the Good Ol' Days
PETER: If you must know, I've gone undercover to get rid of the toad problem, so your school can be safe and innocent. Like the good ol' days.
    (Flashback to a one-room schoolhouse, where a classroom full of Puritan Children sits quietly at their desks. The stern-looking Schoolmaster looks on as a Puritan Girl answers a math question.)
PURITAN GIRL: . . . negative B, plus or minus radical B squared, minus four A-C, over two A.
SCHOOLMASTER: That's correct. A girl answered a math problem. You know what that means . . . A WITCH!
OTHER PURITAN STUDENTS: Witch! / Witch! / Witch!
    (The schoolmaster and students quickly take out rocks and pelt the girl.)

Way to Not Blow That Cover
MEG: Oh, yeah? If I'm such a loser, how come I'm going to the Winter Snow Ball with Lando?
    (Everyone gasps and looks to Lando expectantly.)
PETER: Meg, you got a date?! Oh, wait'll I tell your mother— *(realizing)* —who I'm looking forward to meeting. *(then)* And I hope is making Steak-Umms tonight.

Reliving the Glory Days
PETER: I tell ya, Lois, high school's a lot more fun this time around. And it's a lot safer now that all of the kids have guns. Oh, oh, and and today in study hall, I tried to fart real loud on purpose, you know, to make the guys laugh, and swear to God, it was so heinous Susie Johnson ralphed up her salisbury steak.
    (Stewie throws his spoon down.)
STEWIE: Oh, I'm sorry! Is this really proper dinner conversation?!

Peter Griffin, Pouty Teen

LOIS: Okay, this whole thing is ridiculous! I forbid you from going to that dance.

PETER: You can't tell me what to do! You're not my real mom!

LOIS: End of discussion.

PETER: Thank you for ruining my life! You don't remember what it's like to be my age!

(Peter marches upstairs.)

LOIS: I'm two years younger than you!

Missing the Point

LOIS: Honey, he didn't mean to hurt you. And you know, you could still go to the dance.

MEG: Alone? Why don't I just tattoo a big L on my forehead while I'm at it?

LOIS: Now, Meg, you know my feelings on tattoos.

Peter Picks Up His Date

(Mr. & Mrs. D'Amico are uncomfortably sitting on the couch with Peter, who is stuffing potato chips in his mouth.)

MR. D'AMICO: So, uh, Lando, how old did you say you were again?

PETER: Seventeen. And-and a half.

(Connie enters.)

PETER: Sweet statutory, you look beautiful.

(Connie smiles. Peter starts out, then turns to the D'Amicos.)

PETER: Don't worry, I'll take good care of your kid. I got a daughter of my own, ya know.

(They exit, leaving Connie's stunned parents speechless.)

STUFF THAT MIGHT HAVE SLIPPED BY

■ The cargo plane seen flying through the sky at the opening of the episode is labeled "Overnight Express Delivery." High winds peel off the sticker of the word "Overnight" to reveal "Colombian" painted underneath it. Then the "Express" sticker flies off, revealing the word "Cartel." Next, the word "Delivery" comes off, revealing the word "Delivery."

■ The pilots of the plane speak Spanish, but are subtitled in Chinese characters.

■ The pilots' dialogue translates to English as "When the boss hears about this, we're dead," and "Do you remember if I closed the garage door this morning?"

■ Meg has a Hanson poster in her room.

■ The poster in the principal's office shows a boy with webbed hands and reads "My mom did toad during pregnancy. Thanks, Mom."

■ When Peter is acting as Lando, he is seen spray painting "Thompson Twins Rule!" on a wall.

■ The final shot of Peter's silhouette is a reference to the ending of *The Breakfast Club*.

Episode
DAMMIT, JANET!

SUMMARY

When Stewie demonstrates that he's not very good around other children, Lois decides to put him in daycare. However, Lois soon becomes bored and, seeking some excitement, decides she'd like to take on a part-time job. Peter doesn't want Lois to work . . . that is, until he learns that the husbands of flight attendants can travel for free, at which point he strongly encourages Lois to become a flight attendant. Meanwhile, Stewie becomes smitten with a little girl named Janet.

Lois soon discovers that life as a flight attendant is far from glamorous and is, in fact, very tiring. At the same time, Peter is traveling far and wide, unbeknownst to Lois. When she tells Peter she's thinking of quitting her job, Peter encourages her to continue on so he can still reap the travel benefits of being her spouse. But when Peter ends up on the same flight as Lois, she discovers what he's been up to and becomes furious with him. She drags him off to the lavatory to discuss the matter just as the plane is being hijacked to Cuba. Meanwhile, Stewie gets closer to Janet and even spells out his affection for her in a song.

All the passengers are returned home safely, except for Lois and Peter, who went unnoticed in the locked lavatory. They end up being stuck in Cuba for two weeks waiting for their passports to arrive. They try unsuccessfully to buy some passports on the black market, but ultimately resort to boarding a raft filled with refugees. At this moment, Lois realizes she has no need for the excitement she was seeking, because being married to Peter provides plenty of it. Meanwhile, Stewie falls even harder for Janet and tries to make her jealous when she shows interest in another boy. When Janet finally expresses interest in Stewie, he is elated, but then he realizes she's only been interested in him for his cookies. Stewie is crushed, trying hard to hold back his tears.

EPISODE NUMBER: 2ACX09

ORIGINAL AIRDATE: 6/13/00

WRITERS: Mike Barker & Matt Weitzman

DIRECTOR: Bert Ring

EXECUTIVE PRODUCERS: Seth MacFarlane, David Zuckerman

MEMORABLE MOMENTS

Does Not Play Well with Others

STEWIE: I say, Jeffrey, be a sport, will you, and go get that sifter so we can build our sand village.

(*Stewie points, Jeffrey starts toward the sifter.*)

STEWIE: That's right, a little farther.

(*Suddenly the sand below Jeffrey gives way and he plummets out of view. Stewie walks over and looks into a pit.*)

STEWIE: Everyone, meet Jeffrey, the newest member of the Club of Forgotten Children.

(*Four Frightened Children stare up at him.*)

Not Exactly Mr. Involved Dad

LOIS: Stewie needs to learn how to socialize with other children. Maybe we should put him in daycare.

PETER: Lois, his answers are out on the open road. I say we give him a hobo pack on the end of a stick, a can of beans, and a pocket full of dreams.

LOIS: Peter . . . Do you even know which one of our children I'm talking about?

PETER: Uh, Gordon?

So, That's What Those Kravitzes Were Up To

LOIS: Chris, stop it! What will the neighbors think?!

(Across the street, Gladys Kravitz peeks out her front window.)

GLADYS: Abner! Abner! The Griffin boy just killed a plastic reindeer!

(Abner Kravitz sits on the couch, naked, a bowl of popcorn on his lap.)

ABNER: Gladys, it took me two hours to work up the courage to rent this porno. Now, you gonna watch it with me or not?

Gotta Pass the Time Somehow

LOIS: Oh, I'm so bored. Without Stewie around I have nothing to do.

BRIAN: Well . . . we could get hammered.

LOIS: Oh, it's too early for me. But you go ahead.

Busy Work

LOIS: Peter, this is a new chapter in my life. The kids are growing, the nest is emptying. I need some excitement.

PETER: What are you talking about? Your life is plenty exciting. For example.

(Peter pulls out a blowtorch and sets the drapes on fire.)

PETER: There you go. G'night.

Figuring Out How to Play

STEWIE: Oh, let's see now. Duck . . . duck . . . duck . . .

(When Stewie gets to Janet, he smiles and smacks the top of her head, hard.)

STEWIE: Goose!

(Janet starts crying.)

STEWIE: Oh, come on now, I barely touched you. Really, stop it, stop your boo-hooing. Stop it, I say. Stop it! You see? This is exactly why people don't respect the WNBA!

Busted

BRIAN: Well, well, well. Looks like someone's in love.

STEWIE: Ha! That's so funny I forgot to laugh. Excluding that first "ha."

BRIAN: Uh-huh. Face it, you're a sucker for a woman with blue eyes.

STEWIE: A-ha! Her eyes are green!

BRIAN: A-ha! Thank you for proving my point.

STEWIE: Damn!

Kinda Loose Rules on That Airline

(Lois enters the cockpit.)

LOIS: Hey, fellas, I hope you're hungry—AHH!

(The Pilots are dead with bloody knives sticking out of their heads and chest.)

Scene Stealers

JANET

Cookies

WHO SHE IS
Stewie's daycare playmate and huge crush

TURN-ONS
Cookies

THE REAL REASON SHE LIKES STEWIE
Cookies

THE MOST PROMINENT WORD IN HER VOCABULARY
Cookies

STUFF THAT MIGHT HAVE SLIPPED BY

■ As Stewie rakes sand back over the Club of Forgotten Children, he sings "Another One Bites the Dust" by Queen.

■ The sign outside Stewie's daycare facility reads "Hugs and Kisses (the Good Kind) Day Care."

■ After Peter builds a fort in the airplane seats, he hangs a sign outside his fort that reads "No Girls Allowed."

■ **Stewie panics as Janet walks toward him and he notices that his blocks spell out "MY LOVELY JANET." He scatters the blocks, but then they read "I LONG FOR YOU." He scatters them again, and they spell out "RIDE THAT PONY."**

■ As Peter flips through photos of his travels, we see shots of Peter standing in front of the Washington Monument, smiling and waving; Peter standing in front of Mt. Rushmore, smiling and waving; and Peter, standing in front of several starving Ethiopians, smiling and waving with a hot dog in his hand.

■ On the street in Cuba, Peter lights his cigar on a passing Cuban man's burning American flag.

■ When Peter and Lois are in the black market, several Cubans rummage through a bin. One of them eyes a T-shirt featuring the Taco Bell Chihuahua.

LOIS: Oh, my God! What am I gonna—!! Somebody— Help! Help! HELP!
(One of the pilots lets out a stifled laugh. Then the other pilot cracks up as they sit to reveal their prank.)
PILOT: That was great. Look at, look at her, she's still shaking!
(Lois exits, disgusted.)
LOIS: Bastards.
PILOT: Oh, that was beautiful. *(to co-pilot)* Hey, throw me a beer, would ya?

Sometimes It's Hard to Tell the Difference
STEWIE: Unhand me, woman. I don't have gas, I'm in love.
(Stewie emits a huge belch.)
STEWIE: Well, then, I guess it's both.

Parental Advice
LOIS: Well, I guess I'll give it a little more time. It's like I always tell the kids, "A quitter never wins" and "Don't trust whitey."

Hazards of the Job
ARAB SHEIK: *Mumkin tukuni miratti?*
LOIS: Excuse me?
ARAB SHEIK: I said, "May I have a blanket?"
LOIS: Oh, yes, of course—
ARAB SHEIK: Ha! I really said, "Will you be my wife?" And you said "Yes," so now it is official! Let me touch your face.

A Little Griffin History
LOIS: Where are you going? You're never going to find the black market.
PETER: Oh, that's what you said about that back-alley abortionist. Don't get me wrong, I'm glad you changed your mind. The point is, I found the guy.

Stewie Tries to Make Janet Jealous
STEWIE: That is, that is absolutely classic! Melinda, you're an utter delight! *(then)* Oh, hello, Janet. Yes, yes, you know Melinda. Yes, it seems she's um— *(to Melinda)* Oh, what'd we figure out, dear, was it, was it one? No, two. Yes, she's two weeks younger than you. Just look at that butt.
(Stewie slaps her behind.)
STEWIE: That is a tight butt!

A Little More Griffin History
PETER: There it is, the black market. Lois, if we don't make it out of here alive, I-I should tell ya, I-I promised my first girlfriend we'd meet up in Heaven. I was lying, but-but just so you know, it's something we might have to deal with.

Episode

THERE'S SOMETHING ABOUT PAULIE

EPISODE NUMBER: 1ACX10

ORIGINAL AIRDATE: 6/27/00

WRITER: Ricky Blitt

DIRECTOR: Monte Young

EXECUTIVE PRODUCERS:
Seth MacFarlane,
David Zuckerman

GUEST VOICES: Alan King as the
Don, Michael Chiklis as Big Fat
Paulie, Jon Cryer as Kevin

SUMMARY

Lois complains to Peter that having only one car is an inconvenience to the family, so Peter and Lois go to the car dealership to buy a new one. After they get conned into buying a lemon, Peter is approached by a member of the Mob who offers to get rid of his car for him so that Peter can collect on the insurance. Peter takes the guy up on his offer and enjoys his nice, new car, but fails to realize that this now entitles the mob to ask a favor of Peter at any time. When the mobster returns and tells Peter the Don wants to talk to him, Peter panics.

Peter goes to see the Don, who only asks that Peter spend some time with his annoying nephew, Big Fat Paulie, by taking him to the movies. Peter does so, but just when Peter thinks he's off the hook, Paulie wants to hang out with Peter some more. Scared, Peter agrees to bring Big Fat Paulie home for dinner, where he annoys Lois to the point that she tells Peter he can't hang out with him anymore. Peter attempts to convey this to Paulie, but instead Paulie understands Peter to be saying that Lois is the only obstacle between the two of them being friends. So, Big Fat Paulie puts out a hit on Lois. After a few unsuccessful attempts on Lois's life, Peter figures out what's going on. When Peter asks Big Fat Paulie to call off the hit, he agrees to do so, but before he can make the phone call to do it, he is shot dead.

Lois finds out what is going on and is furious. Peter talks to the mobster who originally stole his car for him, and he suggests that Peter speak to the Don at the wedding of the Don's daughter. Lois remembers that in *The Godfather*, the Don grants favors on the day of his daughter's wedding, so Peter attends to ask him to call off the hit on Lois. But, Peter gets sidetracked by the taste of the Don's tiramisu and loses his opportunity to make a special request. Fortunately, Peter offers up some important marital advice to the bride and groom right when they could use it and the Don is happy to repay Peter's deed by calling off the hit. The one casualty, though, is the Griffins' new car, which explodes before the hit could be fully retracted.

MEMORABLE MOMENTS

There's No Reasoning with Him

PETER: Geez, Lois, what are you doing lyin' on the couch at this hour? Have you been drinkin'?

LOIS: Peter! You know I never drink.

PETER: Oh, yeah. Just like you never dodged the draft.

LOIS: What are you talking about? I'm a woman.

PETER: Sure you are. Now.

Urban Legend?

PETER: Oh, no, Lois, no. A guy at work bought a car out of the paper. Ten years later, *bam!* Herpes.

Scene Stealers
BIG FAT PAULIE

WHO HE IS
The Don's annoying
and disgusting nephew

HIS IDEA OF FUNNY
Greeting Peter by putting
him in a painful wrestling
hold, sneezing on his tie,
then pouring a carton of
milk down his pants

HOW HE GETS THE
SEAT HE WANTS
Shooting the guy
who's in it

You're still a minor,
huh? How'd you like
to be a coke mule?

Not Reading Her Signals
PETER: Lois, this is crazy. There's no way we're gonna be able to have
"maritals" with you lying all the way over there.
LOIS: I am very upset with you right now.
PETER: Okay, so I tried on your bra. Geez, the fellas were putting on a
show! I-I didn't think I'd make a good Gigi, either, but God help me,
I was flattered.

This Is Exactly Why the House Always Wins
LOIS: Peter, I'm upset because you never listen to me. This is Atlantic
City all over again.
    *(Flashback to a casino, where Lois stands behind Peter at a black-
jack table.)*
DEALER: You've got twenty.
PETER: Hit me.
LOIS: Peter, don't.
PETER: Hit me. *(The dealer hands him an ace.)*
DEALER: Twenty-one!
PETER: Hit me.
LOIS: Peter . . .
PETER: Hit me. *(The dealer gives him another card.)*
DEALER: That's thirty.
PETER: Hit me.

Not Helping His Case
LOIS: I'm tired of being left out of all our decision-making.
PETER: Okay, honey.
    *(Peter turns off the light, leaving them in darkness. There is the
sound of a laughing chimpanzee.)*
PETER: By the way, I bought a chimp.

A True Gift
LOIS: I just wish my opinion mattered to you.
PETER: Well, the important thing is, it matters to you. And that's the
greatest gift of all.

One Trick <Soviet> Pony
PETER: Hey, Cleveland, come here, check out my on-board computer
navigation system. *(clicks a dial)* Standard.
CAR COMPUTER: Left turn ahead.
    (Peter clicks the dial.)
PETER: Spanish.
CAR COMPUTER: *(Spanish accent) Va a la izquierda alla.*
    (Peter clicks the dial.)
PETER: Yakov Smirnoff.
CAR COMPUTER: *(Russian accent)* In Soviet Russia, car drives you.

Scared Straight

DON: I have asked you here tonight so that you may perform a service—

PETER: *(rambling nervously)* Aaahh, what, what, what are you gonna make me do, whack a guy, off a guy, whack off a guy, 'cause I'm married—

Peter Covers Badly

LOIS: Uh, do you mind?

BIG FAT PAULIE: As a matter of fact, I do, you crazy broad, heh.

LOIS: I am not a "crazy broad" . . .

PETER: Oh, uh, no, no, Lois, see he didn't mean you're crazy-like, Elizabeth Taylor, you know. He, he meant you're crazy, like, ah, like that glue, heh. You stick to things. Heh, you know, like an adhesive, heh. That's-that's all he meant.

It Is What She's Known For . . .

STEWIE: Yes, good heavens! Who taught you how to eat, Mickey Rourke? . . . Why do I know that name? Damn you, *Entertainment Tonight*! *(Cutaway to the set of* Entertainment Tonight, *where Bob Goen sits at his desk.)*

BOB GOEN: Hi, I'm Bob Goen. And these are Mary Hart's legs. *(A pair of Disembodied Shapely Legs sits next to Bob.)*

BOB GOEN: Mary, you recently spent some time with Julia Roberts, didn't you? *(Mary's right leg stomps twice like a horse.)*

BOB GOEN: Mary says yes.

Everyone's a Critic

LOIS: Peter, how can you sleep? I was almost killed!

PETER: Aw, c'mon, Lois, the only victim tonight was the work of Arthur Miller.

They're Such Easy Targets

PETER: Look, don't worry. I got it all worked out. We'll move to England, heh? The worst they got there is, ah, drive-by arguments. *(Cutaway to a British Street, where two Englishmen are driving in their car.)*

ENGLISHMAN #1: I say, Jeremy, isn't that Reginald B. Stiffworth, the young upstart chap who's been touting the merits of a united European Commonwealth?

ENGLISHMAN #2: Why, yes, I daresay that's the fellow.

ENGLISHMAN #1: Oh, let's get him. *(Cut to a London Street Corner, where a third Englishman stands at a bus stop. The car pulls up alongside him and Englishman #1 rolls down the driver's side window.)*

A View from
Behind the Scenes

"We take a few shots at the Mafia in this episode, but I just want to say that I have nothing but respect for them. Please don't kill me."

—SETH MACFARLANE, CREATOR AND EXECUTIVE PRODUCER

STUFF THAT MIGHT HAVE SLIPPED BY

■ The GPS screen in Peter's new car shows streets in town called Clam Street and Quahog Drive.

■ **While Lois is being pursued by the hitman, she is seen through what appears to be the scope of a rifle when she is in fact merely shopping at a grocery store called "Bullseye Market."**

■ The headline on *The Quahog Informant* announcing Big Fat Paulie's murder reads "Big Fat Mobster Gunned Down."

■ The storefront where Peter finds Kevin is covered with a makeshift sign that reads "Pet Store. That's It, Pet Store."

ENGLISHMAN #1: Oh, Reginald!
    (Englishman #3 turns his head to look.)
ENGLISHMAN #1: I disagree!
    (The car speeds away.)

The Man's a Little Slow

LOIS: Didn't you see *The Godfather*? The Don can't refuse a favor on the day of his daughter's wedding.
PETER: So?
LOIS: So? We can ask him for a favor.
PETER: So?
LOIS: So? We ask him to call off the hit.
PETER: So?
LOIS: So? Peter, I-I don't know how to explain it any clearer than that.

Has He Seen the Show Before?

PETER: I don't know about this, Lois. What if something happens to you? I'm too old to start dating again.
    (Cutaway to the set of The Dating Game, *where a young attractive Contestant asks the questions.)*
CONTESTANT: Okay, Bachelor number one, I'm an ice cream cone. How are you gonna eat me?
BACHELOR #1: *(sexy)* I'd invite my friend Rudy over, and the two of us would give you a double dip.
    (The audience whoops it up.)
CONTESTANT: Ooooh, okay. Bachelor number two?
BACHELOR #2: *(sexy)* Well, I'd lick off all the cream and give you my special whipped topping.
    (The audience whoops it up.)
CONTESTANT: Sounds good. Bachelor number three?
    (Pan to Bachelor #3, Peter.)
PETER: *(sexy)* Well, I would try to eat you really fast before I got flaccid.
    (The audience is dead silent.)

Too Little, Too Late

    (Their car blows up.)
PETER: Hehehe. Oh, my God! Our car!
    (The Groom runs over to Lois and Peter, who stand wide-eyed with disbelief.)
GROOM: Oh, man, am I glad I caught you. I almost forgot, don't start your ca—
    (He notices the burning car.)
GROOM: Hey, thanks for coming.
    (He turns around and returns to the party.)

Episode

HE'S TOO SEXY FOR HIS FAT

EPISODE NUMBER: 2ACX10
ORIGINAL AIRDATE: 6/27/00
WRITER: Chris Sheridan
DIRECTOR: Glen Hill
EXECUTIVE PRODUCERS:
Seth MacFarlane,
David Zuckerman

SUMMARY

At the grocery store, a Security Guard mistakenly thinks Chris is trying to shoplift a couple of hams, but realizes it only appears that way due to Chris's sizable girth. Later, the Griffins' house is overrun with fleas, causing them to call an exterminator and vacate the house for a few days. Brian, feeling responsible for the mess they're in, offers to put the entire family up in a hotel. At the hotel pool, Chris seems unwilling to take his shirt off. When Lois asks him about it, Chris admits it's because he thinks he's fat.

Peter helps Chris work out in an attempt to shed some pounds, but to no avail. When Peter complains to Cleveland about how Chris hasn't lost any weight, Cleveland suggests that Chris see Cleveland's brother, Broderick, a cosmetic surgeon who performs liposuction. Peter and Chris go to see Broderick, but when they return home, it's not Chris who is pounds lighter—it's Peter! Meanwhile, in an attempt to make Chris envious of what he can no longer eat, Stewie begins to gorge himself, gaining weight in the process.

Peter, who thoroughly enjoys his new thin self, has even more cosmetic surgery to fix other imperfections. Lois hates what he is doing, but can't help feeling attracted to the new handsome Peter. Meanwhile, Peter is approached by a member of the Quahog Beautiful People's Club, where he finds an entire underground of attractive people enjoying the perks of being beautiful. All this time, Stewie is getting fatter, to the point that he can barely function. When Peter turns Chris away from the Quahog Beautiful People's Club, Lois reaches her limit. Peter, still wrapped up in himself, becomes so distracted by his own reflection while driving that he crashes the car off a cliff and lands into a giant vat of lard. Peter has no choice but to eat his way out of the lard. The combination of the car accident and the lard consumption return Peter to his normal appearance and, with his family at his bedside, he apologizes for his behavior but admits to not learning any sort of lesson whatsoever.

MEMORABLE MOMENTS

Carrying an Extra Five Pounds?

SECURITY GUARD: All right, son, I'm gonna need those two hams back.

CHRIS: Wh— I-I don't have any hams.

SECURITY GUARD: Lift up your shirt, son.

CHRIS: I need an adult! I need an adult!

(The Security Guard lifts Chris's shirt up. He has no hams.)

SECURITY GUARD: You're not a shoplifter. You're just a fat kid. Heh? Sorry about that, fatty fat fatty.

(He tousles Chris's hair and chuckles. The Guard calls off.)

SECURITY GUARD: Hey, Tom, he's just a fat kid. *(to Chris)* Aren't ya, Fatty? You're just a big ol' fat kid. *(gives him a candy bar)* Here's some chocolate, Fatso.

Always with the One-upsmanship

Lois: Stewie's covered with fleas!

Peter: Oh, that's nothing. Once, when I was a kid, I was covered with ticks.

Lois: Peter, it's not a contest.

Peter: Well, it was back then.

(On Peter's night table is a loving cup trophy that reads "Most Ticks—1965.")

The Real Story

Stewie: That's it. Time for doggy to go the way of Ol' Yeller.

(Cutaway to Ol' Yeller's House, where Yeller and The Boy sit at the table, eating sandwiches. Mom enters.)

Mom: Ol' Yeller, did I get a call from Tony?

Ol' Yeller: Oh. Yeah. He— ah, he left a message. I forgot to tell you.

Mom: Is it on the machine?

Ol' Yeller: *(wincing)* I erased it.

(Mom frowns, resigned, and grabs a gun off the wall.)

Mom: All right. Out back.

Boy: No, Ma. Yeller's my dog. I'll do it.

(The Boy takes the gun and nudges Yeller toward the door.)

Ol' Yeller: Aw, c'mon, he'll call back.

Or We Could Do It Her Way

Meg: Out of my way, wide load. Mom, there's fleas all over the house.

Peter: There's only one thing to do. Learn the language of the fleas, earn their trust, then breed with their women, and in time, our differences will be forgotten.

Lois: Call the damn exterminator!

You Gotta Look Beneath the Surface

Lois: Oh, my, what a lovely room. And it's so clean.

Stewie: Well, I think the ultraviolet scanning light will be the judge of that.

(Stewie takes out a handheld ultraviolet scanning light.)

Stewie: I picked this up on *Dateline* from that yummy exoskeleton Maria Shriver.

(The blue ultraviolet light suddenly makes various stains visible on the crib, curtains, and bedspread.)

Stewie: Mmm-hmm, just as I thought. Oatmeal, spittle . . . semen?! This must be where Wilford Brimley was strangled by Bob Crane.

That's Embarrassing, Alright

Peter: What are you hiding under your shirt, Chris? Do you have bruises? Did somebody hit you? Lois! What did you do to my son?!

Lois: Will you keep your voice down. You're embarrassing him.

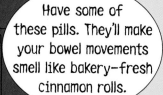

Have some of these pills. They'll make your bowel movements smell like bakery-fresh cinnamon rolls.

PETER: What're you talkin' about? If I wanted to embarrass him I'd do something like this. Hey, hey, everybody, hey, look what Chris Griffin's father Peter Griffin's doing!

(Peter reaches down, grabs his own boob, and starts to lick it.)

That Magic Moment in Every Child's Life

(Stewie is holding on to the side of the pool. He inches himself along trying to get someone's attention.)

STEWIE: I say, hello, you there! I'm ready to get out. Somebody!

(Stewie stops and his eyes widen. He looks down.)

STEWIE: Oh, my. What was that?

(Stewie inches back a few inches and his eyes widen again.)

STEWIE: Well, hello, Mr. Water Jet.

(Meg approaches.)

MEG: Stewie are you ready to—?

STEWIE: Go away!

Just Like the Old Days

PETER: Okay, Chris. Time for some good old-fashioned exercise, like those guys are doing.

(Next to them are a couple of Old-Fashioned Strong Men with bald heads and thick black handlebar mustaches, wearing black one-strap unitards and black lace-up boots.)

BARNABY: I say, Phineus. Great day to be doing squat-thrusts and lifting our huge triangular iron weights.

There Is Another Way . . .

CLEVELAND: Peter, if you're this desperate about Chris's weight, why don't you just suck the fat out?

PETER: Look, if you can find a hole on the boy that you want to put your lips on, be my guest.

CLEVELAND: I'm talking about liposuction. My brother Broderick's a cosmetic surgeon.

PETER: Is-is he good?

CLEVELAND: Well, Nell Carter used to be twice as big before Broderick got through with her. FYI, he used the fat he took out of her to make the two kids from *Good Burger*.

True Story?

LOIS: Meg, for the last time, you're not gettin' plastic surgery.

MEG: Why not? It's totally safe. A lot of famous people have done it.

(Cutaway to an Eskimo village, where the villagers have gathered around a small Eskimo Boy, who stands on an ice raft with his bed-roll.)

A View from Behind the Scenes

"We had gotten into a bad habit at the end of each episode of wrapping up the show with Lois and Peter talking about whatever life lesson they learned that week. We caught ourselves doing it again at the end of this episode, and we all had just had enough of it. So the end of the episode was Lois saying: 'So, Peter, I hope you learned a valuable lesson from this.' And Peter simply responding, 'Nope.'"

—CHRIS SHERIDAN, WRITER OF THE EPISODE

ESKIMO MAN: My son, your place is here in the ice village. You know nothing of Hollywood and its ways.

ESKIMO BOY: But Father, I have dreams, and courage, and the name of an excellent cosmetic surgeon. Fear not, someday word will reach you about the success of me, the great Eskimo actor Jennifer Love Hewitt.

The Strongmen Return

(Stewie falls out of his wagon and rolls into the gutter. Phineus and Barnaby, still in their unitards, walk by.)

PHINEUS: Look, there's a baby in that refuse bin.

BARNABY: Not too close, Phineus. If you touch it, the mother won't take it back.

PHINEUS: Alley, oop!

(Phineus leaps onto Barnaby's shoulder, they jump on one of those bicycles with the huge front wheel, and pedal down the street.)

Vanity Sets In

LOIS: Peter, did you paste a new picture of yourself on our wedding portrait?

PETER: Yeah, I think it looks better.

LOIS: You pasted it over me.

(She holds up the photo. In it, fat Peter is marrying handsome Peter.)

PETER: Yeah, I think it looks better.

Did Not See That Coming

WARREN: Come with me, I've got a lot of tall, statuesque people I want you to meet. *(notices Chris)* What's that?

PETER: Well, that's my son, Chris.

WARREN: He can't come in. Pfff, he's fat.

PETER: Well, let me tell you somethin', buddy. If my son can't come in, then I'll just come in. *(to Chris)* See ya at home.

A Nice Sibling Moment Ruined

MEG: Wow, Chris, did you lose weight?

CHRIS: Um . . . Maybe. I've-I've been working out.

MEG: Well, you look wicked skinny. I'm, like, jealous.

CHRIS: Thanks, Meg. I'm jealous of your mustache.

(He smiles and walks out. Meg turns to Lois.)

MEG: I don't have a mustache. Do I?

LOIS: Oh, honey, it's fine. It makes you look distinguished.

Episode
E PETERBUS UNUM

SUMMARY

When Peter sees all the cool things Cleveland, Quagmire, and Joe were able to buy with their tax refunds, he sets his sights on buying the family a pool for their yard. But instead of a refund, Peter gets audited. So, Peter decides to dig his own pool, knocking out power for the neighborhood in the process. When Peter is informed that city regulations prohibit him from building a pool in his yard, he heads down to City Hall with a head of steam. There, Mayor West informs Peter that upon scrutinizing the town map, he has come to discover that, in an unprecedented anomaly, Peter's property is not part of the town and, in fact, is not even part of the United States. Peter, fed up with bureaucracy, uses this information to declare his own nation called "Petoria."

Peter enjoys being the President of his own country and goes overboard in indulging in his own version of "diplomatic immunity." He even manages to get a seat at the United Nations for his new country, but quickly realizes that he gets no respect there. On the advice of the Iraqi delegate, Peter decides to annex Joe's pool as a way of commanding more respect for Petoria in the U.N. The U.S. government responds with sanctions, meaning that the Griffins' house is immediately surrounded by U.S. military equipment and personnel.

The family is soon in a desperate state. Without electricity or water, the Griffin household degenerates into squalor. Lois, already outraged, becomes even more furious when Peter hosts a cookout for his allies, a cartel of the world's most notorious dictators. She gathers up the family and leaves just as the U.S. military threatens to strike Peter's house. Finally, Peter agrees to negotiate a treaty wherein he consents to rejoining the United States.

MEMORABLE MOMENTS

Peter Griffin, Altruist

PETER: Geez, Cleveland, that musta set ya back, huh? What did ya do, sell your body to science? 'Cause, you know, I've thought of doin' that.
(Cutaway to a Junior High School Classroom, where a Teacher stands next to a skeleton that looks vaguely Peter-shaped.)

TEACHER: All right, uh, Jenny, would you come up here and show us where the femur is?
(Jenny comes up to the skeleton and studies it for a second, then reaches toward the femur.)

PETER SKELETON: AHHH!
(Jenny screams.)

PETER SKELETON: Hehehe. Get outta here ya little bastard. I knew this was the right thing to do.

What Quagmire Blew His Money On

QUAGMIRE: I spent my refund on a Plug-in Playmate!
(Flashback to Quagmire's house, where Quagmire sits across the table from a life-sized electric Sex Doll, which is plugged in and vibrating slightly. The table is set for a romantic dinner.)

EPISODE NUMBER: 2ACX13

ORIGINAL AIRDATE: 7/12/00

WRITERS: Neil Goldman & Garrett Donovan

DIRECTOR: Rob Renzetti

EXECUTIVE PRODUCERS: Seth MacFarlane, David Zuckerman

QUAGMIRE: So, a schoolteacher. That must be interesting.
(The doll and her chair vibrate away from the table, then she topples off the chair.)

Stream of Something

PETER: Well, I'm gettin' something really special, too. An-and-and by "special" I don't mean "special" like that Kleinerman boy down the street. More "special" like-like Special K the cereal. Hey, what do they do with the regular K? And for that matter, whatever happened to Kay Ballard? You know if you said "mallard" and you had a cold it would sound like "Ballard."

BRIAN: Do you even listen to yourself when you talk?

PETER: I drift in and out.

A Little Pathetic

STEWIE: You know, Rupert, the word "gullible" is not in the dictionary. Oh, oh, you don't believe me? Here, look it up.
(Stewie hands the dictionary to Rupert and titters as Rupert "looks it up.")

STEWIE: What? What's that? It really isn't?
(Stewie quickly grabs the dictionary back and discovers that, of course, the word is there.)

STEWIE: Oh, Rupert, touché! Hoisted by my own petard.
(Stewie laughs, then grows silent.)

STEWIE: I am so alone.

So, That's Why They're Married

PETER: All right, now kids, I don't want anyone swimming in this pool unless there's a lifeguard on duty. Hehehehe. Duty. Hehehehe. Diarrhea.
(Lois exits the house carrying a tray of iced tea.)

PETER: Hey, Lois!

LOIS: What?

PETER: Diarrhea!
(Lois laughs.)

LOIS: Peter, I'm holdin' iced tea.

A Bit of Griffin Family History

PETER: Damn government. Tell me I can't build a pool on my own land. And after my grandfather helped create one of this country's most beloved cartoon characters.
(Flashback to a 1940's Conference Room, where A Studio Head sits with a bunch of Cartoonists looking at an easel with a picture of Bugs Bunny.)

STUDIO HEAD: Okay, we've narrowed it down to two possible names. All in favor of "Bugs Bunny"?
(They all raise their hands.)

This just in: I'm tired of all the abuse.

Scene Stealers
ASIAN CORRESPONDENT TRICIA TAKANAWA

OCCUPATION
That's sort of encapsulated in her name, isn't it?

HER SPECIALTIES
News reporter cadences, deflecting anchors' barbs

HER AMBITIONS
Pay her dues in this small TV market, then get plastic surgery and marry Les Moonves

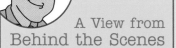

A View from Behind the Scenes

"This is the episode where we really learn why Peter loves Lois so much. After all, isn't that what all us guys are looking for? Just a woman who can laugh with you about the word 'diarrhea.' Ah, romance . . ."

—SETH MACFARLANE, CREATOR AND EXECUTIVE PRODUCER

STUDIO HEAD: All in favor of "Ephraim the Retarded Rabbit"?
(*No hands go up.*)
PETER'S GRANDFATHER: Oh, you can all go to hell!
(*He throws down his sketch pad and storms out.*)

Don't Cross This Guy

(*Peter opens the door and takes a few steps in.*)
PETER: Hello? Uh, is this the—
(*Mayor West pounces on Peter and pummels him with punches. After a moment, he stops his attack.*)
MAYOR WEST: Oh. Sorry. I thought you were the district attorney.

The Man Knows What He Likes

MAYOR WEST: I love this job more than I love taffy. And I'm a man who enjoys his taffy.
(*He takes a piece of saltwater taffy off his desk and pops it in his mouth. He chews on it "mming" and "ohing" for a long, long time.*)

Hail to the Chief

CLEVELAND: Here ya go, Mr. President. Mr. President. Oh, Peter that tickles me in a way that if Loretta tickled me in that way, I'd say, "Oh, yeah, that's nice, that's the spot."
PETER: What're ya talkin' about, I'm a born leader. Like my great, great uncle Ulysses S. Griffin.
(*Flashback to a Battlefield, where Ulysses S. Griffin sits across a table from Robert E. Lee. Each are cheered on by their Troops as they engage in a chug a lug beer-drinking contest.*)
TROOPS: Chug-a-lug, chug-a-lug, chug-a-lug!
(*Ulysses swiftly gulps his entire beer, then puts the empty mug on top of his head as the Union troops cheer.*)
ULYSSES S. GRIFFIN: How's that, Robert E. Lee?
ROBERT E. LEE: (*defeated*) All right, no more slaves. But we still don't have to read books.
ULYSSES S. GRIFFIN: Deal.
(*Both sides cheer.*)

Flouting Authority

QUAGMIRE: Hey, Peter, you can't drink that outside, you're gonna end up in jail, and not the good jail like on Cinemax, the man jail.

Squalor in Petoria

SUSAN SARANDON: Hi. I'm Susan Sarandon. A lot of you know me as Tim Robbins's mother, but I'm actually his girlfriend. And this is Stewie.
(*Susan scoops Stewie up in her arms and brushes the flies away.*)

5

STEWIE: What the deuce?

SUSAN SARANDON: For less than the ticket price of one of my movies about capital punishment or neo-feminism, you can make sure that Stewie never goes hungry again.

(Stewie eyes her ample bosom.)

STEWIE: Yes, and from the look of those sweater cows, so can you.

Stewie's Editorial Comment?

LOIS: Peter, this has gotten way out of hand. Look at what we're reduced to. Our own baby has to use newspapers for diapers.

STEWIE: No-no, no, no, this, this is fine. One second. I'm just about finished with "Family Circus." *(grunts)* There we are, who did that, Jeffy? Not me.

Universally Relatable

SADDAM: . . . And then Jerry guessed that her name was "Mulva."

QADAFFI: That show was so funny. It-it really reminds me of me and my friends, you know, the way we just hang out, before I kill them for worshipping the wrong God.

SADDAM: Yeah, and I love that Kramer guy. He comes in the room like this.

(He awkwardly imitates Kramer.)

SADDAM: Well, I can't do it, but you know.

Set an Example

PETER: Whoa, whoa, whoa, wh-where do you think you're going?

LOIS: America! I've had enough. You can keep this filthy mess you call a country. C'mon, kids.

STEWIE: This is treason! Oh, for God's sake, Peter, make an example of her. Nothing says "Obey me" like a bloody head on a fence post.

Negotiations Begin

MAYOR WEST: Thank you all for coming. We invited Jesse Jackson to open our negotiations with a prayer.

(Everyone "oohs" with anticipation.)

LOIS: Oh, my.

MAYOR WEST: Unfortunately, he couldn't make it, so in his place we have LaToya Jackson.

LATOYA: Thanks, um . . . Rub-a-dub-dub, thanks for the grub. Yay, God!

MAYOR WEST: How very inappropriate, thank you.

STUFF THAT MIGHT HAVE SLIPPED BY

■ Lois's attire while she's being interviewed by Tricia Takanawa is intended to be reminiscent of Jacqueline Kennedy.

■ At the U.N., Peter is seated in the back row, next to the delegate from Albania.

■ After Peter annexes Joe's pool, the headline on *The Quahog Informant* reads "Petoria Invades U.S."

■ At Peter's cookout, one of the dictators mans the grill wearing an apron that reads "Cooking with Mustard Gas."

Episode

THE STORY ON PAGE ONE

EPISODE NUMBER: 2ACX14
ORIGINAL AIRDATE: 7/18/00
WRITER: Craig Hoffman
DIRECTOR: Gavin Dell
EXECUTIVE PRODUCERS:
Seth MacFarlane,
David Zuckerman
GUEST VOICE: Luke Perry
as himself

SUMMARY

The family goes on a visit to Brown (Brian's alma mater) so that Meg can see the campus and speak to the Dean of Admissions. She is informed that her chances of being admitted are very small without more extracurricular activities, so she gets a job on the school paper. On her first day as a reporter she's told to interview Mayor West, a task that proves to be extremely difficult. Meanwhile, Stewie gets the idea that his tiny stature is an impediment to achieving his objectives.

After great effort, Meg finally gets her interview and even manages to uncover a story of government corruption. When Peter hears about it, though, he thinks Meg has misjudged the kind of story that will get her the attention she wants, so he decides to write his own story and substitute it for the one Meg wrote. The next day when the paper comes out, the headline (as allegedly written by Meg) screams "Luke Perry Is Gay." Meanwhile,

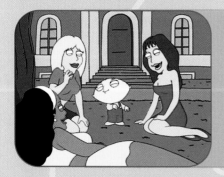

to overcome his issues with being small, Stewie rigs the more sizable Chris with a device that effectively transforms Chris into Stewie's personal robot.

Luke Perry threatens to sue Meg. When Peter sees how upset she is about the situation, he sets out to make things right. But instead of coming clean, Peter plans to get evidence that Luke Perry is gay in order to bolster the article's claim. Peter and Brian seek out Luke and, despite their efforts, aren't able to get any incriminating photos of him. But when Peter's plan is revealed and he explains that he was just trying to help out his daughter, Luke offers to sit down for an interview with Meg. Meanwhile, Stewie's efforts to harness Chris's brawn for his own good take a bad turn, causing Chris to come after Stewie, but fortunately, Stewie is able to fend him off.

MEMORABLE MOMENTS

Stewie Mixes with the Campus Ladies

STEWIE: A veritable bevy of coeds!
(He approaches a couple of Sorority Girls.)

STEWIE: Um, I say, the most recent campus sporting event was most disappointing for our side, wasn't it?

SORORITY GIRL #1: Oh, aren't you adorable! Are you in a fraternity, little boy?

STEWIE: Not yet, but I'm thinking about joining I Felta Thigh!
(The girls giggle.)

STEWIE: Oh . . . So, what do you think of this music television?

He'll Come Around

BRIAN: If I remember correctly, this is the Physics Department.

CHRIS: That explains all the gravity.

Only a Tiny Bit Fourth Wall-ish

DEAN WAGNER: Well, then. Let's take a look at your transcript. "Meg." Hmm. That's not very impressive. I mean, it's just three letters. It's hardly a name at all.

PETER: Well, I-I-I never wanted to call her "Meg." I-I wanted to call her "Twikki." But Lois said kids these days wouldn't get the reference. You know who I'm talking about, right? "Beedeebeedeebeedee."

A Hard Interview to Get

MEG: Excuse me, Mayor West—

MAYOR WEST: How do you know my language?

MEG: Listen to me. My entire future is in your hands.

MAYOR WEST: Are you Sarah Connor?

MEG: No, I'm Meg Griffin. See, I need to interview you and—

MAYOR WEST: You're with the press?

MEG: Yes.

MAYOR WEST: Well . . . you can't interview a dead man, can you?
(He takes three steps and jumps out the window.)

It's True, Just Look It Up

PETER: Aw, this'll never get Meg on the paper. This is old news! There've been scandals in politics ever since Thomas Jefferson.
(Flashback to Monticello, where Thomas Jefferson, his Wife, Martha, and a Couple of Children pose for a family portrait.)

THOMAS JEFFERSON: Oh, oh, oh, hold on, hold on. Honey, let's get all the kids in this.
(Jefferson motions and immediately, thousands of Young Black Children rush into frame and stand around Jefferson, posing.)

Could It Really Be True?

PETER: So what? A lot of these famous types lead secret lives that we don't even know about. Like Ricky Martin.
(Cutaway to a Dressing Room, where screaming Fans claw at Ricky Martin as he fights his way into the room.)

FANS: Ricky, we love you! / Ricky, Ricky! / Ricky we love you!
(Ricky pushes the door shut and locks it, then breathes a sigh of relief. He puts on jeans, a tank top, a long straight, blond wig, and some makeup that makes his skin lighter. A door on the far side of the room opens and a Stage Manager pokes his head in.)

STAGE MANAGER: One minute to curtain, Jewel.
(Ricky, who now looks exactly like Jewel, grabs a guitar and quickly follows the Stage Manager out.)

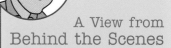

A View from Behind the Scenes

"Luke Perry could not have been a better sport about participating in this episode. In fact, his willingness to be up for pretty much anything was only surpassed by Adam West, who, when informed he'd be doing a scene where he was in bed with Luke Perry, merely responded with, 'Great. Let's do this.'"

—SETH MACFARLANE, CREATOR AND EXECUTIVE PRODUCER

Even if I was gay, come on, I'm Luke Perry. I can get a much better gay guy than Peter.

Scene Stealers
LUKE PERRY

OCCUPATION
Teen heartthrob and target of Peter's libel

HOW HE LEARNS ABOUT THE ARTICLE
From his daily routine of reading every high school newspaper in America to see if he's mentioned

NUMBER OF YEARS HE'S BEEN PLAYING A TEENAGER
30

See, Now That's Just False
MEG: Well, thanks to you, I can put down that I'm a big fat liar who makes up stories about people.
PETER: Hey, it worked for Walter Cronkite. You know that whole Vietnam thing? Never happened.

Can't Say He Doesn't Try to Be a Good Father
PETER: Aw, don't cry, sweetheart. I-I'lll, I'll make it up to you. You remember that pony you wanted when you were six? Well, I bought him and I've been saving him for a time like this. Surprise!
(Peter opens a closet, revealing a Dusty Horse Skeleton. Meg gasps.)
PETER: Oh, oh, God, that's right, ponies—ponies like food, don't they? Oh, boy.

Ah, poor Meg. I know it sounds crazy, but I can't help feelin' like this is somehow my fault.

Hmmm, Let's Think about That . . .

PETER: Ah, poor Meg. I know it sounds crazy, but I can't help feelin' like this is somehow my fault.

Possibly a New Low

PETER: Hey, I've gotten people to believe crazier things.

(Flashback to a Sunday School, where Peter stands in front of a bunch of Little Children, a Bible in front of him.)

PETER: And if you are pure of heart and deed, you'll all go to a beautiful place called "Heaven."

(They all stare up at him intently and nod. Peter starts to titter.)

PETER: I'm yanking you. You just rot in the ground.

Stewie's Experiment Goes Awry

STEWIE: Now look here, you gourd-bellied codpiece, allow me to purchase the provisions I demand or I shall transform your blue collar into a red one and . . . Who the deuce are you? No, I don't have any spare change. Where the hell would I keep it, in my diaper? Get out of here, you hobo. Oh, bloody hell, is this thing still on?

That's Not Really Helping

MEG: Well, there's no way I'm gonna get in now. I'm a felon.

LOIS: Now, that's not true. Libel's not a felony, it's a civil matter.

That's a Possibility, I Suppose

PETER: I'm telling you, "Dark Side of the Moon" totally syncs up with *The Wizard of Oz.*

LUKE PERRY: Really? Shannen Doherty told me that once, but I thought she was just being a bitch.

That Was the Plan? Really?

BRIAN: Uh, Peter, I think it's time for plan B.

PETER: Way ahead of you, Brian.

(Peter tears off his shirt, revealing that he's wearing a backpack over a T-shirt. He reaches behind him and pulls a rip cord. A parachute pops out and simply wafts down behind him.)

PETER: Don't worry. I packed my own back-up chute.

(Peter pulls another rip cord. A smaller parachute falls out in front of him.)

PETER: Aw, crap.

And Everyone Learned a Nice Lesson

LOIS: Won't you drop the lawsuit? Please, Dylan?

LUKE PERRY: Aw, what the hell. But, hey, you gotta print the real story. And this time I want to talk to the real reporter. Let's go, Meg.

PETER: See, Meg? Things always work out if you just do whatever you want without worrying about the consequences.

STUFF THAT MIGHT HAVE SLIPPED BY

■ The names in the "Sherry and the Anus" credits are various combinations of the first and last names of different *Family Guy* writers.

Co-Producer
Matt Barker

■ When Stewie tells the Zoltar machine he wishes he was big, the machine responds with a printed card that reads "I wish I could weigh people."

■ The *TV Guide* cover has a sidebar headline that reads "If you can read this, *Family Guy* is on the air."

■ The name of Meg's school paper is the *James Woods Bugle.*

■ Luke Perry's pool is the shape of his own head.

■ The name of the hotel where Peter and Brian find Luke Perry is The Five Seasons.

■ The headline of the article that Meg ultimately writes about Luke Perry reads "Luke Perry Is Straight, but It Didn't Do Me a Damn Bit of Good."

Episode
WASTED TALENT

EPISODE NUMBER: 2ACX15
ORIGINAL AIRDATE: 7/25/00
STORY BY: Dave Collard & Ken Goin
TELEPLAY BY: Mike Barker and Matt Weitzman
DIRECTOR: Bert Ring
EXECUTIVE PRODUCERS: Seth MacFarlane, David Zuckerman
GUEST VOICES: Michael McKean as Pawtucket Pat, Adam Carolla as Death

SUMMARY

The mysterious Pawtucket Pat, owner of the Pawtucket Patriot Brewery, announces a contest whereby the finders of four scrolls (randomly distributed into beer bottles) will each win a tour of the brewery. Peter is dead-set on winning, so he goes on a beer-drinking binge in an attempt to find one of the scrolls, but to no avail. Meanwhile, Lois is frustrated that none of her piano students show much promise, putting her in the likely position of losing this year's piano competition to a student of her annoying rival, Alexis Radcliffe. Tom Tucker falsely announces that the last scroll has been found, but when his story is corrected, Peter makes one more attempt to find it—and he does!

Peter and Brian show up for the tour of the brewery and have a great time, but are soon kicked out for not keeping up with the group. Peter returns home drunk and sits down at the piano where he plays beautiful renditions of old TV theme songs. Lois is thrilled, realizing she may have found the pupil who will enable her to beat Alexis Radcliffe. However, she is thrown by the fact that Peter's talent appears to wear off whenever his buzz does. That is to say, Peter can only play the piano proficiently when he is wasted. Determined to beat Alexis this year, Lois tells Brian to get a case of beer for Peter.

Lois keeps the beer flowing right up until the time of the competition when she is informed that all the liquor stores are closed, forcing them to crash a high school party, where Peter gets smashed. They head back to the competition and Peter wins, finally giving Lois the victory over Alexis that she'd been hoping for.

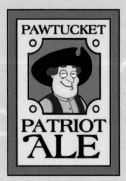

MEMORABLE MOMENTS

Friends Don't Let Friends Walk Home Drunk
(Peter enters with a case of beer.)

PETER: Oh, Lois, thank God it's you. The last three houses I went to were very rude.

A Place for Everyone
LOIS: Why do you care so much about touring a stupid brewery?

PETER: Lois, everyone has their sanctuary. The Catholics have churches, fat people have Wisconsin, and I have the Pawtucket Brewery! Now-now, help me drink these beers.

That Does Make a Certain Kind of Sense

LOIS: You're drunk again!

PETER: No, I'm just exhausted because I've been up all night drinking.

There Are Scents for Those?

(Alexis exits. Lois looks livid. Doctor Rubin starts to leave, but stops and leans in to Lois with a mischievous smile.)

DR. RUBIN: Don't let her get to you. She asked for "pine forest." I gave her "new car."

Sour Grapes

TOM TUCKER: It's true. The final scroll has been recovered. The lucky recipient has declined to be interviewed for safety reasons, but I'm sure you're all with me when I say, "Congratulations, you son of a bitch."

I Guess That Kinda Captures It

PETER: Aw, it's like I died and went to Heaven, but then they realized it wasn't my time and so they sent me back to a brewery.

Real Sensitive

BRIAN: Maybe we should stick with the group.

PETER: Beer that never goes flat. Do you know what that means, Brian? This beer will still be carbonated long after you die of old age and-and we buy another dog to help the kids, you know, forget about ya.

Desperate Housewife

(Peter and Brian enter.)

PETER: Lois, take a letter. Dear Pawtucket Pat. I hate you! You are a bad man! And you made me cry. Furthermore—

LOIS: Not now, Peter. Meg and I are havin' a little girl time.

MEG: Help me—!

(Lois quickly covers Meg's mouth.)

LOIS: Go on. No boys allowed.

PETER: Geez, Lois, still with the piano? What's a guy gotta do to get a little attention around here?

(Peter bangs noisily on the keys, but the banging soon turns into a rhapsodic, classical version of the theme from Dallas.*)*

LOIS: Peter?! That's incredible! I don't understand how— You're like that idiot from *Shine!*

Scene Stealers
PAWTUCKET PAT

HIS GREATEST SECRET
The formula for Perma-Suds

HIS GREATEST PERFORMANCE
Pretending to be shot by Cheech Marin

HIS GREATEST FAULT
Not having handicapped access ramps at the brewery. And grossly underpaying the Chumba Wumbas.

The beer may be free, but you're just renting it from me.

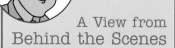

A View from Behind the Scenes

"This episode was obviously a nod to Willy Wonka and the Chocolate Factory. *Except without the six old people all sleeping in the same bed."*

—SETH MACFARLANE, CREATOR AND EXECUTIVE PRODUCER

STUFF THAT MIGHT HAVE SLIPPED BY

■ Meg is seen reading *Popularity for Dummies.*

■ The group of people who win the tour of the brewery includes two characters who look a great deal like Charlie Bucket and his grandfather from *Willy Wonka and the Chocolate Factory.*

■ When Peter wins the piano competition, Mary Tyler Moore is in the crowd to celebrate his victory by tossing her hat in the air.

■ The last shot in the show is of Stewie hitchhiking, re-creating the closing scene of the TV series *The Incredible Hulk.*

Still Felt Pretty Good

LOIS: Peter, talent doesn't disappear just like that.

PETER: Well, sometimes it does. I mean, I mean, you-you were pretty bad in bed Saturday night.

(Flashback to Peter and Lois's bedroom, where it's almost pitch black. There is some movement under the covers.)

PETER: Come on, Lois, move or something. Geez, it's like doin' it with a pillow.

(Cut back to the Griffins' den.)

LOIS: Peter, I stayed at my mother's that night.

PETER: Oh.

Way to Lay on the Guilt

PETER: Aw, geez, this hangover's killing me. I haven't felt this crappy since the time I went to that museum.

(Flashback to a Museum of Natural History, where a twelve-year-old Peter, his Classmates, and a Museum Guide stand around a Brontosaurus Skeleton.)

PETER: Why did all the dinosaurs die out?

MUSEUM GUIDE: Because you touch yourself at night.

(Peter hangs his head in shame.)

Good Point

LOIS: Oh, my God, you can only play the piano when you're drunk.

PETER: That's not true. I can also vomit, fall down, and make dirty calls to your sister when I'm drunk.

Lois Orders Peter More Beer

LOIS: Well, how much harm can one more pitcher do?

BRIAN: This is all for the sake of "art," right?

LOIS: Don't start with me, Brian. This may not be my proudest moment but, dammit, I wanna win.

Episode
FORE, FATHER

SUMMARY

Peter and Chris accompany Joe, Kevin, Cleveland, and Cleveland Jr. on a father-son camping trip. Joe's gung ho ways and his derisive remarks, coupled with Chris's inability to be responsible for the campsite, cause Peter to doubt his influence on Chris. Peter decides he has to teach Chris some responsibility. Meanwhile, Stewie goes to the pediatrician for his physical. He endures it quite well until he has to get his immunizations, at which point he regresses into being a terrified toddler.

Peter decides that the best way to teach Chris some responsibility is to get him a job as a golf ball shagger at the public golf course. Having done that, Peter believes himself to be the model father, prompting him to take Cleveland Jr. under his wing. Cleveland Jr. has such natural athletic talent and a knack for golf that Peter showers attention on him, essentially forgetting about Chris. Meanwhile, Stewie gets a fever from the immunizations, which Brian convinces him was actually an injection of a mind control serum. Stewie's fears about what nefarious deed Lois is trying to perpetrate on him with these shots combined with the fever result in a series of wild hallucinations.

Chris, feeling abandoned by Peter, begins to hang out with Quagmire, who tries to show Chris a good time. While they're at a strip club, Chris tells one of the dancers why he's so glum and she encourages him to give his dad another chance. Meanwhile, Peter and Cleveland Jr. decide to enter a "man-boy" golf tournament. But just when Cleveland Jr. is on the verge of winning, he loses focus. Cleveland tells Peter that perhaps he's better off tending to his own son, which leads to a heartfelt (and deadly) reconciliation between Peter and Chris.

EPISODE NUMBER: 2ACX16
ORIGINAL AIRDATE: 8/1/00
WRITER: Bobby Bowman
DIRECTOR: Scott Wood
EXECUTIVE PRODUCERS:
Seth MacFarlane,
David Zuckerman

MEMORABLE MOMENTS

Leave Well Enough Alone

(Meg and Lois are dusting. Lois comes across a box of memorabilia and pulls some items out.)

LOIS: Aw, look, Meg. It's your little baby booties. Oh, and your little bronzed hat. And your tail . . .

MEG: My what?!

LOIS: Nothing.

Really Putting Her to the Test

PETER: Lois, you know I swore I'd never clean again, not after Bounty dropped me as their spokesman.

(Flashback to a Diner, where Peter stands across the counter from Rosie. He pours a glass of liquid on the counter.)

PETER: Wait a second, Rosie, I've just poured this glass of warm yellow liquid on the counter and you're telling me that Bounty can pick it up in five seconds?

ROSIE: What is this?

PETER: Four seconds.

ROSIE: Is that—?

PETER: Three seconds.

ROSIE: That smells like—

PETER: Clean my pee!

Thanks for That, Cleveland

JOE: You guys wanna come along?

Scene Stealers
PATTY TANNINGER

OCCUPATION
Caddy Manager (Yeah, it rhymes. Big whoop. You wanna fight about it?)

WHY HE'S HAPPY
Business has picked up because everyone wants to hit the fat kid

HOW HE GETS AROUND THE DRIVING RANGE
Secret tunnels, like in *Hogan's Heroes*

Love. Jealousy. Forever. Passion. Obsession. Calvin Klein.

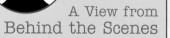

A View from
Behind the Scenes

CLEVELAND: Hmm. It would be nice to get out of the house. This is the time of the month when Loretta is visited by her Aunt Flo. Loretta likes to personify her menses in humorous ways.

Some Things Are That Delicious
STEWIE: I say, Rupert, this paste is quite delicious. It's almost worth the bowel obstruction.

Not a Bad Idea, Actually
CLEVELAND: You remember that short-lived sitcom *Fish*? They shoulda put that on before *CHiPs*. The marketing practically writes itself.

Quite a Grift
JOE: Let's go, Chris. Your dinner isn't gonna catch itself.
CHRIS: I don't wanna go. I had a bad experience with a fish once.
(Flashback to Chris's Bedroom, where Chris enters, carrying his book bag. He walks up to his desk and stops at the sight of an empty fish tank.)
CHRIS: Huh. Oh, my God! My fish is gone!
(Chris's eyes follow a trail of water leading over to a smashed piggy bank then to an open window.)
CHRIS: And he robbed me!

Comments Like That Hurt
DOCTOR: Hmmm, twenty-nine pounds. That's big for your age.
STEWIE: Well, forgive me for not being one of those anorexic babies from those diaper commercials.

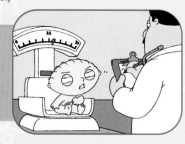

That Is Pretty Bad
CLEVELAND: I can't believe how terrible the fishing was.
PETER: Yeah, all we caught was a tire, a boot, a tin can, and this book of cliches.

Consulting the Fourth Wall
LOIS: Peter, you can't force-feed maturity. He needs to learn it on his own. Why, why don't you get him a job or something?
PETER: Whoa! Freeze-frame!
(The action, except for Peter, freezes.)
PETER: *(to camera)* That's it! I can teach Chris responsibility by getting him a job! Isn't she great? Now you see why I married her. Go away now. I'm gonna do stuff to her.

Tired of the Tedium
LOIS: Oh, Stewie, are you okay?
STEWIE: Oh, must we make small talk every time we pass?

Drama Queen

STEWIE: I should have known. Her treachery knows no limits! I— Oh, my . . . Getting dizzy!

(*He leans against the couch for support.*)

STEWIE: Oh, fight it, Stewie! "Do not go gentle into that good night," to quote Bob Dylan.

(*He puts the back of his hand to his forehead and faints like Scarlett O'Hara. Then he sits up, abruptly.*)

STEWIE: No, no, Dylan Thomas!

(*He faints again.*)

The Competitive Spirit Still Lingers

PETER: Boys, I'm a miracle worker. I have used all my parenting skills to change my son from a lazy slacker into a working man.

JOE: Nice going, Peter.

PETER: Yeah, up yours, Joe.

JOE: What?

PETER: Thanks.

Checkered Past

MEG: Why is he freaking out like that?

LOIS: Oh, he's having a little hallucination from the fever. Just like when you were three and you accidentally ate those adult brownies I was saving for the Doobie Brothers concert.

A Slice of Quagmire's Life

(*A Uniformed Delivery Woman rings Quagmire's doorbell. He opens the door unshaven, wearing a tank top and boxers.*)

DELIVERY WOMAN: Package for Glenn Quagmire.

(*Quagmire glances down at what he's wearing.*)

QUAGMIRE: Oh, oh, ex-excuse me.

(*He shuts the door. A beat later, it opens. He's now completely naked.*)

QUAGMIRE: Heh, I've got a package for you, too. All right.

(*The Delivery Woman pulls some mace from her belt and sprays it directly into Quagmire's face. He doesn't even flinch.*)

QUAGMIRE: Nice try, but I've built up an immunity.

Just Finding the Limits

PETER: Hey, great shot, Cleveland Junior.

CLEVELAND JR.: Thanks, Mr. Drummond.

PETER: Listen, for, uh, for today . . . Can you, can you switch and call me Mr. Popodopolos?

CLEVELAND JR.: You got it.

PETER: And would you, would you hate me if I called you Webster?

CLEVELAND JR.: That's the line.

PETER: Okay, sorry.

STUFF THAT MIGHT HAVE SLIPPED BY

■ Quagmire's license plate reads "BUSHMAN."

■ The name of the strip club that Quagmire takes Chris to is "The Fuzzy Clam."

■ The sign outside the strip club reads "Minors Welcome."

■ When Quagmire runs out of cash, he pays his stripper by sliding his ATM card through her butt crack.

Season Three

Episode
THE THIN WHITE LINE

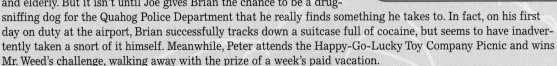

SUMMARY

When Brian tells his therapist that he is in a bit of an emotional rut, his doctor suggests that he may be too inwardly focused and that perhaps doing some volunteer work might be a good idea. Brian takes him up on his advice, serving as a guide dog for the blind and elderly. But it isn't until Joe gives Brian the chance to be a drug-sniffing dog for the Quahog Police Department that he really finds something he takes to. In fact, on his first day on duty at the airport, Brian successfully tracks down a suitcase full of cocaine, but seems to have inadvertently taken a snort of it himself. Meanwhile, Peter attends the Happy-Go-Lucky Toy Company Picnic and wins Mr. Weed's challenge, walking away with the prize of a week's paid vacation.

Brian continues to excel as a member of the police force, but his problems with cocaine mount until he ends up with a full-blown addiction. After he shows up at the house high on drugs and with a crack whore in tow, the family decides to stage an intervention. Ultimately Brian agrees to enter rehab. Meanwhile, Peter and the family have to cancel the cruise they had planned until after Brian's treatment. Peter, disappointed at not being able to sail the seas in style and in awe of the fancy amenities at Brian's rehab facility, decides to fake his own addiction in order to "vacation" at the detox clinic.

Before long, Peter's obnoxious behavior attracts the attention of the clinic's head doctor. And despite his initial attempts to ignore Peter, Brian gets sucked into Peter's antics. When the doctor claims that Peter is the "X factor" responsible for driving Brian to his addiction, Brian indignantly exits rehab (along with Peter). Back at home, the family celebrates Brian's return, but he drops a bombshell on them. Saying his experience has shown him that everyone is responsible for his own destiny, Brian says he's off to follow his own personal journey. And with that, Brian hails a cab, drives off, and the audience learns that this story is "To Be Continued . . ."

EPISODE NUMBER: 2ACX17

ORIGINAL AIRDATE: 7/11/01

WRITER: Steve Callaghan

DIRECTOR: Glen Hill

EXECUTIVE PRODUCERS: Seth MacFarlane, David Zuckerman

GUEST VOICE: Leif Garrett as himself

MEMORABLE MOMENTS

Thank God for Doctor-Patient Confidentiality

BRIAN: I, uh, I-I notice you got a new receptionist. Nice little body on her, huh?

DR. KAPLAN: That's my daughter. *(A long, awkward silence.)*

BRIAN: Well, we could probably call this an early day, huh?

Matchmaker, Matchmaker . . .

PETER: Hey, Derek, how ya gettin' to the picnic?

DEREK: I don't know. I don't have a ride.

(Peter turns to John, another handsome young employee.)

PETER: Hey, John, you got a two-seater, don'tcha? Hey, Derek, maybe, maybe you go with John. Huh? Huh?

DEREK: For the last time, I'm not gay. *(Derek gets up and leaves, annoyed.)*

JOHN: Thanks anyway, Peter.

PETER: *(smiles)* Hey, we'll get 'im.

That Guy Is Lucky He's Blind

(Brian, working as a Seeing Eye dog, sits beside his Blind Guy in a movie theater. Brian watches the screen then turns to the man and speaks in a hushed tone.)

BRIAN: Okay, they're-they're in the woods . . . the camera keeps on moving . . . Uh, I think they're, they're looking for some witch or something, I—I don't know, I wasn't listening . . . nothing's happening, nothing's happening, something about a map, nothing's happening, it's over, a lot of people in the audience look pissed.

A Quahog Star Is Born

(A Few Dozen Employees crouch in a wide circle surrounding a clearing with a cage in the center.)

PETER: Oh, this is my favorite event: catch the greased-up deaf guy.

MR. WEED: Go!

(Mr. Weed pulls a rope, opening the cage. A greased-up Deaf Guy in a bathing suit springs out and leaps about erratically as Peter and the other contestants rush in, trying unsuccessfully to grab him.)

DEAF GUY: *(mockingly)* You're never gonna catch me. You're wasting your time. Forget about it. Go do something else.

(Peter lunges for the guy and grabs him, but he's too slippery for Peter to hold on. The guy runs through the crowd and disappears into the woods.)

DEAF GUY: See ya'll next year.

What Would That Look Like, Exactly?

(Stewie watches Peter run.)

STEWIE: Look at him. He runs like a Welshman. Doesn't he? Doesn't he run like a Welshman?

Psyching Out the Competition

(Brian sits next to Toucan Sam in folding chairs outside a door marked "Casting." They are each holding pages.)

TOUCAN SAM: *(Rehearsing)* Follow your nose. Follow your nose. Follow your nose.

(Brian laughs. Toucan Sam looks up.)

BRIAN: Oh, I, uh, I'm sorry. I-I. No-no, that-that-that was good. I-I just, I-I-I didn't think you were going to go so "cartoony" with it.

TOUCAN SAM: Well, how-how would you read it?

BRIAN: Oh, I-I don't know. I was thinking of doing it, you know, good. Like, like an actor. But, you know, your-your way's good, too.

(Toucan Sam slides down in his chair, clearly shaken.)

Guess Again, Quagmire

JOE: Say hello to our newest narc. He's a natural.

QUAGMIRE: Oh yeah? How good are ya?

(Brian looks at Quagmire and gives a quick sniff.)

BRIAN: You're back from Manila. You had lumpia for dinner. Then you made love to two Filipino women. *(sniffs)* And a man.

QUAGMIRE: You mean three Filipino women!

(Brian just looks at him. A look of horror slowly comes over Quagmire's face.)

QUAGMIRE: Nooo!!

My blind guy is in the bathroom.

You're never gonna catch me. You're wasting your time. Forget about it. Go do something else.

A View from Behind the Scenes

"This episode is 'To Be Continued' because it was originally conceived as a season finale that would be resolved in the following season's premiere. But then, FOX changed our air schedule again. For the fifth time."

—SETH MACFARLANE, CREATOR AND EXECUTIVE PRODUCER

Way to Burn the Midnight Oil

PETER: Hey, hey, Brian, if cops are pigs does that make you a Snausage?
BRIAN: Heh, clever, Peter. Did you stay up all night writing that?
PETER: Nah, I got to bed around two, two-thirty.

Where Does She Get This Stuff?

BRIAN: You know what Joe said the street value of that cocaine would've been?
LOIS: Uh, let's see, four-and-a-half kilos, uncut Nicaraguan? Uh, one point seven mil, that area.
BRIAN: Uh, yeah. That's-that's, that's right.

Show-Off

BRIAN: Oh, c'mon, stop it, you guys. It's nothing, really. *(sniffs)* Oh, Lois, your toast is ready.
(The toast pops up in the toaster.)
LOIS: Well!
(All but Stewie applaud lightly, ad-libbing approval.)
BRIAN: Uh, Meg's using a new conditioner.
MEG: He's right!
(All but Stewie applaud lightly again, ad-libbing approval.)
BRIAN: And it's time to change Stewie.
STEWIE: Oh, that's preposterous. I haven't— Oh, there it is.
(They all applaud lightly again, ad-libbing approval.)

A Pat on the Back, Sort Of

(Joe stands with Brian, surrounded by a bunch of admiring cops.)
JOE: Nice work, Rookie!
COP #1: You're a credit to the force!
COP #2: Additional generic cop compliment, Brian!

Home from Work, High as a Kite

LOIS: So, how was your day?
BRIAN: My day? Un-freakin'-believable. First-first we nailed this bastard who had the gall to hide his stuff in his daughter's doll. Her doll, for God's sake. Oh, where's the line anymore? Well, I got news for you: it's-it's-it's-it's-it's not even on the radar screen! The days of decency and virtue are gone, honey. *Bam!* Freakin' evaporated like a dingy, stinkin' mud puddle. One-one day you-you–you see your reflection in it, and the next day it's-it's a, it's a, it's a damn oil spot on your cracked driveway, staring back at you, mocking you, blah blah blah, knowing the perverted truths that rot in the pit of your soul! That's how my freakin' day was.
(The family looks at Brian, stunned, for a long time.)
PETER: You know what I haven't had in a while? Big League Chew.

Cancer? What's Cancer?

PETER: Now Chris, before you go on a cruise, you gotta build up a base tan.

CHRIS: But, Dad, I heard that if you use tanning beds you can get something called "melanoma."

PETER: Oh, that's just fancy talk for "sexified." Now climb in.

Not Quite Getting the Concept of a Book, Eh?

LOIS: Oh, *The Old Man and the Sea*. I see you're getting in the mood for our cruise.

PETER: Yeah, stupid fisherman. Sitting out there in a boat, yammering to himself. He doesn't even know I'm watching him.

The Family Intervenes

BRIAN: Hey, Doc. What the hell are you doing here?

DR. KAPLAN: Your family has something they'd like to say to you.

(Meg reads from a piece of paper.)

MEG: Brian, I know I don't speak up much, and it's-it's really hard for me to talk about my feelings, but—

DR. KAPLAN: Why don't we start with someone more interesting? Peter?

Stewie Craves the Spotlight

LOIS: Good luck, Brian. I just know you're gonna get clean.

PETER: Heh, shouldn't be too hard to get clean with all these mineral baths and Jacuzzis.

(Everyone except Stewie laughs. Stewie scowls.)

STEWIE: Oh, oh, I see. The fat man makes a pun and everyone wets themselves. I give you gold and I get squat. *(then)* I'll be in the car.

Lie Thwarted

DOCTOR HORTENSE: I'll be keeping my eye on you. What's your name?

PETER: Uh, my-my name? . . . uh . . .

(Peter nervously scans the lunch room and lands on a dirty dish with one green pea on it.)

PETER: Uh . . . "Pea— "

(Peter scans the room some more and settles on the face of a Girl who is crying and has a single tear running down her cheek.)

PETER: — "Tear— "

(A Gryphon flies across the room, squawking loudly.)

PETER: "Gryphon." Yeah, yeah, Peter Griffin! *(realizing)* Aw, crap.

That's Sort of Touching . . .

PETER: Brian, it's moments like this that make me sad you're going to die fifty years before I do.

STUFF THAT MIGHT HAVE SLIPPED BY

(and one thing you wouldn't have known)

■ The newspaper announcing Brian's heroism and showing a picture of him riding in a ticker tape parade has a subheadline that reads "Scientists Mystified by Paper Rain."

■ When Joe and Brian break up the drug ring of midgets posing as a Sunday school class, a poster on the wall shows Jesus in a baggy jacket and sunglasses, striking a gangsta pose. The caption reads "It's Cool to Love Jesus."

■ When Brian is speaking to the school assembly, a banner hangs above him that reads "Welcome, McGriffin, Quahog's Cuddliest Soldier in the War on Drugs."

■ Gerald the Happy and Abstinent Police Clown originally sang a song that got cut for time. It was to the tune of "If You're Happy and You Know It," and the lyrics are, "IF YOU DON'T HAVE THE CLAP, LET'S CLAP. IF YOU DON'T HAVE THE CLAP, LET'S CLAP."

■ Peter and Chris go to a tanning salon called "U.V. Ray's."

■ The sign in front of Brian's detox clinic reads "Providence Rehab Clinic—Because, dude, it's time."

Episode
BRIAN DOES HOLLYWOOD

EPISODE NUMBER: 2ACX20

ORIGINAL AIRDATE: 7/18/01

WRITER: Gary Janetti

DIRECTOR: Gavin Dell

EXECUTIVE PRODUCERS:
Seth MacFarlane,
David Zuckerman

GUEST VOICES: Jenna Jameson as
herself, Ron Jeremy as himself

SUMMARY

The Griffins get a letter from Brian in which he describes his life as an aspiring screenwriter in Hollywood. The reality, though, is not all that rosy as Brian clearly struggles to make inroads in the Hollywood community. Meanwhile, Lois takes Stewie to an audition for *Kids Say the Darndest Things*, figuring that if Stewie gets on the show he'd get a free trip to Los Angeles for the whole family and, therefore, a chance to visit

Brian. Stewie jumps through just the right hoops and is selected to be on the show, sending the Griffins off to Hollywood.

When they arrive they immediately contact Brian. Since Brian is still struggling career-wise, he's all prepared to lie to the family about the success he's found, but then Brian's cousin Jasper hooks him up with a pro-ducer who hires Brian as a director on a low-budget film. Feeling good about his prospects, Brian shows off for the family and even invites them to the set of his film. It's only when he shows up for his first day of work that he discovers he's been hired to direct a porn movie.

Brian manages to convince himself that perhaps he can infuse the film with a bit of creativity, but when the Griffins arrive, he becomes embarrassed about what he's doing. He shoos them away, causing the family to think that Brian is too big for them now and that he can't be bothered to hang out with them. Meanwhile, Stewie goes on *Kids Say the Darndest Things*, thinking it will be his opportunity to brainwash the viewing masses, but his plan is disrupted by the barely intelligible antics of host Bill Cosby. Brian is nominated for an Adult Movie Award, but he is still too ashamed to invite the family. At Jasper's request the Griffins show up for Brian's big night anyway and show him that while he thought he needed to get away from the family to find out what was missing in his life, the only thing missing was his family.

MEMORABLE MOMENTS

Careful, There
STEWIE: Aw! Easy! Massage the scalp. You're washing a baby's hair, not scrubbing vomit off your Christmas dress, you holiday drunk!

Easily Placated
MEG: You guys, we got a letter from Brian.
PETER: *(whispering)* Tell-tell him I'm not here.
LOIS: Ooh, let me see.
(She picks Stewie up and sets him on the counter next to the sink. He sits bolt upright.)

STEWIE: Aaaaahhhh! Aaaaahhhh!

(He stands up, removing a fork from his thigh.)

LOIS: Oh, I'm sorry, sweetie.

(Lois kisses Stewie's thigh.)

LOIS: There, all better?

STEWIE: You know, you are some piece of work, lady. If you— Well, actually, yes, it is.

Brian Works the Room

BRIAN: Keanu Reeves, wow. Huh, you know, I don't usually gush, so you'll have to forgive me.

(A Woodpecker alights on Keanu's head and starts pecking.)

BRIAN: But, uh, but when I was writing *Coast Guard*, oh, uh, that's what I do, I'm a writer, anyway, when I was writing *Coast Guard*, I couldn't think of anyone other than— Uh, uh there's a woodpecker on your head.

KEANU REEVES: Yeah, he comes and goes.

We Know How That Turned Out

PETER: Geez, I haven't been to California since I lived with my other family.

(Flashback to a Rundown Ranch, where Charles Manson sits amid a bunch of other Wild-Looking Hippies on the floor. Peter runs in, excited.)

PETER: Guys! I just got invited to a party at Sharon Tate's house. You guys can come. But ya gotta promise not to embarrass me.

Playtime with Stewie

(Stewie slaps a stuffed Kermit the Frog, who is tied up to one of the legs of the crib.)

STEWIE: Talk, damn you. I know you've been plotting to foil my plans of world domination. Who're you working for? The Libyans? The French? *(then)* Very well, if torture won't work, perhaps a little tenderness will.

(Stewie takes a stuffed Miss Piggy from his toybox and lovingly puts his arm around her in front of Kermit.)

STEWIE: Mmmm, I like your taste in women. Yes, I think she and I are going to have a good time together.

(He stands behind Miss Piggy, fondling her as he looks at Kermit.)

STEWIE: Yes, you like this, don't you. *(BEAT)* Oh, God, look at me, having sex with a pig. I've become my father.

Pretty Much Sums Him Up

MICHAEL EISNER: What's your name?

BRIAN: Brian.

MICHAEL EISNER: Let's see . . .

(He reaches into his coat pocket, rummages around, then

Scene Stealers
JASPER

WHO HE IS
Brian's cousin

WHAT HE LIKES
Filipinos and sex and the city (not the TV show)

THE IRONY ABOUT HIM
He doesn't like bitches (the dog kind), but he is one (the catty kind)

I know, I know, I'm a rice queen.

pulls out a mouse ear hat with the name "Brian" embroidered on it. He sets it on Brian's head.)

MICHAEL EISNER: There we go. Brian.

(He rubs Brian's head.)

MICHAEL EISNER: See you at Disneyland. Bring money.

At a Loss for Words

PETER: Did you hear that, Lois, we're going to Hollywood! Where the people are sexy, and clever, and they always say something funny right before the commercial break.

(There is a long, long, long pause. Peter looks like he's about to speak, but changes his mind.)

That'll Teach You to Prejudge

(The Griffins file down the aisle of the plane. A Grumpy-Looking Man sees that Lois and Stewie sit down behind him. He rolls his eyes.)

GRUMPY MAN: Oh, great. I always end up sitting next to a damn baby.

STEWIE: What? What did you just say?!

(Stewie struggles to get out of Lois's arms.)

LOIS: Stewie, stop fussing.

STEWIE: Not now, Lois.

(Stewie jumps onto the tray table and starts smacking the back of the man's head with his open palm.)

STEWIE: Hey, big man, turn around. If you've got something to say, say it to my face.

(The guy looks annoyed then goes back to reading his paper.)

STEWIE: Oh, you can't hear me now? *(then)* All right, that's it, I was going to watch the movie, but forget it. For the next five hours you're my bitch.

(Stewie gets on his back and viciously kicks the back of the man's seat.)

STEWIE: Wah! Wah! My ears are popping and there's no way to console me! I'm hungry and possibly teething! Maybe I'm wet! Who knows? I'm a baby! Wah! Wah!

The Griffins Do Some Sightseeing

(Lois, Peter, Chris, Stewie, and Meg are by the curb. Meg reads a tourist map.)

MEG: Ooh, it says here that this is the actual gutter where the policeman fell over laughing after Eddie Murphy told him he was just giving the transvestite a ride home.

Thanks?

BRIAN: Oh, boy, this is great. All that searching, that-that emptiness I felt back home— Gone. I think I've finally found my life's calling, y'know?

LOIS: How wonderful! Y'know, Brian, I've always found your writing to

---

A View from Behind the Scenes

"It was a real pleasure working with Jenna Jameson and Ron Jeremy on this episode. But let's just say that after Ron reached into the jar of mixed nuts in the kitchenette, well, we pretty much had to just throw that thing away."

—SETH MACFARLANE, CREATOR AND EXECUTIVE PRODUCER

be a little hackneyed and stilted, but I guess that's why I'm not working out here in Hollywood, huh? Oh, congratulations on all your success!

Brian Drinks the Kool-Aid

(Zack hands Brian a script.)

BRIAN: You know, this isn't bad.

ZACK: It's kinda like *Bang the Drum Slowly*. Except the drum's a chick.

Brian Gives Some Direction

BRIAN: Uh, okay, uh, nice take Jenna, but, uh, l-let's try giving the lines a little subtext this time. Your husband's always away on business, and you feel increasingly isolated and unloved, so you begin to think maybe you should go back to graduate school and finish your dissertation. And that's when you notice the cable man has taken his pants off.

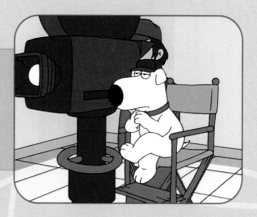

Vanity Sets In

MAKEUP ARTIST: You're gonna look so handsome.

STEWIE: Oh, look at these crow's-feet. My God, you stay up past seven-thirty and you pay for it in the morning.

Jasper Dishes It

JASPER: Brian, they're your family. They'll love you even if you made a couple of crappy movies. I mean, Blythe Danner still loves Gwyneth Paltrow. Oooh, score one for me!

The Griffins Arrive to See Brian's Big Moment

LOIS: Brian, why didn't you tell us?

BRIAN: I thought you'd be ashamed of me.

PETER: Eh, you kiddin'? I oughta knock you out for not bringin' me here sooner. Look at the pair on that one, Lois. Bigger than your head.

Indecent Proposal

MAN: *(to Lois)* You got a nice wiggle, baby. You wanna be in a movie, huh? A little girl-girl action, maybe?

LOIS: Oh, Peter!

PETER: *(to the guy)* Heh, good luck, buddy. I've been barkin' up that tree for seventeen years.

STUFF THAT MIGHT HAVE SLIPPED BY

■ When Brian is searching for a lie to tell the Griffins, he says he's been invited to the premiere of a new movie. As he searches for an actor to claim is in the movie, he glances at a *Movieline Magazine* with Val Kilmer on the cover and pushes it aside, revealing an *Entertainment Weekly* with Kevin Costner on the cover. Then he chooses to go with the more believable choice, Val Kilmer.

■ Ron Jeremy announces the nominees for Best Original Score in an Adult Film, including Ron Jones and Walter Murphy, the names of the *Family Guy* composers.

■ Brian's "Woody" award is blurred out, because it actually is a "woody."

Episode
MR. GRIFFIN GOES TO WASHINGTON

SUMMARY

Peter plays hooky from work in order to take the family to a baseball game. He runs into Mr. Weed at the game and is told to show up in Mr. Weed's office the next morning. But when Peter comes to see Mr. Weed, he informs Peter that the Happy-Go-Lucky Toy Company has been bought by a huge corporation and Mr. Weed has been fired. Soon, the toy factory is filled with all sorts of perks to placate the employees, all of whom are unaware that the new owner intends to use the toys produced by the factory to get kids addicted to cigarettes.

put me through to the pentagon!...

Peter returns home and tells the family he got a raise and shows off some of the new prosmoking toys the factory is now turning out. Lois disapproves of the changes in the company and tells Peter to voice his concerns to the new management. When Peter does so, they offer to make him president of the company and extend a variety of perks to the family in order to shut Peter up. The perks do the trick for everyone except Brian, who remains disgusted that the Griffins could be bought off so easily. In fact, Brian decides to give up smoking in protest. When the company executives learn about antismoking legislation that is being considered by the "idiots" in Washington, they decide to send someone who they believe speaks the same language as the politicians to defeat the bill. They send Peter.

In Washington, Peter soon wins friends in Congress. But back at home, Lois sees Stewie about to light up a cigarette and realizes how irresponsible she's been. She quickly gathers up the rest of the family and races to the Capitol to stop Peter. Just as Peter is addressing Congress and seemingly on the verge of killing the anti-smoking legislation, he notices the effects cigarettes have had on Stewie and changes his tune, resulting in a huge fine for the cigarette company. The family heads home, none of them happier than Brian, who can now give up his hiatus from smoking.

EPISODE NUMBER: 2ACX11

ORIGINAL AIRDATE: 7/25/01

WRITER: Ricky Blitt

DIRECTOR: Brian Hogan

EXECUTIVE PRODUCERS:
Seth MacFarlane,
David Zuckerman

GUEST VOICE: Alyssa Milano
as herself

MEMORABLE MOMENTS

Street Smarts

LOIS: Peter, you can't just pull the kids out of school for a baseball game.

PETER: Ah, there's nothing these kids learn in school they can't learn on the street.

(Cutaway to an Inner-City Street, where Two Teenagers are on the corner. The younger one checks his watch.)

YOUNGER TEENAGER: It's three o'clock, where the hell is Louie?

OLDER TEENAGER: Well, you tell me. Louie left his house at two-fifteen

and has to travel a distance of six point two miles at a rate of five miles per hour. What time will Louie arrive?

YOUNGER TEENAGER: Depends if he stops to see his ho.
(The Older Teenager tousles the Younger Teenager's hair, pleased.)
OLDER TEENAGER: That's what we call a variable.

Calling in Sick, Sort Of

MEG: Dad, don't you have to work today?
PETER: It's nothin' a little phone call can't take care of.
(Peter picks up the phone and dials.)
MR. WEED: Hello?
PETER: Mr. Weed? I can't come to work today. I was in a terrible plane crash. My entire family was killed and I am a vegetable. I'll see you tomorrow.

Just Stating an Opinion

PETER: I'm tired of Mr. Weed treating me like a common doormat. I want him to treat me like one of those deluxe ones from Pottery Barn with the fancy straw.
BRIAN: Hmm. I don't care for Pottery Barn.

It Probably Made More Sense in His Head

CHRIS: Can't we eat? I'm so hungry I could ride a horse. *(then, confused)* I don't get it. I could ride it to the store, I guess.

The Changes Begin

PETER: And check out the new toys we're makin'.
(Peter hands them each a toy.)
MEG: "Baby Smokes-a-lot."
(She pushes a button on the back of the doll. The doll takes a drag from a cigarette, exhales, then says:)
BABY SMOKES-A-LOT: Tastes like happy!
CHRIS: Cool! That's imitatable!

Persona Non Grata

PETER: Don't you worry, Lois, I'll set 'em straight. Just like I did with Chris.
(Flashback to a Whale Watching Boat, where Peter and Chris look out at the ocean as a whale breaches the surface.)
CHRIS: Dad, what's the blowhole for?
PETER: I'll tell you what it's not for, son. And when I do, you'll understand why I can never go back to SeaWorld.

Close, but No ...

PETER: You shoulda seen the way they were treating me. I've never gotten that kind of respect before.
(Flashback to the Community Pool, where Peter, wearing a shirt that says "Coach" and a whistle around his neck,

A View from Behind the Scenes

"Peter's 'writers' in this episode are drawn to resemble Family Guy *writers Mike Barker and Matt Weitzman. And, well, let's just say that once or twice I've hired them to follow me around just like that in my own life."*

—SETH MACFARLANE, CREATOR AND EXECUTIVE PRODUCER

> We just need these bastards to see what kind of fun-loving people the tobacco industry's really made of.

Scene Stealers
MR. HARRISON

OCCUPATION
El Dorado Cigarette Company executive

HOBBIES
Selling cigarettes to kids, killing puppies, tennis

WAYS HE'S TRIED TO INFLUENCE WASHINGTON POLITICIANS
Harvard lawyers, lobbyists, wise-cracking leprechauns

talks to Bobby, a ten-year-old who is pulling himself up out of the pool.)
PETER: Great workout, Bobby.
BOBBY: Up yours, sack breath.
PETER: That's *Mister* Griffin.

Bring On the Perks

PETER: After all these years, the company finally thinks I'm worth something. Oh, just wait 'til you see all the perks we're gonna get!
(Cut to James Woods High School, where Meg is at her locker. She closes the door, revealing a very Ugly Girl standing there.)
MEG: Um . . . hi? Can I help you?
UGLY GIRL: Yeah, some company hired me to stand next to you all day so you'd look better by comparison.
MEG: That's ridiculous. I don't need—
(A passing Student calls to Meg.)
STUDENT: Hey, Meg. Did you get less ugly?
(Meg pulls the girl closer to her.)
MEG: Yeah!

Everyone Should Have One of Those

PARKING LOT ATTENDANT: Oh, you don't need to park here, Mr. Griffin. You have an executive parking space now.
PETER: Well, that looks exactly like my old space.
PARKING LOT ATTENDANT: Yeah, but this one comes with your own company suck-up.
(The attendant indicates an energetic young Suck-Up wearing a suit standing beside the parking space.)
SUCK-UP: Morning, Mr. Griffin. Nice day.
PETER: Eh, it's a little cloudy.
SUCK-UP: It's absolutely cloudy. One of the worst days I've seen in years. So, good news about the Yankees.
PETER: I hate the Yankees.
SUCK-UP: Pack of cheaters, that's what they are. I love your tie.
PETER: I hate this tie.
SUCK-UP: It's awful, it's gaudy, it's got to go.
PETER: *(leading)* And I hate myself.
SUCK-UP: I hate you, too. You make me sick, you fat sack of crap.
PETER: But I'm the president.
SUCK-UP: The best there is.
PETER: But you just said you hated me.
SUCK-UP: But not you the president, the you who said you hated you. You-who, love, hate, Yankees, clouds—
(His head explodes.)

Peter's Checkered Past

PETER: Washington? Ah, sweet! Hey, I'm your man. But I gotta warn ya, I've made some enemies on Capitol Hill.

(Flashback to a Senate Hearing Room, where Peter is seated at the Senate witness table in the packed hearing room.)

PETER: And that's when Clarence Thomas forced me into his chambers and showed me lewd pictures.

SENATOR: Mr. Griffin, we have indisputable evidence that not only have you never been in the same room as Clarence Thomas, you've never been in the same state. How do you respond to that?

(Peter's eyes shift back and forth a few times. He then grabs the microphone with both hands.)

PETER: Bababooey, Bababooey, Howard Stern's penis, Bababooey, Bababooey . . .

(He continues shouting "Bababooey" as Security Guards try to peel him off the mic.)

That'd Be One Use for It

CHRIS: Hey, Mom, the school janitor said that Dad's working for the bad guys. And he said it through a hole in his throat!

LOIS: Well, that doesn't make him right.

CHRIS: If I had a hole in my throat, I'd put pennies in it!

Imagine How Long That Was Building Up

LOIS: Oh, God, what have I done? I knew smoking was bad but-but I still sold my soul . . . and for what? Martha Stewart?! C'mon, kids, we've gotta put a stop to this. Now!

(Lois leads the family quickly out the door. Martha Stewart looks around for a beat, then sighs.)

MARTHA STEWART: Finally.

(She lets out a long, loud fart and exhales.)

Way to Take a Stand

SENATOR #1: Mr. Griffin is right! Smoking is a horrible vice. It shortens life expectancy and pollutes our air. And according to recent polls, air is good.

SENATOR #2: Cigarettes killed my father. And raped my mother!

SENATOR #1: Gentlemen, I propose we send a message to tobacco companies everywhere by fining the El Dorado Cigarette Company infinity billion dollars!

SENATOR #3: That's the spirit, Frank. But I think a real number might be more effective.

STUFF THAT MIGHT HAVE SLIPPED BY

■ The montage that follows Mr. Harrison's decision to send Peter to Washington is a parody of the opening credits of the TV series *That Girl*.

■ The series of magazine ads featuring Peter includes one of Peter drawn as Joe Camel.

■ **The strip club that Peter takes the politicians to is called The Oval Orifice.**

■ In the Capitol building lobby a sign reads "Today's Agenda: Tobacco Vote. Tomorrow: Gay Friday."

Episode
ONE IF BY CLAM, TWO IF BY SEA

EPISODE NUMBER: 2ACX19

ORIGINAL AIRDATE: 8/1/01

WRITERS: Jim Bernstein
& Michael Shipley

DIRECTOR: Dan Povenmire

EXECUTIVE PRODUCERS:
Seth MacFarlane,
David Zuckerman

SUMMARY

A hurricane bears down on Quahog, causing all the residents to hunker down. After the storm passes, Peter, Quagmire, Joe, and Cleveland are out and about, surveying the damage, when they come across Horace, owner and bartender of the Drunken Clam. Horace tells the guys that he sold the bar so he wouldn't have to worry about getting wiped out by storms like the one that just blew through. But to the shock and horror of Peter and the guys, their beloved bar has been transformed by the new owner into a British pub.

Peter comes home to complain to Lois about what's happened to the Drunken Clam and is introduced to the Griffins' new neighbor, Nigel Pinchley, the Brit who bought the bar and turned it into a pub. Frustrated, Peter and the guys try finding a new hangout, but are unsuccessful. Taking a cue from their forefathers, the guys stage a

"Quahog Tea Party" as a form of protest, but instead just end up getting really drunk. Peter returns home the next morning to learn that the British pub has been burned down and he is immediately arrested as one of the prime suspects. Meanwhile, Stewie accepts Brian's challenge to teach their new, unrefined toddler neighbor, Eliza, how to act and speak like a lady.

After the guys are all sent to prison, their wives come to suspect that Nigel burned down the pub himself in an effort to collect an insurance payout. They try to trap him into admitting his culpability, but stumble. Finally, they're able to get the guys off the hook just as the guys are scheduled to be slain by another inmate. Also, Stewie succeeds in turning Eliza into a woman, but only temporarily, inviting mocking remarks from Brian.

MEMORABLE MOMENTS

Just Covering His Bases
QUAGMIRE: Yeah, here's to the Drunken Clam, boys! Where they don't ask for proof of age and neither do I!
CLEVELAND: Quagmire. You forgot to say "oh."
QUAGMIRE: You sure? I think I did. *(then)* Well, just to be safe. Oh!

Does He Even Know What That Word Means?
CHRIS: Mom, I'm afraid if I fall asleep, the hurricane's gonna sneak up on me and give me a vasectomy.

Aftermath of the Storm

(Peter has a fence board sticking straight through his torso.)

PETER: Aaaagh! Aaaagh! Aaaagh! For the love of God, do something!

(The stunned family pulls the board off, revealing it to be a "gag" board like Steve Martin's arrow through his head.)

PETER: Gotcha! See kids? Natural disasters have their lighter sides, too. You just have to be creative.

CHRIS: Yeah, like my dead rat marionette theater.

(Chris pulls out two dead rats attached to puppet strings.)

CHRIS: *(as rat)* I'm so stressed. Life sure is a "human" race.

(The family laughs.)

STEWIE: Right, that's brilliant.

They Can't Believe Their Eyes

QUAGMIRE: Hey guys! There's no more girlie magazines in the can! All they got is this David Copperfield.

PETER: Wa-wa-wait. Any pictures of his girlfriend?

(Quagmire thumbs through the book.)

QUAGMIRE: No! No pictures at all!

(They all gasp in horror.)

CLEVELAND: I think we should go.

PETER: Yes, this is a dark and evil place.

Humor from Across the Pond

(Two Stuffy Englishmen, Biggles and Caruthers, are seated in comfy chairs, reading The Times of London.*)*

BIGGLES: I say, Caruthers . . .

CARUTHERS: Mmmm.

BIGGLES: You know what's very, very funny? A man dressed in women's clothing.

CARUTHERS: Mmm, yes, quite. Ripping good laugh.

BIGGLES: Yes.

CARUTHERS: Mm.

(They nod and continue to read.)

That Did It

NIGEL: Yes, and I'm afraid I'm the limey bastard who's purchased your bar. A bit of an awkward moment, really.

PETER: Awkward moment? I'll give you an awkward moment. Onetime during sex I called Lois "Frank." Your move, Sherlock.

Very well, then. If you refuse to go peaceably, I'm afraid we'll have to use our superior linguistic skills to convince you to leave.

Scene Stealers
NIGEL PINCHLEY

OCCUPATION
Pub owner and creepy British perv

HIS CRIMES
Arson and a bad sense of humor

HIS PUNISHMENT
Hanging

A View from Behind the Scenes

"One of our Color Artists, Cynthia MacIntosh, was a professional dancer for sixteen years before getting into animation, so when the script called for the guys in prison to be practicing some 'Fosse moves,' I went into her office with a pencil and paper and had her hit some poses for me. Peter, Quagmire, Cleveland, and Joe were all drawn over those original sketches of Cynthia."

—DAN POVENMIRE, DIRECTOR
OF THE EPISODE

A View from Behind the Scenes

"We thought Greg the Weather Mime might have turned into a recurring character, but that hasn't happened just yet. Don't worry, though. I'm sure that when we're completely out of ideas in season seventeen we'll dust off that 'Greg the Weather Mime Has a Baby' story I have in my desk."

—SETH MACFARLANE, CREATOR AND
EXECUTIVE PRODUCER

Bust Out Those Encyclopedias

LOIS: Why are you acting like this? Nigel's charming. All British men are.
PETER: Yeah, right. That's what they said about Benjamin Disraeli.
(Cutaway to 10 Downing Street, where Benjamin Disraeli looks up from the brief he's writing, seemingly annoyed at the interruption.)
BENJAMIN DISRAELI: You don't even know who I am.
(Disgusted, he returns to his work.)

Stewie the Classist

LOIS: Stewie, look, it's an invitation to little Eliza's birthday party.
STEWIE: You mean that horrid girl who talks like a scullery maid? I didn't realize she'd been born. I assumed she'd simply congealed in a gutter somewhere.

The Gauntlet Is Thrown Down

STEWIE: I accept your challenge! At the celebration of her birthday, I shall pass that guttersnipe off as a lady! What are the stakes of this wager?
BRIAN: Why don't you shut up for about a week?
STEWIE: Very well. And if I win?
BRIAN: No, I-I-I wasn't betting. Why don't you just shut up for about a week?

At Least Somebody's Responsible

(The door flies open and Peter stumbles in.)
LOIS: Peter! We-we waited up all night. Where were you?
PETER: *(tipsy)* Wh-where was I? Where-where were you?
LOIS: Out drinkin', but I was back by two.

The Kids Love a Good Pun

TRICIA: One thing is certain, the pain here is palpable. For many, this charred portrait of Elizabeth the Second gives poignant new meaning to the phrase "Hey, check out that flaming queen."

Those Are His Best Moves?

NIGEL: Oh, Lois, I'm so sorry this terrible tragedy has befallen you.
LOIS: Oh, thank you, Nigel, you're very kind.
NIGEL: Can I touch your bum once?
LOIS: What?
NIGEL: Now I expect to see you at Eliza's birthday bash. And I won't take "no" for an answer, unless the question is, "Do you not like me?" *(laughs dorkily)* Get it? Double negative, you know.

Not Getting It

STEVE: Well, well. Officer Swanson. You and your friends are dead! You're all dead!
(Steve walks away.)

PETER: *(relieved)* Oh, good, he thinks we're zombies, he'll leave us alone.

Not Exactly the Star Pupil

STEWIE: Now, listen to me, you tin-eared piece of baggage, we've got five days left and I'll not lose my wager. Now, repeat after me, "Hello, Mother, have you hidden my hatchet?"

ELIZA: "'Ello, Mother, 'ave you 'idden moi 'atchet?"

STEWIE: Oh, God, no. It's an "h" sound, you moron. "H." Hha-hha-hha-hha.

ELIZA: Ewwww! Your breaf smells like kitty litter.

STEWIE: I was curious!

Lois Plays Nigel

LOIS: Oh, Nigel! Since Peter's been gone I've been searching for someone new. Y'know, someone with a sense of danger and . . . adventure.

NIGEL: I once played a game of cricket without shin guards.

LOIS: Ooh, I love a reckless man.

NIGEL: One time, I went up to this bloke's flat, rang the bell, and ran like Sebastian Coe.

(Lois oohs and purrs and pulls Nigel's tie seductively through her fingers.)

LOIS: More! Tell me more!

NIGEL: I burned down my pub for the insurance money and framed your husband!

Stewie Lashes Out

STEWIE: Don't give me that smug look. *(then)* Fine. Well, you have extra-sensitive hearing. Hear this.

(Stewie looks side to side then mouths two syllables, the second looking like "you.")

BRIAN: I'm telling.

(He starts to walk off.)

STEWIE: I, no-no, I said "vacuum"!

Inspiring, Peter

(Peter, Joe, Cleveland, and their wives and Quagmire sit at a booth, drinking.)

PETER: Here's to our wives. They may not be as hot as the women you see on TV, or as entertaining . . . But, um, you know, I don't know, I don't know where I'm goin' with this, but thanks anyway.

A View from Behind the Scenes

"There was a joke I liked in the first draft about the Three Musketeers winning fights because their opponents would become so disoriented over the fact that there were actually four of them. It's probably good that some stuff gets cut because then you can convince yourself that some joke you wrote would have been total utter genius if only it had been voiced and animated."

—MICHAEL SHIPLEY, ONE OF THE WRITERS OF THE EPISODE

Episode
AND THE WIENER IS . . .

Oh, my God, that's not your leg.

SUMMARY

Peter continues the competitive dynamic that he and Chris have always shared, unwilling to believe that there will come a day when Chris will best him at something. He feels particularly victorious in his latest competition with Chris, a game of one-on-one basketball, until they both enter the locker room and Peter discovers that Chris's penis is far larger than his own. Meanwhile, Meg makes it onto the flag girl squad at school, thinking this will be her ticket to the popular clique. However, at her first performance, the popular kids pelt her with stinky, raw slabs of meat.

Peter is now very insecure about his inability to measure up to Chris and takes it out on Chris in a variety of passive-aggressive ways. After trying to conceal his inadequacy, Peter looks for ways to compensate, including buying a fancy sports car. Finally, Peter joins the National Gun Association, where he finds many other overcompensating men like him. Meanwhile, Meg follows Lois's advice—trying to win over her enemies with kindness—but is then informed by Lois that doing so is only the first step in exacting revenge on the kids who humiliated her.

Peter revels in his new gun ownership and the distraction it provides from his other inadequacy. But when he takes Chris on a hunting trip and they are attacked by a bear, it's Chris who scares the bear off while Peter stands by helplessly, proving to Peter that Chris possesses other traits that really do make him a man. Peter confesses his insecurity to Chris and reassures him that he'll never have to suffer the feelings of inadequacy that Peter felt. Meanwhile, Meg can't go through with the plot to get back at the popular kids so Lois is left to get revenge with the help of Quagmire's lecherous ways.

EPISODE NUMBER: 2ACX22

ORIGINAL AIRDATE: 8/8/01

WRITERS: Mike Barker & Matt Weitzman

DIRECTOR: Bert Ring

EXECUTIVE PRODUCERS: Seth MacFarlane, David Zuckerman

GUEST VOICE: Patrick Duffy as Jack Green

MEMORABLE MOMENTS

A Little Friendly Competition

PETER: Hey Chris, you wanna race? Onyourmarkgetsetgo!
(Peter takes off. Chris skates after him. As Peter skates, he points to a marker at the far end of the pond.)

PETER: *(as he skates)* First one to the marker where that Pakistani girl fell through the ice after coming to the States to get treatment for her severely burned face, which she got when the man she refused to marry dumped sulfuric acid on her wins—I win!

A Little Less Friendly Competition

PETER: What are you talkin' about? I'm better than Chris in everything. You name it . . . sports, video games, even magic tricks.
(Flashback to the Griffins' Living Room, where Lois, Peter, and Chris are watching TV. Chris playfully reaches for Peter's nose.)

CHRIS: Ha-ha. I got your nose.

PETER: Oh, yeah?
(Peter reaches over and pulls Chris's entire face off his skull, leaving a flat flesh patch behind.)

PETER: *Well, I got your face. Hehehe.*
> *(Peter holds Chris's face up.)*

CHRIS: Ahhhhhh!
> *(Chris runs around the room, screaming.)*

LOIS: Calm down, Chris. It's only a trick.

Way to Spoil a Nice Moment

JOE: I remember the first time Kevin beat me. I was so proud of him. I gave him a little congratulatory punch in the arm. And then another, and then everything got a little hazy, Kevin went to live with a foster family for a while— Anyway, it's inevitable.

PETER: Ah, don't feel bad, Joe. I-I-I think I know why your son beat you. Apparently you're a, you're a twelve-year-old prepubescent girl. Which is good, 'cause I finally have someone to give this training bra to.
> *(Peter pulls a small training bra out of his back pocket. He straps it on Joe.)*

PETER: Here you go, Josephina. Does that feel good on your new budding bosoms? Eh? Eh?
> *(Peter grabs Joe's cheeks and presses them together to make Joe's lips move.)*

PETER: *(high-pitched voice)* It sure does—

JOE: GET THE HELL OFFA ME!!!

Technically Correct, but Not the Answer We Were Looking For

MEG: Hey, everybody, guess what I am?

STEWIE: Oh, the end result of a drunken backseat gropefest and a broken prophylactic.

No Respect

> *(Stewie purposely exhales to see his breath. He then mimes smoking a cigarette and exhales the "smoke.")*

STEWIE: Look at me! Look at me! I'm smoking! Dog, dog, look, look.
> *(Stewie "smokes" at Brian who takes a nip from a flask.)*

STEWIE: You know, alcohol doesn't really make you warmer. In fact, it constricts the blood vessels, causing—

BRIAN: Shut up.
> *(Stewie turns to Lois, aghast.)*

STEWIE: The dog just told me to shut up. I demand to know what you plan to do about this.
> *(Stewie tugs on Lois's scarf)*

STEWIE: Hey! Hey! The dog just told me—

LOIS: Be quiet, Stewie!
> *(Stewie stares at her incredulously, then turns and mimes taking another drag from a "cigarette.")*

STEWIE: Freezing my nips off out here.

Scene Stealers
JACK GREEN

OCCUPATION
President of the National Gun Association

PERSONAL ASSETS
His enormous gun collection

PERSONAL LIABILITIES
He's tiny down there

A man's only as big as the gun he carries.

Does He Ever Think?

PETER: No foul?! Aw, that's a stupid call! And I know something about stupid calls.
> *(Flashback to the Griffins' Living Room, where Lois sits on the couch. The phone rings and Lois picks it up.)*

LOIS: Uh, hello?

PETER: Uh, Lois, I can't take out the garbage because I'm at the office and, and they're making me stay late.

LOIS: Peter, the Caller ID says you're calling from the kitchen, in fact . . .
> *(She turns toward the kitchen. We can see that Peter is in the kitchen eating a turkey leg.)*

LOIS: I can see you.
> *(Peter sees Lois looking at him and quickly takes a step backward so he's out of her line of sight.)*

PETER: Can you see me now?

LOIS: No.

PETER: Okay, now I'm at the office.

Genetics 101

PETER: Thanks to you, our son has a huge wang.

LOIS: Thanks to me?

PETER: Well, he didn't get it from me!

Not the Best Comparison

LOIS: Oh, Peter, I care as much about the size of your penis as you care about the size of my breasts.

PETER: *(distraught)* Oh, my God!
> *(Peter runs out of the room.)*

Insult to Injury

STEWIE: Oh, Megan, you must try the brisket. Allow me to serve it in the manner to which you're accustomed.
> *(Stewie flings a fork of brisket at Meg, splattering her face. Meg runs out in tears.)*

Not as Kinky as It Sounds

MEG: Hey, you guys want tomorrow's biology test?

SCOTT: Whoa, how'd you get that?

MEG: I spent the night with Mr. Berler.
> *(Flashback to Mr. Berler's bedroom, where Mr. Berler is in bed, clutching a large crucifix and a string of garlic. Meg sits in a chair next to the bed, fighting to stay awake. Meg holds a wooden stake and a mallet. The sun rises in the window. Mr. Berler sits up in bed, relieved.)*

MR. BERLER: Oh, the sun's up. I'm safe for another night. Thanks, Meg.

That's No Help

BRIAN: Look, Peter, you're-you're overreacting to this Chris stuff. I mean, I mean, mine goes inside of me when I stand up. How do you think I feel?

Peter Gets a Gun

LOIS: Peter, what the hell are you doing with that thing?

PETER: You wanna touch it? Go on. Gotta be careful, though. We don't want it to get too excited and go off in your hair.

That's One Way

LOIS: Okay, listen up. Connie D'Amico's house is two stories. Now, if we set up booby-traps here, here—

MEG: How'd you get these blueprints?

LOIS: *(mischievously)* Oh, your mother has her ways. She has her ways.

(Flashback to City Hall, where Lois walks up to a clerk.)

LOIS: Can I have the blueprints to the D'Amico house?

CLERK: Sure, here you go.

(He hands her the blueprints.)

Back to Nature

PETER: Shh, Chris, look! Tracks. There must be a deer around here.

CHRIS: Well, those are snowmobile tracks.

PETER: Shh, there he is.

(Nearby, a Deer sits on a parked snowmobile. He drinks coffee from a thermos. Peter steps on a twig. The deer bolts up, tosses his coffee, and takes off in the snowmobile.)

PETER: Ah, such grace . . .

Plan B

MEG: Mom, you were right! I should've just stuck to the plan.

LOIS: Well, I figured you might get soft on me, so I hired an old friend to scar them for life.

(Meanwhile, at Connie D'Amico's House, the doorbell rings. Connie opens it, revealing Quagmire.)

QUAGMIRE: Hi, there, Sweetie. How old are you?

CONNIE: Sixteen.

QUAGMIRE: Eighteen? You're first.

CONNIE: Mom?

QUAGMIRE: I like where this is going. Giggedy-giggedy-gigg-a-dee.

Quick Thinking

(Peter is still paralyzed with fear at the sight of the bear. Chris steps in front of him.)

CHRIS: Dad, I know what to do! I saw it on Fox's *When Bears Attack*.

(Chris plants his feet apart and starts waving his arms.)

CHRIS: Go away! Go on, get! Stay tuned for an all-new *Ally McBeal!*

(The bear backs off and walks away, intimidated.)

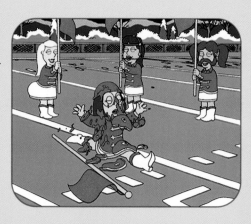

Episode
DEATH LIVES

SUMMARY

It's Peter and Lois's wedding anniversary and Lois is hoping for a very special gift from Peter. But Quagmire has arranged for a tee time for all the guys at a very exclusive golf course and Peter would rather golf than worry about their anniversary. To buy himself time for the round of golf, Peter arranges an elaborate scavenger hunt for Lois to follow, but what he doesn't count on is a rained-out game. Peter, determined to continue playing, stays out on the course and is struck by lightning, causing Death to appear on the scene.

Death informs Peter that he's actually having a Near-Death Experience, from which he's expected to derive a revelation that could save his otherwise doomed marriage. Peter is reluctant, even as Death walks Peter through the important milestones of Peter and Lois's shared past. In fact, Peter's stubbornness makes Death so late for his next appointment that Death brings Peter along. Death's appointment is actually with his own nagging mother who reveals to Peter that Death himself is lacking in the romance department. Just when Death appears to have given up on Peter and is about to force him to live through his future divorce with Lois, Peter realizes he couldn't tolerate that and offers to help set Death up with a woman if Death will, in exchange, help Peter come to the revelation that will save his marriage.

Peter has limited success helping Death score with the ladies until Death confides that he has a secret crush on a young woman who works at a pet store. Peter takes Death to her, where Death ultimately gets his date. Meanwhile, Lois runs into Cleveland and Loretta, who tell her that Peter was playing golf today. Lois is furious that Peter would spend their anniversary playing golf and decides to confront him on the golf course. Meanwhile, Death helps Peter with his revelation. When Peter realizes that he once gave up a huge sum of money to be with Lois, he realizes how far his attitude has shifted since then and that he needs to pay more attention to his relationship with her. So, with Death's help, Peter gets Peter Frampton to accompany him to the golf course where he plays Peter and Lois's special song in honor of their anniversary. Lois is moved and Death finally has his date with the girl from the pet shop, only to find that they have no chemistry at all.

EPISODE NUMBER: 2ACX21

ORIGINAL AIRDATE: 8/15/01

WRITER: Mike Henry

DIRECTOR: Rob Renzetti

EXECUTIVE PRODUCERS:
Seth MacFarlane,
David Zuckerman

GUEST VOICES: Peter Frampton as himself, Adam Carolla as Death, Estelle Harris as Death's Mom

MEMORABLE MOMENTS

Watch What You Say in Front of the Kids

LOIS: This year, instead of exchanging gifts, I told him it'd be nice if we could just spend a romantic day together.

STEWIE: Oh, dear. I think we all know what that means. *Boing*! Gross.

No Love for Mother-in-Law

CLEVELAND: Sorry, fellas, I'm not gonna be able to play. Loretta's mother is in town and we have to go buy new sheets for the dog bed.

LORETTA: Cleveland!

CLEVELAND: I mean the pull-out sofa bed.

Wonder If That Would Work

LOIS: I can't believe your father organized this. Usually he can't even handle simple tasks.

(Flashback to the Griffins' Living Room, where Lois looks at a lamp, quizzically.)

LOIS: *(calling off)* Peter, why is there a diaper in the lamp socket?

(Stewie enters, naked, with a lightbulb protruding from behind him at ass-level.)

STEWIE: *(angry)* Lois, he's done it again! *(then)* Wait a minute.

(He rubs his feet on the carpet, then touches his nose. The bulb lights up.)

STEWIE: Ha!

Itsy, Bitsy, and Annoying

PETER: Aw, c'mon, there's worse things in life than rain. Like a, like, like spiders.

(Flashback to a Movie Theater, where Lois and Peter are watching a movie. A Small Spider is on the seat next to them, smoking.)

SPIDER: Owp, he's behind the door.

LOIS: *(whispering)* Peter, he's bothering everyone. Say something.

PETER: *(whispering)* Say something? I'll kick his ass, someone oughta kick his ass.

SPIDER: *(calling to screen)* Don't go in there!

LOIS: Peter.

PETER: Awright, awright, gimme a Kleenex.

(She hands him a tissue.)

SPIDER: I knew he was bad! I knew—argh!

(Peter squeezes him to death in the Kleenex.)

Peter Doesn't Want Any Part of It

PETER: Aw, the hell with this, I'm goin' home.

(Peter grabs hold of his body's mouth and opens it as wide as he can. He puts both feet in the mouth and starts pulling the body up like a wetsuit.)

DEATH: What are you doing? You can't get in that way.

PETER: Well, I'm sure as hell not going in the back door.

Fun with Silly Names

CHRIS: What's Mom doing?

STEWIE: I'll tell you what she's doing. She's screwing up my six-two quinella! Dammit!

(Down on the track, Lois, at full sprint, is bearing down on the pack of dogs.)

TRACK ANNOUNCER: My Nose out in front, followed by Sea Biscuit, followed by Some Crazy Lady, followed by Middle-Aged Housewife, followed by Wait a Minute Who's That, followed by Silver Dasher. And now it appears there's a woman chasing the dogs.

Scene Stealers

AMY

OCCUPATION
Pet store employee and
Death's crush

WHERE SHE BOUGHT HER SHOES
On the Internet

WHY
Because they don't
test on animals

CAUSE OF DEATH
Her intensely boring
personality

Animals never have war. War is an invention of mankind.

Guessing Games

PETER: Wait a minute, I got it, I got it. I figured out my revelation. Uh . . . God loves a workin' man.
DEATH: No.
PETER: The Shadow is in reality Lamont Cranston, wealthy young man about town.
DEATH: No.

Quite a Catch

YOUNG LOIS: Oh, Peter, you look so wonderful. You aren't nervous about meeting Daddy are you?
YOUNG PETER: Oh, you'll know when I'm nervous.
CARTER: Lois?
(Young Peter makes a high-pitched fart.)
YOUNG PETER: Now, Lois, take the rap for this. I only get one chance to make a first impression.
(Carter Pewterschmidt approaches them. He wrinkles his nose, curiously sniffing.)
YOUNG LOIS: Hi, Daddy, that was me and this is Peter.

Just Planning for the Future

YOUNG PETER: And I'm taken with her. I mean look at this, huh, huh? Show us front and back there, Lois.
(Young Lois does a turn.)
YOUNG PETER: *(to Carter)* There ya— Don't-don't think I don't know where that comes from. That's some world-class juice you got brewin' in the old flesh balloon down there, Carter. Huh? Huh? Okay.
(Carter just stares at him.)
YOUNG LOIS: I'm gonna go get my purse.
(She exits.)
YOUNG PETER: All right. *(to Carter)* Hey, uh, ba-ba-based on what you've seen with your wife, what-what can we expect in terms of droopige, here? We talkin' a slight slope or the full-blown fried-eggs-hangin'-on-a-nail thing?

Death Quits

PETER: Whoa, whoa, whoa, wait—what-what are— What are you saying?
DEATH: The revelation, jackass! It coulda helped you save your marriage, uhp, but too late. Oh and uh, by the way, when the lightning hit you, you soiled yourself. Enjoy.

Crotch Fun

YOUNG QUAGMIRE: I'm taking you out for some shore leave.
(Quagmire gestures to his own crotch.)
YOUNG QUAGMIRE: Does this look like a Q to you?
YOUNG PETER: No.

(Quagmire tilts one hip to the side.)

YOUNG QUAGMIRE: How 'bout now?

YOUNG PETER: Sorry, Quagmire, your crotch just looks like Lois to me.

YOUNG QUAGMIRE: Well, let's ask her then. *(to his crotch)* Hey, Lois, should Peter sit around and mope all night?

(He shifts his hips back and forth.)

YOUNG QUAGMIRE: Or should Peter go out with his buddy and have some fun?

(He shifts his body up and down.)

YOUNG QUAGMIRE: All riiight!

Death's Crush

PETER: Ah, you don't know what it's like when you're in love.

DEATH: Oh, yeah?

(Death pulls out his Velcro wallet and shows Peter a picture.)

DEATH: Her name's Amy. She works at a pet store. I met her last summer when her dad hung himself, but I was too shy to ask her out.

PETER: Ahh! What's with that mustache?!

(Death takes it from him.)

DEATH: Huh? Let me see that. *(then)* Sorry, that's Edward James Olmos.

(He takes out another picture.)

DEATH: Here, this is her.

(Peter looks at the new photo.)

PETER: Hey, nice ass.

(Death leans over and looks at the picture.)

DEATH: Oh, sorry, no, no, that's Edward James Olmos's ass. I guess I don't have a photo of her, but trust me she's cute.

PETER: Well, let's go get her!

DEATH: I'm gonna need that picture of Olmos's ass back.

Still No In-Law Love

LOIS: What are you doing here?

CLEVELAND: Loretta's mom was hankering for a snack so we had to pick her up some Kibbles 'n Bits.

LORETTA: Cleveland!

CLEVELAND: I mean Cheez-Its.

Death Does a Favor

DEATH: Pe-ter . . .

(Peter Frampton, startled, drops a dish and turns around.)

DEATH: Pe-ter Framp-ton.

PETER FRAMPTON: Oh, no. God, please, no. I'm too young to die! Are you sure you're not supposed to be at Keith Richards's house?

A View from Behind the Scenes

"We thought it was an interesting device to revisit the character of Death like this in order to reveal back story that otherwise— Ah, who am I kidding? By this point, we were burning these things off in August and figured Family Guy already had one foot in the grave."

—FOX EXECUTIVE

Episode

LETHAL WEAPONS

SUMMARY

Quahog is invaded by hordes of New Yorkers who have come to view the fabulous autumn foliage. The out-of-towners wreak havoc on the place, though, and are such a nuisance to Peter that he makes a couple of lame attempts to scare them off. But when Peter gets into a fight with one of the New Yorkers, it's actually Lois who kicks some ass to break it up, using techniques she's picked up from Bonnie's Tae-Jitsu class. Lois is worried that Peter will feel emasculated about the incident, but is surprised instead to see Peter charging passers-by money for a chance to take on his "ass-kicking wife."

Lois was going to tell her Tae-Jitsu instructor that she was going to quit, but Peter's obnoxious behavior pushes her into continuing. As she becomes more proficient at martial arts, she also becomes more aggressive, both to strangers in the park and to Peter in the bedroom. Peter sees the new Lois as an effective means to getting rid of the leafers (which she does, through violence). But it isn't until Lois sees Stewie strike Peter into unconsciousness with a baseball bat that she realizes she's inadvertently brought a climate of aggression into her home and feels like the worst mother ever for allowing this to happen.

Peter and Lois take Stewie to a child psychologist to try to get to the root of his behavior. What the doctor uncovers is that there appears to be a great deal of unresolved anger in the Griffins' household, so the Griffins try out a variety of suggested techniques to alleviate tension with one another. Their various attempts fail and finally degenerate into an extended, all-out, bare-knuckle brawl between all the family members. In the end, the cathartic effect of the melee actually brings relief to the family, who ultimately realize that sometimes violence can be a solution.

EPISODE NUMBER: 2ACX18

ORIGINAL AIRDATE: 8/22/01

WRITER: Chris Sheridan

Director: Brian Hogan

EXECUTIVE PRODUCERS:
Seth MacFarlane,
David Zuckerman

GUEST VOICE: Peter Gallagher as
Jared Fellows

MEMORABLE MOMENTS

Is That a Compliment?

PETER: *(to Bonnie)* Wow, you musta had a great body before it went all funhouse mirror on ya.

The Leafers Arrive

BRONX GUY #1: Yo, Matty, check out those colors. Yellow like a taxi, orange like the ball in a Knicks game, and red like the sauce on my mama mia's goo-gots.

BRONX GUY #2: Yeah. And brown, like the guys I don't pick up in my cab.

BRONX GUY #1: Be-yootiful.

Way to Welcome the Out-of-Towners

DIANE: Good evening. Tonight's top story, Quahog is infested. With loud, hairy creatures also known as New Yorkers.

TOM: They migrate north every autumn to see the foliage, and I think I speak for all of us when I say that New York and everyone from there can fornicate themselves with an iron stick.

Don't Fight Nature

PETER: Lois? Brothers and sisters fighting is as natural as a white man's dialogue in a Spike Lee movie.

(Cutaway to Sal's Pizza Place, where A Black Man walks up to the counter.)

BLACK MAN: Whatsup? Can I get two slices of pepperoni?

(A White Man behind the counter snarls like an animal.)

Giving a Plug Where a Plug Is Due

(A kindly Old Lady sitting in the back pew sees Stewie peering over the back of the pew in front of her. She smiles at Stewie.)

OLD LADY: Aren't you precious!

(Stewie ducks back down, then pops up wearing a pair of devil horns, makes a horrible face, and hisses at her satanically. She faints. Stewie laughs, gleefully.)

STEWIE: Some of my novelty items were provided by Jack's Joke Shop of South Attleboro, Massachusetts. Remember, "If it ain't funny, it ain't worth Jack."

Merry Poppin's?

LOIS: I'm really cutting loose. Just like Julie Andrews in that movie where she showed her breasts.

(Cutaway to the Banks Children's Bedroom, where Jane and Michael Banks sit on their beds as Mary Poppins stands before them.)

MICHAEL BANKS: Oh, Mary, you'll never leave us, will you?

(Mary Poppins lifts her shirt, flashing her breasts to the children.)

MICHAEL BANKS: Yes, those are lovely, but it doesn't quite answer our question.

Quagmire Misreads the Situation

QUAGMIRE: Hey, honey, why don'tcha turn around and show me the Lower East Side?

(The lady stands. She towers over Quagmire.)

LADY: *(deep male voice)* Sure.

QUAGMIRE: Whoa! Transvestite. Back off! *(then)* Wait a sec. Pre-op or post-op?

LADY: Pre-op.

QUAGMIRE: Whoa! Transvestite. Back off!

Can't Wait to Hear This

PETER: Don't worry, I've got an idea. An idea so smart, my head would explode if I even began to know what I was talking about.

Not Sure That's the Expression

PETER: Come one, come all! She floats like a butterfly and stings like when I pee!

Scene Stealers
QUAGMIRE

OCCUPATION
Part-time airline pilot, full-time pervert

HIS < NOT SO > SECRET CRUSH
Lois

NUMBER OF WOMEN HE'S SLEPT WITH
A top-notch team of scientists is still calculating it

Hello, 911? It's Quagmire . . . Yeah, yeah, yeah, it's in a window this time.

153

Weekend Warrior

STEWIE: Ooo, damn! Must've pulled something playing hoops last week.
(Flashback to a City Park Basketball Court, where Stewie plays a game of three-on-three with Five Black Guys. An opposing player tries to get open, but Stewie sticks with him by chest bumping his shins each step of the way. The player gets the ball. Stewie waves his arms.)

STEWIE: I know you're not putting that rock up from here. You ain't got no J.
(The player makes his move toward the basket. Stewie subtly trips the player who falls to the ground, and the ball rolls out of bounds. The player, gets up and he and Stewie walk up to each other and stand toe to toe.)

PLAYER: Yo, man, that's tripping!

STEWIE: Brother, please! You're the one who's trippin'. Go on, go cry home to your momma. She waitin' for ya.

PLAYER: Now, don't make me put my size thirteens up your narrow ass—

STEWIE: I don't sweat you. Bring it on, bitch. Now how you gonna act?
(The Player turns and walks away. Stewie walks back up the court.)

STEWIE: Sheee. Bringing that trash in here. This is my house.

Sibling Rivalry

(Meg and Chris are raking leaves.)

CHRIS: Hold it, Meg. Those two are mine.

MEG: What?

CHRIS: *(pointing to two leaves)* That's Randy. And that's Fred. Randy's the messy one. Fred's very neat. And when you get 'em together, oooh-whooo, hold on to your sides!
(Meg picks up the leaves.)

MEG: Nice to meet you both.
(She rubs the leaves together, grinding them into dust.)

CHRIS: Murderer!

Stewie Watches Lois Do Tae-Jitsu

STEWIE: Go, Lois! Pummel him with your powerful fists of female fury. And then when he's weary, emasculate him with your incessant nagging.
(Stewie turns to a Nearby Man.)

STEWIE: Eh, women.
(Stewie mimes a mouth with his hand.)

STEWIE: Yackity-yack-yackity-yack-yack-yack.
(Stewie nudges the guy and points to him.)

STEWIE: Heh. You know, huh? Enjoy the fight.

Stewie Wears a Wire

LOIS: I'm the worst mother in the world.

STEWIE: Aha!

(Stewie rips his shirt open to reveal that he has a tape recorder strapped to his chest.)

STEWIE: I got it all on tape.

(He removes it from his chest, hits rewind, then hits play. He sets the tape recorder on the table.)

STEWIE: *(on tape)* Okay, um, this is me interviewing Ed Sullivan: What-what's new, Ed? *(Stewie as Ed Sullivan)* Well, Stewie, tonight we have a really big show. *(Stewie as himself)* Okay. Okay. And now a word from our sponsors . . . It takes a very steady hand. Don't touch the sides. *(Stewie makes a buzz sound)* Butter fingers.

(Stewie punches the stop button.)

STEWIE: I-I was making radio shows for fun, ever-everybody does it. At least e-everybody I know, do—Shut up!

Damn you and such!

The Kid's Got an Active Imagination

DOCTOR MORIN: Now, Stewart, I want you to take this mommy doll and this daddy doll and show me how they act together.

STEWIE: Oh, yes, very well. All right. Um . . . *(holding up man doll)* You see, Margaret, after twenty odd years of marriage, your curious indiscretions no longer faze me. *(holding up woman doll)* Really? And I suppose you think I enjoy hanging on to those hammocky deposits of gin-sugars you call buttocks.

(The doctor writes something on his pad. Stewie stops playing.)

STEWIE: What was that? What did you just write there?

(Stewie snatches the pad out of the doctor's hand. He runs to the other side of the room.)

DOCTOR MORIN: Give me that.

STEWIE: *(reading)* "Insecurity?" "Gender confusion??!" Oh, I'll give you something to write about.

(Stewie starts to eat the paper.)

STEWIE: Look at me. I'm insane! I'm Martin Lawrence on a bender.

(Stewie latches on to the doctor's face and starts chewing on his ear.)

Quite a Gift

DOCTOR MORIN: Mr. and Mrs. Griffin, does Stewart have a history of aggression?

LOIS: No, no, hitting Peter is the first violent thing he's ever done.

STEWIE: Well, technically, the first act of violence was that time bomb I left ticking in your uterus before I came out. Happy fiftieth birthday, Lois.

A View from Behind the Scenes

"The idea for this episode came from writer Chris Sheridan who, being from the east coast, used to experience the phenomenon of New Yorkers invading his town each fall. And, of course, it didn't hurt that Chris happens to be an extremely brutal and violent individual."

—SETH MACFARLANE, CREATOR AND EXECUTIVE PRODUCER

Cathartic, Isn't it?

LOIS: Okay, the psychologist wants us to try an exercise called role reversal, where we pretend to be the person who makes us angry. I'll go first. *(as Peter)* Don't listen to your mother, kids. She's worthless and dumb and ignore her and only listen to me . . . Peter.

(Lois shoots Peter a look. He glares back.)

PETER: *(imitating Lois's voice)* I'm Lois, I brake for yard sales. But I don't let Peter buy anything he likes, like that Narragansett Beer sign where the hot chick has two mugs for jugs. *(his own voice)* It was eight freakin' dollars and we have a dozen places to put it.

STEWIE: Ooh, oooh, me next, me next! *(as Brian)* I'm the dog. I'm well read and have a diverse stock portfolio. But I'm not above eating grass clippings and regurgitating them on the small braided rug near the door.

BRIAN: *(as Stewie)* I'm a pompous little Anti-Christ who will probably abandon my plans for world domination when I grow up and fall in love with a rough trick named Jim.

What's the Opposite of Pen Pals?

MEG: *(reading a letter)* "Dear Meg. For the first four years of your life, I thought you were a house cat." Dad!

STEWIE: *(reading)* "Dear Stewie, get out." *(to Peter)* Oh, that's nice.

LOIS: Mine just says "Dear Lois." And after that, it looks like someone just spit on the paper.

Getting to the Root of the Problem

BRIAN: Man, I'm glad we got that out of our systems.

MEG: I wonder what came over us.

CHRIS: Maybe people are just naturally violent.

LOIS: I don't believe that. I think it's all the TV we watch. Ah, there's so much violence.

PETER: Yeah, TV is dangerous. Why the hell doesn't the government step in and tell us what we can and can't watch? And shame on the network that puts this junk on the air!

LOIS: Uh, Peter, Peter, may-maybe you shouldn't say anything bad about the network.

PETER: Oh, why? What are they gonna do? Cut our budget? Feh! I'm gonna get a beer.

(A still drawing of Peter slides crudely across the screen toward the kitchen.)

Episode
THE KISS SEEN 'ROUND THE WORLD

SUMMARY

When Tom Tucker shows up at Meg's school to report on the arrest of a teacher, Meg develops a huge crush on him, which inspires her to apply for an internship with the Channel 5 News Team. But after landing the gig, she's horrified to learn that her internship partner is Neil Goldman. Meanwhile, Stewie is giddy over getting his first tricycle.

Later, as the Mass Media Murderer strikes downtown Quahog, Tom Tucker fearfully sends interns Meg and Neil to cover the story in his place. When the two arrive at the scene they discover that Hugh Downs has been taken hostage. In the ensuing confusion, the criminal shoots down the Channel 5 Newscopter. As Meg and Neil descend to what they assume will be their deaths, they share a kiss. Later, when Neil is filing his report on the day's events, he downplays the crime and instead repeatedly runs the footage of his kiss with Meg, much to Meg's horror. Meanwhile, a neighborhood bully named Charlie takes Stewie's tricycle.

Meg is further mortified to discover that not only is Neil distributing T-shirts at school bearing the image of the now-famous kiss, but that Peter and Lois have invited Neil's parents over for dinner. In response, Meg goes on the Channel 5 News and delivers a scathing report that humiliates Neil. When Neil threatens to hurl himself off a building Meg feels awful and finally realizes that her crush, Tom Tucker, is only interested in ratings and his own on-screen persona. Finally, Stewie tortures his bully in order to get his tricycle back.

EPISODE NUMBER: 3ACX02

ORIGINAL AIRDATE: 8/29/01

WRITER: Mark Hentemann

DIRECTOR: Pete Michels

EXECUTIVE PRODUCERS:
Seth MacFarlane,
Daniel Palladino

GUEST VOICES: Hugh Downs
as himself, Abe Vigoda
as himself

A View from Behind the Scenes

"In addition to writing this episode, Mark Hentemann also provided the voice of Chief McKenzie and the 'phony' guy—something he likes to shout at people in real life, too."

—SETH MACFARLANE, CREATOR AND EXECUTIVE PRODUCER

MEMORABLE MOMENTS

Peter Shows Off His "Talents" at the Toy Store

(Peter pushes the demo button on a Casio keyboard and it starts playing a jazz music piece. Peter puts his fingers on the keys and pretends he's playing it.)

PETER: Hey, look at me, Chris. I'm Yanni, sans the attitude.

(A Toy Store Customer walks up next to Peter and stares in awe.)

TOY STORE CUSTOMER: My God, that's amazing. You are so talented!

(Peter looks up and stops playing. The music, however, continues.)

PETER: Huh?

TOY STORE CUSTOMER: Wait a second. Something's not right here. You were just making it look like you were playing! You're a phony! *(to everyone around him)* Hey, this guy's a great big phony!

Stewie Gets a New Toy

PETER: Hey, come on, Stewie, your mom and I have somethin' for you.

STEWIE: Oh, let me guess, you've picked out yet another colorful box with a crank that I'm expected to turn and turn, until, ohp, big shock, a jack pops out, and you laugh, and the kids laugh, the dog laughs, and I die a little inside.

Chris Amuses Himself at the Toy Store

CHRIS: When I stick this army guy with the sharp bayonet up my nose, it tickles my brain! *(he does so)* Aha-ha-ha-ha— Ow! Oh, now I don't know math.

A Teacher Is Hauled Away by the Cops

PRINCIPAL SHEPHERD: What in God's name—? Mr. Lazenby, what the hell's going on here?

MR. LAZENBY: *(annoyed)* Apparently there's some "law" against teaching the evolutionary theory that Gil Gerard used a time machine, went back, and ejaculated into the primordial ooze.
(The principal shakes his head bitterly.)

PRINCIPAL SHEPHERD: This stupid country.

Peter Doesn't Quite Get It

MEG: Oh, my God, I'm missing the news!

PETER: We all miss The News, Meg. But Huey Lewis needs time to create, and we have to learn to be patient.

You Heard It on Channel 5

DIANE: And in entertainment, Mary Tyler Moore is sixty-four years old today.

TOM: Really? Sixty-four?

DIANE: Yes.

TOM: Now, I thought she was dead.

DIANE: Nope, she's alive.

TOM: Fantastic. And now this . . .

Job Interview from Hell

TOM TUCKER: All right, question number one: Would you consider growing a mustache?

STUDENT: I guess so.

TOM TUCKER: Question number two: Look at my mustache. Do you think it tickles women when I kiss them?

STUDENT: I . . . I don't know.

TOM TUCKER: Wrong. The answer is: Only slightly. Only slightly. Next!

Peter Sees the Beauty in the World

(Peter videotapes Stewie on his tricycle. Suddenly, the wind carries a plastic bag into the frame. Peter continues filming the bag,

losing sight of Stewie in the process. The bag "dances" in the wind à la American Beauty.)

PETER: Look, it's dancing with me. It's like there's this incredibly benevolent force that wants me to know there's no reason to be afraid. Sometimes there's so much beauty in the world, it makes my heart burst.

(Pan up to God, standing on the clouds, looking down.)

GOD: It's just some trash blowing in the wind! Do you have any idea how complicated your circulatory system is?

Narcissus Would Be Proud

TOM TUCKER: I'm sorry, but there's a handsome man in my spoon. You'll have to come back later.

The Mass Media Murderer Holds Hugh Downs Hostage

HUGH DOWNS: Hey, why me? Why the media?

MEDIA MURDERER: I've got my reasons. *(bitterly)* Dan Rather thinks he can just condense a whole day's worth of events into a half hour.

HUGH DOWNS: Oh, don't get me started on Rather, that arrogant jerk.

MEDIA MURDERER: Really? You know him?

HUGH DOWNS: I'm Hugh Downs. I know everybody. In fact, *(points)* he's right down there.

MEDIA MURDERER: Where?

(The Media Murderer looks down to the street. Hugh Downs knocks the gun out of his hand and runs off.)

HUGH DOWNS: Ha, ha! See ya later, sucker! And by the way, Rather's an okay guy in small doses!

Meg and Neil's Last Regrets

MEG: Oh, my God, we're gonna die! There's so much of life I haven't experienced. I never even got the chance to be some drunk college guy's last resort.

NEIL: My years of expensive orthodontic work will be a total waste!

Meg Is Humiliated

MEG: I just wanna kill myself. I'm going upstairs right now and eat a whole bowl of peanuts. *(off Peter and Lois's blank looks)* I'm allergic to peanuts.

(They just look at her, dumbfounded.)

MEG: You don't know anything about me!

(She storms off.)

PETER: Who was that guy?

Meg Confronts Neil at School

NEIL: Hello, lover!

Scene Stealers
HUGH DOWNS

OCCUPATION
Part-journalist, part-hero

HOW TO CONTACT HIM
Blow a whistle or call John Stossel's cell phone

KINDEST TRAIT
Willingness to tolerate Dan Rather (in small doses)

WHAT HE WAS DOING IN QUAHOG
Still unclear

Hugh Downs awaaaaaaaaaay!

STUFF THAT MIGHT HAVE SLIPPED BY

■ The toy store the Griffins are shopping at is called Toys 'R' Overpriced.

■ Tom Tucker has a photo of himself in his office.

■ The Mass Media Murderer shows up again in "To Love and Die in Dixie," to rob a convenience store and threaten Chris.

■ Charlie reads *Bully Weekly,* which features articles such as, "Wedgie Tips."

A View from Behind the Scenes

"This is the first appearance of Neil Goldman's parents, Mort and Muriel. This family is based on that of Family Guy *writer Neil Goldman, with our apologies."*

— MARK HENTEMANN, WRITER OF THE EPISODE

MEG: Neil, what are you doing? I am not your lover! I don't even like you!

NEIL: Meg, I strongly suggest you hold my hand, lest you look like a slut.

Talk About High Pressure

(Stewie sits in the office of a gym across from a Buff Sales Guy.)

BUFF GUY: So what were you wanting to work on, cardio, upper body, what?

STEWIE: Upper body, definitely, I-I need to get buff so I can get my tricycle back.

BUFF GUY: Yeah-yeah, well, lucky we're running a special right now for the next seventeen minutes.

STEWIE: Uh, okay, well, that's-that's a little unusual, but, uh, okay, well, tell me.

BUFF GUY: Okay, well, the normal plan is seventy-eight months at forty a month and two hundred down. Watch this, forget the down, are you watching?

STEWIE: Yeah, yeah, yeah.

BUFF GUY: Good-bye forty a month, let's do thirty-five.

STEWIE: Okay, thirty-five, all right, now-now that's the cheapest?

BUFF GUY: Yeah, hang on, hang on. *(calling off)* Hey, Trace, can you bring me some of those free gym bags? Thanks!

STEWIE: Gosh, you know, I-I-I, you know, I could probably just do some push-ups at home.

BUFF GUY: Okay, well, let's start you off with the complete body fat test, maybe a heart rate—

STEWIE: You're actually not hearing me. Yeah, I don't think it's for me, um, thanks anyway, and, um, for the future, *(whispering)* you came on a little strong.

Moving a Little Too Fast

LOIS: We invited Neil's family over for dinner.

MEG: You what?!

PETER: Yeah, we wanted to get to know them better . . . y'know, seeing as how the two of you will one day bless our home with the pitter patter of sweet little grandchildren as ugly as sin.

Meg Reaches Her Limit

MEG: Excuse me. I'm gonna go throw up.

(She storms out of the room.)

MR. GOLDMAN: Please flush the toilet twice. Once for the bulk and again for the remainder. Thank you. *(to Lois and Peter)* Oh, she's a dear.

Episode
MR. SATURDAY KNIGHT

SUMMARY

After Peter is humiliated at Career Day in front of Chris's class, he becomes depressed about his work situation. Brian encourages Peter to invite his boss, Mr. Weed, over for dinner in order to make an impression on him. Peter does invite Mr. Weed over, but just as he offers Peter a promotion, Mr. Weed accidentally chokes to death in the Griffins' dining room.

Peter is further devastated when he learns that Mr. Weed's will dictates the demolition of the toy factory. Now jobless, Peter tries out one new job after another, all ending in failure. Finally, Lois encourages Peter to pursue his lifelong career dream of becoming a jouster in the Renaissance Faire.

During his training to become a jouster, Peter gets scared off by the one man who originally inspired his jousting dream: the Black Knight. But when Lois sees Peter giving up so easily, she tells him to get back out there. At the jousting tournament, Peter challenges the Black Knight to a battle and emerges victorious. But, when offered the chance to continue jousting, Peter realizes he's already lived his dream, and that his real place is with his family.

EPISODE NUMBER: 3ACX04

ORIGINAL AIRDATE: 9/5/01

WRITER: Steve Callaghan

DIRECTOR: Michael Dante DiMartino

EXECUTIVE PRODUCERS:
Seth MacFarlane,
Daniel Palladino

GUEST VOICES: Will Ferrell as the Black Knight, Adam Carolla as Death, Jimmy Kimmel as Dog Death, R. Lee Ermey as the Jousting Coach

MEMORABLE MOMENTS

Peter Speaks to Chris's Class on Career Day

PETER: Hey, kids! Ey, ey, ya know what I do? I work in a toy factory! And ya know what I do there?

KID #1: I bet you're just one of those low-level assembly-line guys who stand there all day screwing heads on dolls! Ooh, is it on straight? I don't know! BOOOOOO!
(Peter stares for a beat, then lunges for the kid.)

PETER: Why, you little snot-nosed—
(Ms. Patterson restrains him from behind.)

MS. PATTERSON: Mr. Griffin! *(whispering)* He plays kickball in the park after school. Get him there. *(to class)* So does anyone have any questions for Mr. Griffin?

A View from Behind the Scenes

"The only reason we were allowed to say 'Cleveland Steamer' is that Seth told our censors that it was just a non-sense phrase. But by the time they learned otherwise, the show had already aired. Needless to say, they don't trust Seth as much these days."

—STEVE CALLAGHAN, WRITER OF THE EPISODE

Stewie Does Mad Libs with Rupert

STEWIE: All right, Rupert, are you ready to hear our Mad Lib? *(reading)* "Cinderella had three wicked step watermelons who were very smelly to her. So, her fairy God toilet turned a pumpkin into a fanny and sent her off to the poop." *(laughs)* Oh, my, how ruthlessly absurd!

The Family Tries to Cheer Peter Up

PETER: Oh, it was terrible. Everyone else there had some big, important job and was way more successful than me.

BRIAN: Hey, c'mon, you-you-you have a— You have a great job.

STEWIE: Yeah, you're, you're doin' . . . you're doin' . . . You're doin' good.

Mr. Weed Chokes to Death

BRIAN: He's dead!

(They all gasp in unison. Suddenly, Margot Kidder bursts through the door, screaming.)

MARGOT KIDDER: Ahhhh, ahhhhhh! *(calmly)* Forgot my purse. *(crazed)* Ahhhh, ahhhh!

(She upends the table, smashes through the window, and once again runs screaming into the night.)

Death Comes for Mr. Weed

(Lois opens the door, revealing Death, holding his scythe.)

DEATH: H-ha! Gotcha! It's just me, Death. I'm here for the body.

LOIS: Peter, it's okay. It's just Death.

(Peter enters, holding Mr. Weed's body.)

PETER: Oh, thank God.

(A small cloaked Dog Skeleton on all fours steps into the doorway next to Death.)

DOG DEATH: Uh, hey, did someone choke on a roll in here?

BRIAN: Oh, no, no, no, I spit it up.

DOG DEATH: *(nods)* Ah.

Stewie Scopes Out the Other Babies at the Funeral

STEWIE: . . . I'd do her . . . do her . . . wouldn't do her . . . uh, who hasn't done her . . . do her . . . lose the pigtails and we'll talk.

Peter Begins His Job Search

(Peter sits across from an empty desk. A Job Placement Counselor enters, studying some papers.)

JOB PLACEMENT COUNSELOR: Okay, we've got your typing test here, and all the pertinent data about your, um, um, you know, your background and, and, um, uh, skills, uh, and . . .

(He trails off.)

PETER: And?

JOB PLACEMENT COUNSELOR: Y'know, I-I gotta be honest with you. I-I only have another week and a half here and I-I have completely checked out.

PETER: Oh.

JOB PLACEMENT COUNSELOR: Yeah.

PETER: Well, what should I do?

JOB PLACEMENT COUNSELOR: Ahhhhhhm . . . *(exhales hard, then shrugs)* Chef?

Peter's Job Search Hits Rock Bottom

(Peter approaches the Griffins' car, dressed as a trashy prostitute.)

PETER: *(to Lois)* Hey! Looking for a good time, sweet cheeks?

MEG: Oh, my God!

LOIS: Peter, get in the car!

PETER: Okay, but it'll cost you. What do you want, a Cleveland Steamer?

LOIS: I said get in the ca— *(curious)* What's a "Cleveland Steamer"?

BRIAN: It means that he'll—

PETER: *(whispers)* Whoa, whoa, be cool, be cool.
(A cop slowly drives by.)

PETER: *(covering)* Yeah, so go to, uh, Maple Street and then take a left and then, uh . . . you go, uh . . .
(The cop rounds the corner.)

PETER: Okay, so you wanna party or what?

Stewie's Keen Eye

(Stewie keeps glancing back and forth between Peter, still dressed as a trashy prostitute, and Meg.)

STEWIE: It's eerie, isn't it? Like looking into the future.

Lois Tells Peter to Pursue His Dream

PETER: Wow. You know, since, since money's getting tight, I was gonna suggest that we eat the kids, you know, I mean like jokingly at first, but then I was gonna gauge your reaction and, and if you were cool with it, then, uh, you know, we could go from there, but this is a much better idea.

Peter Runs into Mort Goldman at the Renaissance Faire

PETER: Hey, you're gonna be a jouster, too?

MORT GOLDMAN: Yes, I'm trying to overcome my fear of swords because a man in a pirate suit stabbed me in the ear when I was five. And then again when I was thirty. What about you, the same?

The path to knighthood is paved with strength and nobility, not LSD and sideburns.

Scene Stealers
THE BLACK KNIGHT

OCCUPATION
Alpha-jouster at the Renaissance Faire

MODES OF TRANSPORTATION
A horse (of course!) and his kick-ass, totally tricked-out Hyundai

GIRLFRIEND
"Trophy Wench" Maid Madeline

ACTIVITIES FOR WHICH HE REMOVES HIS HELMET
None

A View from Behind the Scenes

"This was the second time we did something resembling a two-parter. We figured, 'It worked so well for Batman . . . what the hell, you know?'"

—SETH MACFARLANE, CREATOR AND EXECUTIVE PRODUCER

STUFF THAT MIGHT HAVE SLIPPED BY

■ One of Chris's classmates seen in this episode shows up again in "To Love and Die in Dixie" as Chris's crush, Barbara.

■ The *Match Game* bit actually features an animated Richard Dawson and Charles Nelson Reilly.

■ The booth that Peter buys his food from at the Renaissance Faire is called Mutton Jeff's.

A View from Behind the Scenes

"The joke about Diane's cleavage being like a grandmother's was my pitch, inspired by my Grandmother Rose, who well into her eighties wore low-cut dresses that scarred me for life."

—DAVID GOODMAN, CO-EXECUTIVE PRODUCER

No One Said Jouster Training Would Be Easy

COACH: You find something funny, maggot?!
PETER: Sir, no sir!
COACH: You love the Middle Ages, don't you?!
PETER: Sir, yes sir!
COACH: The concept of a geocentric universe gets you sexually excited, doesn't it?!
PETER: Sir, yes sir!
COACH: You wanna make sixteenth-century mathematician Johannes Kepler your bitch, don't you?!
PETER: Sir, yes sir!

Lost in Translation

PETER: *(to Renaissance Faire vendor)* Uh, yeah, two mutton joints, please.
RENAISSANCE GUY: Oh, thou wishest to feast on the appendage of the humble ovine.
PETER: Listen, you freak, we don't all watch *Frasier*, okay? Now get me two mutton joints.

Close Call

(Peter shoves his suit of armor in a trash can.)
LOIS: Peter, what are you doing? I spent hours soldering that costume for you.
PETER: I don't need it anymore, Lois. I quit the team.
LOIS: Quit the team? But you can't quit jousting. The big meet is today, and I thought you were—
PETER: *(laughs)* Did you— Did you just say "big meet?"
LOIS: *(giggling)* Oh, my God, I did. Oh, we almost missed that one.
PETER: I know. That was a close one.

Tom Tucker Never Misses a Shot

DIANE: Well, it's an exciting day for all, here at the Renaissance Faire jousting meet. Wouldn't you say, Tom?
TOM: Diane, I'd say it was a perfect day if you weren't reminding us all of our grandmothers' cleavage.

Stewie Tries One Last Time to Cheer Peter Up

STEWIE: Hey. *(he pats Peter on the knee)* How ya doin' there, big guy? *(no answer)* You holding up all right? *(still no answer)* You want a soda? Hmm? *(then)* Ah, screw it. I tried.

Episode
A FISH OUT OF WATER

SUMMARY

After an extended period of unemployment (and weight gain) Peter decides to become a fisherman. He buys a boat at a police auction for $50,000 and sets out to find a way to pay back the loan before Lois and Meg return from a Spring Break trip at a local spa. But, when Peter begins his fishing career, he soon develops a rival in the form of Hennessey, a fellow fisherman who doesn't exactly welcome the competition.

Before long, the bank takes all of the Griffins' belongings and even prematurely sells their house to another couple. Meanwhile, Lois takes Meg on a detour on their way home, thinking that what Meg really wants is the traditional, rambunctious Spring Break experience, but it's Lois who gets caught up in the debauchery, not Meg. Peter, who has completely run out of ways to pay back the bank, decides to try killing the legendary and deadly bluefish known as Daggermouth in the hope of collecting the price on his head.

The guys join Peter in his quest for Daggermouth, but ultimately discover that the terror fish is merely a legend created by Hennessey's old partner, Salty. Salty pays Peter the $50,000 reward just to keep his mouth shut. Meanwhile, Lois inadvertently gets herself and Meg arrested after Meg flashes a crowd of other Spring Breakers, teaching Meg a lesson about enjoying life in the process.

MEMORABLE MOMENTS

Worst Family Trip Ever
(The Griffins stand at the edge of the orca tank at SeaWorld. The whale suddenly leaps out of the water and kisses Lois on the cheek. Peter punches the whale and turns to Lois.)
PETER: And how long has this been going on?!

Peter Is Fat Beyond Comprehension
TOM TUCKER'S SON: *(sees Peter)* What's that, Daddy?
TOM TUCKER: Well, that's Mercury, Jake. The planet closest to the sun. What it's doing down here by the wharf, I haven't the foggiest, but we should probably ask a scientist—
PETER: I'm a guy, you jackass!

Peter Announces He's Going to Become a Fisherman
CHRIS: Dad, if you catch a mermaid can I chop off her top half? 'Cause I already have those legs I found out by the train tracks.

EPISODE NUMBER: 3ACX05

ORIGINAL AIRDATE: 9/19/01

WRITERS: Alex Borstein and Mike Henry

DIRECTOR: Bert Ring

EXECUTIVE PRODUCERS: Seth MacFarlane, Daniel Palladino

GUEST VOICES: Michael Chiklis as Hennessey, Brian Doyle-Murray as Salty

Scene Stealers
DAGGERMOUTH

OCCUPATION
Legendary creature of the sea and merchandising cash cow

WHERE YOU CAN SEE HIM
In his hideout in Fish Stench Cove (as well as with his wacky cohort, Boom-Boom, on their own incredibly lame Nickelodeon show)

AMOUNT PAID FOR KILLING HIM
$50,000

AMOUNT PAID FOR DAGGERMOUTH T-SHIRTS AND COFFEE MUGS
Let's just say a lot more than that

Oh, dear. Would you mind holding still for a moment? These antique pistols take about ten minutes to reload.

At the Police Auction
AUCTIONEER: Welcome. We open today's bidding with this pair of panties confiscated from a prostitute—
QUAGMIRE: Fifty bucks!
AUCTIONEER: She had nine STDs.
QUAGMIRE: Forty-five bucks.
AUCTIONEER: And when we caught her, she wet herself.
QUAGMIRE: Fifty bucks.
CLEVELAND: Excuse me, are you gonna sell anything that's not gross?

Peter Applies for a Loan
PETER: Oh, wow, so you can really give me a loan?
SALESMAN: I sure can. You see, Mr. Griffin, what sets us apart from other banks is that other banks are banks. Now I trust you have collateral.
PETER: Uhm, I-I got three kids. Hehehehe.
SALESMAN: I'll take 'em. *(chuckles)* Just kidding. Or maybe I'm not. Sign this.

What Fine Print?
BRIAN: Peter, did you read the fine print on this loan contract?
PETER: Um, if by "read" you mean imagined a naked lady, then yes.

Mother-Daughter Bonding Time
LOIS: Meg, did I ever tell you that if you're on birth control and you take an antibiotic, it makes it not work? *(laughs)* Because no one told me. *(laughs)* I thought you should know.

Who Needs Kevin Bacon?
(Peter and Brian are sitting on milk crates where the sofa usually is.)
BRIAN: Well, that's the last of the furniture.
PETER: No TV. I miss my friends. John Ritter, and Florence Henderson, and Alfonso Ribeiro.
BRIAN: Is he the guy from *Silver Spoons*?
PETER: Um, uh, no, well, he was on *The French Prince of Bel Air*.
BRIAN: *Fresh Prince*.
PETER: *Fresh Prince of Bel Air*. But, you know, I don't know if he was also on— Hey, Alfonso!
(One of the movers turns to them.)
ALFONSO: Yeah?
PETER: Were you on *Silver Spoons*?
ALFONSO: Yes, I was.
PETER: Oh, there you go.

Sick and Tired
CARSON DALY: All right, now, let's go to Tom Green, who's gonna do something really outrageous!
(Cut to a supermarket, where Tom Green is on his back under-

neath a cow, sucking the udder. He wears nothing but a tutu. He stops and looks at the camera.)

TOM GREEN: Does anyone out there like me yet? Can I stop this?

Stewie Holds Court at a Party

STEWIE: All right, all right, I've-I've-I've got, I've got one. I've got one. Um, okay, two men are standing at the pearly gates . . . *(to himself)* Oh, God, wait, how did that one go? *(gives up)* Oh, well, anyway, it turns out they're Siegfried and Roy. Ugh, I'm no good at telling jokes.

Nice Reference

(Chris enters with the phone.)

CHRIS: Dad, it's Mom.

PETER: Oh, God, please be Somerset Maugham, please be Somerset Maugham. *(into phone)* Hello?

LOIS: Peter?

PETER: Damn!

Quagmire Brainstorms

PETER: Oh, man, I am screwed. I'm gonna lose my house and my boat and everything. How am I gonna come up with fifty grand by tomorrow?

QUAGMIRE: Well, you could whore yourself out to a thousand fat chicks for fifty bucks a piece. Or-or fifty really fat chicks for a thousand bucks. What? Don't look at me like that. Fat chicks need love, too. But they gotta pay.

The Cops Shut Down Spring Break

POLICE OFFICER: All right, everybody. This party's over.

TREVOR: Hey, why do you cops always have to kill our buzz?

POLICE OFFICER: He used a teenage colloquialism. Get the tear gas.

Creepy Legends

JOE: I heard that when Daggermouth eats you, he devours your guts first.

CLEVELAND: I heard he doesn't just eat you, he eats your soul.

PETER: I heard that one of Shannen Doherty's eyes is off-center 'cause it's trying to escape.

Lois Home at Last

LOIS: Oh, Peter, I'm so glad being a fisherman is working out for you. You know, I've got to admit, I half-expected to come home and all our stuff would be gone, and we'd owe somebody a whole lot of money.

PETER: How can you half-expect something?

LOIS: I don't know. It's just a turn of phrase.

PETER: How do you turn a phrase?

LOIS: Oh, God, you're dumb. Thank God for that ass. Now, come here and kiss me.

A View from Behind the Scenes

"Getting Michael Chiklis for this episode was a big coup for us. Because, let's face it, the kids love The Commish.*"*

—FOX Executive

STUFF THAT MIGHT HAVE SLIPPED BY

■ In their hotel, Meg is reading *The Bell Jar*.

■ The wharf bar where the guys are drinking is called The Poopdeck.

■ Peter gets a loan from the same Salesman who conned him in various other episodes.

Episode
EMISSION IMPOSSIBLE

SUMMARY

Peter and Lois go to visit Lois's very pregnant sister, Carol, who has recently been dumped by her husband. They leave the kids with Quagmire, who doesn't have the slightest idea how to entertain or even look after children. While Peter and Lois are with Carol, she goes into labor and has her baby. The profound experience of being in the delivery room with Carol inspires Peter and Lois to try to have another baby of their own.

When Stewie catches wind of Peter and Lois's plan, he worries about being replaced by the new baby and vows to prevent Peter and Lois from conceiving. But after several unsuccessful attempts, Stewie realizes his only option is to shrink himself to microscopic size, enter Peter's body, and kill off all his sperm from the inside.

Once inside Peter's testicles, Stewie begins killing sperm until he confronts what appears to be a formidable foe named Bertram. With Peter and Lois enjoying a romantic evening, Stewie has only a short amount of time to dispense with Bertram, until Stewie learns that Bertram, too, hates Lois. This shared bond changes Stewie's mind, who now looks forward to the prospect of having Bertram as a partner in killing Lois. But as Stewie makes his way out of Peter's tear duct, he overhears Peter and Lois deciding not to have another baby after all.

EPISODE NUMBER: 3ACX01

ORIGINAL AIRDATE: 11/8/01

WRITERS: Dave Collard & Ken Goin

DIRECTOR: Peter Shin

EXECUTIVE PRODUCERS: Seth MacFarlane, Daniel Palladino

GUEST VOICES: Wallace Shawn as Bertram, Carol Kane as Carol

MEMORABLE MOMENTS

Cheap Entertainment
(Lois enters to find Peter sitting and staring intently at the spinning clothes in the dryer.)
LOIS: Peter, why are you staring into the dryer?
PETER: Ah, I'm watching the latest episode of *Laundry Theater*. See now, now those are Chris's socks, right? Now, they don't know that Stewie's shirt is having an affair with Meg's trousers. Ooh, it's fun to watch rich people be naughty!

Spousal Support
PETER: Oh, come on, Lois. When have I not been there for you?
(Flashback to a city street at night. Lois and Peter are at a stoplight. Lois is driving. Two thugs put a gun in Lois's face.
THUG #1: Get out of the damn car! Now!!
THUG #2: Scream and you're dead!
(Peter calmly opens the passenger-side door and gets out.)
PETER: *(to Lois)* Thanks for the ride, lady!
(Peter quickly walks away.)

Bad Timing
(Lois and her sister, Carol, are in the backseat of the car. Carol is doing her Lamaze breathing. She moans loudly as Lois holds a wet washcloth to her temple.)
LOIS: Don't worry, Carol. We're almost there.
(She notices that the car is not moving.)

LOIS: Peter, why are we stopped?
(We see that they're in line at a fast-food drive-thru window. Peter speaks into the clown's head.)
PETER: Um, yeah, I-I'll have three cheeseburgers.
LOIS: Peter! For God's sake, she's having a baby!
PETER: Oh, that's right . . . a-and a kids' meal. And, uh, I-I guess I'll have fries. *(to backseat)* I-if I have fries is anybody else gonna have any? 'Cause, you know, I-I-I don't want to be the only one eating them. I'll feel like a fatty.

Wait Your Turn

(Peter and Lois help Carol into a wheelchair and wheel her inside the emergency room, up to the Check-in Nurse.)
LOIS: Nurse! This woman is in labor!
(Mayor West steps in front of them.)
MAYOR WEST: *(to Lois)* Excuse me. I was here first. *(to Nurse)* My leg is asleep.

Chaos in the Delivery Room

(The doctor falls out of frame, unconscious.)
CAROL: Oh, my God, who's gonna deliver my baby?
LOIS: Honey, do something!
(Peter peeks his head underneath the sheet.)
PETER: Well, no baby, but it looks like Carol's blowing a bubble.
LOIS: Peter, that's the head. Push! Push!
PETER: I am! It won't go back in!

House Training

PETER: H-hey, look at this, Lois. It's our Pet Rock. Ah, I remember the first day we brought it home.
(Flashback to the Griffins' living room, where Lois stands by as Peter shoves the Rock into a stain on the carpet.)
PETER: (to Rock) See that? Huh?! Huh?! Bad Rock! BAD!! We do that outside! *(to Lois)* Look at him, he knows what he did.

Stewie Moves In

(Stewie runs into Peter and Lois's bedroom and jumps on the bed, causing Peter and Lois to break their embrace.)
STEWIE: Waah! Waah! Mommy, Daddy, I had a bad dream. I-I-I saw the-the-the boo— Oh blast, what the devil is that name again? Uh, boo-boo-boo- Boogeyman! Yes, that's it! I saw the Boogeyman!
(Lois scoops Stewie up and puts him in between them.)
LOIS: Ooh, did someone have a bad dream? Hmm, why don't you sleep with Mommy and Daddy.
(Stewie smiles to himself, flips over the pillow, fluffs it, and lays his head down. Peter makes a move toward Lois.)
LOIS: Peter, for God's sake, Stewie's right here!
PETER: Come on, Lois, we can still do it. He'll just think I'm hurting you.

Scene Stealers
BERTRAM

POSITION
A sperm in Peter's testicle

DISTINGUISHING FEATURE
An intellect to rival Stewie's

TURN-ONS
Doing away with Lois

TURN-OFFS
People who use the word "guesstimate," guys who wear socks with sandals, Jason Patric

You seen that little gleam in the fat man's eye? That twinkle? That's me, plotting my escape.

STUFF THAT MIGHT HAVE SLIPPED BY

■ In the first scene of the show, Lois is reading *The Bailiff* by John Grisham.

■ Quagmire's doorbell is in the shape of a woman's head with her mouth open.

■ Stewie's access code for the keypad on his bedroom wall is 3-5-1-5.

A View from Behind the Scenes

"This episode contains one of at least three Incredible Hulk references in the first three seasons of Family Guy. Part of that was my being a big fan of that show; the other part was utter laziness."

—SETH MACFARLANE, CREATOR AND EXECUTIVE PRODUCER

Brian Helps Peter Assemble a Crib

BRIAN: Okay, insert rod support A into slot B . . .
(Before Peter can speak, Brian cuts him off.)
BRIAN: If you say, "That's what she said," one more time, I'm gonna pop you.

Stewie Keeps Up His Efforts to Prevent Conception

(Stewie peeks around the corner. He sees Peter and Lois enter their bedroom.)
STEWIE: Oh, my God, they're at it again! *(sigh)* All this time spent keeping people from having sex. Now I know how the Catholic Church feels . . . Ba-zing!

A Romantic Evening, At Last

LOIS: *(sexually)* You know, I'm not wearing any panties.
PETER: *(just as sexually)* Don't worry, we can always throw that chair out.

Stewie Meets Bertram in Peter's Testicle

STEWIE: Well, it seems you're out of ammunition.
BERTRAM: As are you, Stewart.
STEWIE: *(gasp)* You know my name!
BERTRAM: I know many things.
STEWIE: Indeed.
BERTRAM: Quite.
STEWIE: Yes.
BERTRAM: Mm.
STEWIE: Well, perhaps we should exchange monosyllabic expressions of arrogance in person.
BERTRAM: Ahh.
STEWIE: Mm.
BERTRAM: Yes.

Stewie and Bertram Part Ways

BERTRAM: I guess this is good-bye.
STEWIE: For now.
(Stewie and Bertram shake hands.)
STEWIE: Oh, when you're born, don't let the doctor slap you on the ass. It degrades us all.

Lois Has Second Thoughts

(Lois pulls back from kissing Peter.)
LOIS: Oh, Peter, wait. I-I've been thinking . . . It's been a long time since we had such a wonderful night. And it's gonna be impossible to spend time together like this if we're raising another child.
PETER: Well, I-I thought uh, you know, Brian would kinda do a lot of the work.

Episode
TO LOVE AND DIE IN DIXIE

SUMMARY

Chris's crush from school, a girl named Barbara, invites a very nervous Chris to her birthday party. Chris gets a paper route to pay for a birthday gift for her, but is still clumsy and awkward around Barbara when he presents the gift to her. Later on his paper route, Chris witnesses a robbery at a local convenience store. At the police station, Chris identifies the thief. But when the criminal later escapes from jail, he vows to hunt down Chris and kill him.

The FBI relocates the Griffins to a town in the Deep South called Bumblescum. As the family explores Southern life, Chris befriends a kid named Sam and Peter becomes the town sheriff. But when Peter questions the revisionist history of Bumblescum's Civil War reenactment, the townsfolk turn on him and even forbid Chris to spend time with his new friend. As Chris and Sam share their sadness over not being able to hang out together anymore, Sam stuns Chris by giving him a giant kiss.

Back in Quahog, the thief shows up at the Griffins' house and manages to learn the Griffins' location from the FBI. Meanwhile, Chris discovers that Sam is not a boy after all, but, in fact, a girl! Chris is now awkward around Sam . . . that is, until Sam points out that Chris had no problem talking to her when he thought she was a boy. Chris realizes what Sam says is true and they happily head off to be together. When the thief catches up to them, Sheriff Peter (along with his deputy, Brian) arrives to save the day, but, of course, bungles saving Chris. Finally, one of their fellow Southerners bails them out by killing the thief, enabling the Griffins to return to their lives back in Quahog.

EPISODE NUMBER: 3ACX09

ORIGINAL AIRDATE: 11/15/01

WRITER: Steve Callaghan

DIRECTOR: Dan Povenmire

EXECUTIVE PRODUCERS:
Seth MacFarlane,
Daniel Palladino

GUEST VOICE: Waylon Jennings
as himself

MEMORABLE MOMENTS

Nervous Much?

BARBARA: I'm having a birthday party next week. I was hoping you could come.
> (*She hands Chris an invitation.*)

CHRIS: Oh, no! Someone peed in my pants!

Brainstorming on Gift Ideas

CHRIS: I wanna get Barbara a really nice gift. What kinds of gifts have boys gotten for you, Meg?

MEG: Oh . . . well, my boyfriend, Prince William, got me this beautiful watch (*she holds out her empty wrist*) and this diamond tiara (*as if she's wearing one*) and this wonderful scepter.
> (*Meg laughs a little insanely, bursts into tears, and runs out of the room.*)

STEWIE: She needs to get laid—big time.

PETER: Listen, Chris, I read a book saying that women are from Venus. All right, so here's what you get her: thick layers of sulfuric acid, viscous surface rock, and coronae, which seem to be collapsed domes over large magma chambers. Here's five dollars.

A View from Behind the Scenes

"The Thief's line, 'Well, I hated T.J.Hooker. And I never actually saw McMillan and Wife . . . although I was aware of it,' came thirty percent out of trying to write a joke and seventy percent out of simply expressing how I felt about both those shows as a kid."

—STEVE CALLAGHAN, WRITER OF THE EPISODE

Not Your Average Wacky Sitcom Neighbor

HERBERT: Well, hey there, young fella, bringin' me good news today?

CHRIS: What?

HERBERT: C'mon over here, son. Hand me the paper so I don't need to use my grabber.

(Chris approaches Herbert and hands him a paper.)

HERBERT: Mmmm. That's a nice muscley throwin' arm you got there.

CHRIS: Uh, thanks.

(Herbert jingles some coins in his pocket.)

HERBERT: Got a nice tip for you right here in my pocket. But my arthritis . . . Why don't you reach in there and fish it out for yourself?

Better to Give Than Receive

CHRIS: I hope you like it.

(Barbara unwraps the gift. It's a small bottle.)

BARBARA: Wow! Perfume! That is so sweet.

CHRIS: It'll make you smell like Elizabeth Taylor. I guess that means you'll smell like bourbon and Vicodin.

Blowing Chris's Cover

(Peter enters the line-up room with the criminals Chris is picking from.)

PETER: Hi, uh, excuse me, you guys. Uh, yeah, I'm here to pick up my son, Chris Griffin. Uh, he's here to finger the guy who held up that convenience store. Maybe you've seen him. His name is Chris Griffin. Uh, wait a sec, you know, I think I got a picture of him somewhere. Here you go.

(Peter pulls out a photo of Chris, which the Thief studies intently.)

PETER: Yeah, you can go ahead and hang on to that. I got a ton of 'em at home. In fact, I was gonna throw that one out anyway, 'cause Chris messed it up by writing his school schedule and a list of his fears all over the back of it.

A Guy Can Dream, Can't He?

LOIS: Oh, we're so proud of you, Chris, for helping to put that horrible man in jail.

PETER: Geez, you couldn'ta said it was Celine Dion, huh? Our one chance to put that showboatin' Canadian wench behind bars, and you blow it.

A Guy Can Dream, Can't He?, Part 2

AGENT HARRIS: Yes, ma'am. This criminal will stop at nothing to find your son. So, we're placing your family in the Witness Protection Program.

STEWIE: Oh, is Europe an option? I say, I've always wanted to spend a year in Prague teaching English. You know, slacking off a bit, but really getting to know myself.

What Were You Expecting?

AGENT HARRIS: Well, until we catch this guy, you'll be relocated to the Deep South.

(The Griffins vocalize their dismay.)

PETER: The Deep South?! Isn't that the place where the black guys are really lazy and all the white guys are just as lazy, but they're mad at the black guys for bein' so lazy?

Happy Housewarming

LOIS: Uch. What's that smell?

BRIAN: It's either bad meat or good cheese.

Peter's Southern Dream

PETER: All right, that about does it. Isn't she beautiful, Brian?

(Peter has modified the Griffins' car to look exactly like the General Lee from The Dukes of Hazzard.)

BRIAN: The Duke boys would be proud, Peter.

PETER: Yeah, and you gotta get in through the window, like this.

(Peter takes a running jump and leaps through the open window, landing in the driver's seat.)

Scene Stealers
HERBERT

WHO HE IS
The Griffins' extremely old neighbor

WHAT HE LIKES
Chocolate phosphates, "those talkie pictures," Chris Griffin

Ya like Popsicles? I got a whole freezer full of Popsicles. Mmmm.

A View from Behind the Scenes

"In the script the rednecks show up at the end to shoot the thief to save Chris. Then everybody stands around talking to wrap up the episode and there's never any more mention of the thief. When the board artist brought the sequence to me there was this presumably dead body lying on the bridge for the rest of the scene. Now, I grew up in the Deep South and I know how things work down there so I just drew the rednecks nonchalantly kicking the body into the river during the conversation. It got a huge laugh in the screening and Seth says it's one of his favorite gags in that show. I myself was just going for realism."

—Dan Povenmire, DIRECTOR
OF THE EPISODE

PETER: Okay, now you.
(*Brian takes a running jump and slams into the closed passenger-side window, falling to the ground.*)
PETER: Oh, sorry. I forgot to roll yours down. *(then)* You all right?
(*He looks down at Brian, who remains motionless.*)
PETER: Hello? . . . Wake up, sleepy head.

Misstatements Can Be Funny . . .
PETER: That was great! Next time let's get Meg to be Boss Hogg and Chris can be Anus.
BRIAN: Enos.
PETER: What'd I say?
BRIAN: Anus.
PETER: Hehehehehe.

Meg Is Popular for Once
SOUTHERN TEACHER: All right, class, we have a new student joining us. Everyone please welcome Megan Griffin, *(dramatically)* from the North.
(*All the kids "oooh" and "aaah" and stare at Meg in awe.*)
SOUTHERN KID #2: What's it like up there? Y'all got them talking pictures?
SOUTHERN KID #3: And flying machines?
SOUTHERN KID #1: And perfume for your armpits?
MEG: We sure do.
(*They all "oooh" and "aaah."*)
SOUTHERN TEACHER: All right, class. That's enough questions for Megan. Time to hand back last week's spelling tests.
(*She looks down at the stack of spelling tests.*)
SOUTHERN TEACHER: And it looks like Oinky set the curve again!
(*Reveal a pig, Oinky, sitting at a desk in the front.*)
SOUTHERN KIDS: Aw, dang it. / That is some smart pig. / Good thing I copied offa Oinky.

Peter Logic
LOIS: Well, I'm glad you're having fun, but we need some money coming in. Have you thought about looking for a job?
PETER: Yes, Lois, I have. But I've also thought about getting fired from that job. Is that something you really wanna put our family through?

An Easy Sell
DEPUTY: Y'all interested? We just take turns being the Sheriff. It's real easy. You just hang out here, eat some pie, and get drunk.
PETER: Wait, hold on a second. "Pie"? "Drunk"? "The"? You got yourself a sheriff!

Revisionist History, Southern Style

(On a raised platform are various Actors dressed in costumes, including one dressed as Robert E. Lee, sitting at a table. He checks his pocket watch as Ulysses S. Grant stumbles in carrying a giant bottle of booze.)

ULYSSES S. GRANT: Robert E. Lee, I knew I'd find you here where they seat the sorry-ass losers.

(He laughs drunkenly.)

ROBERT E. LEE: Ulysses S. Grant, you invite me to lunch, then show up an hour late, drunk?

ULYSSES S. GRANT: I was busy looking for your wife, to give her the old—

(He babbles incoherently and grinds his hips.)

ROBERT E. LEE: Sir, this means war.

(Robert E. Lee pushes Ulysses S. Grant to the ground.)

ULYSSES S. GRANT: I am vanquished!

ROBERT E. LEE: I hereby declare victory in the name of the Confederacy!

Let's Settle This Like Southern Gentlemen

HILLBILLY #1: Hee, sure is a ding dang of a hoedown.

HILLBILLY #2: Nuh-uh. This here's a hootenany!

HILLBILLY #1: Hoedown!

HILLBILLY #2: Hootenany!

HILLBILLY #1: Hoedown!

HILLBILLY #2: Hootenany!

HILLBILLY #1: Hoedown!

HILLBILLY #2: Hootenany!

(They immediately fight.)

And Now This Announcement

("Stewie and the Cowtones" finish their song.)

STEWIE: Thank you, thank you very much. Thank you.

(Someone hands Stewie a piece of paper.)

STEWIE: *(reading)* Oh, and, uh, to the owner of a John Deere tractor, you're parked on top of a pig. John Deere tractor, on top of a pig.

We've All Got to Have Heroes

MEG: *(bragging)* You know, my brother is the one he's here to kill.

(The group of kids, including a five-year-old girl, all "ooh" and "aah.")

FIVE-YEAR-OLD GIRL: My daughter'd absolutely love you.

STUFF THAT MIGHT HAVE SLIPPED BY

■ When the Griffins enter Bumblescum, an old man on the side of the road changes the population figure on the sign at the edge of town from "48" to "54."

■ The ATM in Bumblescum is nothing more than a guy in a cardboard box to whom you tell your PIN before he'll hand you some cash.

■ When Peter and Brian are driving through Bumblescum, the radio finishes playing a fictional Merle Haggard song called, "I Kissed My Sweetie with My Fist."

■ In an homage to *The Dukes of Hazzard*, the angle of Peter and Brian's car is at a decidedly less precarious angle after the commercial than it is before the commercial.

■ When the FBI agents are having a party at the Griffins' house, Quagmire runs by in the background.

■ Stewie's band in Bumblescum is named "Stewie and the Cowtones."

■ The Southerner who saves Chris by shooting the convenience store thief very casually kicks the body into the river after the shooting.

■ Peter is attacked by the raccoon four times: as it jumps out of the TV, as it leaps from the refrigerator, as it flies out of Lois's cleavage, and as it escapes from the muzzle of Peter's gun.

Episode
SCREWED THE POOCH

SUMMARY

Peter is dreading an upcoming family trip to the Pewterschmidts' because he and Lois's dad have never gotten along. Quagmire, Cleveland, and Joe suggest to Peter that he find common ground with Carter, so Peter attempts to culture himself. At the same time, Brian experiences some primal urges, directed at his own species, for a change. When Peter and Lois discover Brian pleasuring himself to doggie porn, Lois suggests he join them for the trip to the Pewterschmidts as a way to clear his mind.

At the Pewterschmidts, Carter is, as always, annoyed by Peter's boorish behavior . . . that is, until Peter bonds with Carter over a night of poker and wild pranks with Carter's buddies, Bill Gates and Michael Eisner. However, just when it appears that Peter has finally won Carter over, Brian destroys all of Peter's hard work by having sex with the Pewterschmidt's prize-winning race dog, Sea Breeze.

Carter throws the Griffins out of his house and insists that Brian never see Sea Breeze again. But, Brian, intent on doing right by a now-pregnant Sea Breeze, escapes with her. Together, they hole up in a crappy motel. When Carter finally finds them, Brian decides to sue for custody of his puppies. The verdict comes down, requiring Brian to be neutered in order to retain custody, a condition to which Brian nobly agrees. Just before his surgery, though, it is discovered that Brian is not the father of Sea Breeze's puppies after all, and Brian's gonads are spared.

EPISODE NUMBER: 3ACX08

ORIGINAL AIRDATE: 11/29/01

WRITERS: Dave Collard & Ken Goin

DIRECTOR: Pete Michels

EXECUTIVE PRODUCERS: Seth MacFarlane, Daniel Palladino

GUEST VOICE: Bob Barker as himself

MEMORABLE MOMENTS

Fun at the Zoo

STEWIE: There you are. Oh, don't be such a pig, Mr. Pig. Oh, now, where's Mr. Sheep? Is he being baaaaa-shful? *(laughs)* Uh, oh, that's right, you're all ripe for parody.
BRIAN: Can we go now?
STEWIE: Shut up, I'm having fun!

Worse Than Spam

PETER: Lois is making me visit the in-laws this weekend. I don't know why she even bothers. Me and Lois's old man have never gotten along. *(Flashback to the Griffins' family room, where Peter sits at the family's computer.)*
PETER: Hey, I got an e-mail from Mr. Pewterschmidt. *(Peter clicks the mouse. Suddenly a fist flies out of the screen and punches Peter in the face.)*

French Class

TEACHER: In French, when you want to say "yes," you say "oui, oui!"
PETER: You gotta be kidding me! Oh, my God, that is hysterical. *(laughs)* Oh, man. Hey, what do you say for "no?" "Doo doo?" *(Peter rises.)*
PETER: Hey, I'll be right back. I gotta go take a wicked "yes."

Passive-Aggressive Grandma

MRS. PEWTERSCHMIDT: Oh, look at you all. *(she hugs Meg)* I know some-one who's getting a gift certificate for liposuction in her stocking.

Making a Good Impression

PETER: Bonjour, Monsieur Pewterschmidt.

MR. PEWTERSCHMIDT: Did Peter have a stroke?

LOIS: No, Daddy, Peter's cultured himself. Like Julia Roberts in *Pretty Woman.*

MR. PEWTERSCHMIDT: Oh, so I should treat him like a high-class whore. *(Mr. Pewterschmidt lights a cigarette, takes a puff, then puts it out on Peter's chest.)*

PETER: *(suppressing pain)* That's fine, just no kissing on the lips.

Wine Tasting

WINE TASTING MAN #2: Carter, did you tell your son-in-law he's not supposed to swallow the wine? *(An extremely drunk and naked Peter wanders out.)*

PETER: Hey, hey, where the, where the hell is that Peter Griffin? He said he'd give me a hundred dollars if I took off all my clothes off.

Enough Said

LOIS: Daddy, Peter's been trying really hard to get you to like him. Couldn't you give him another chance? Let him join your poker game tomorrow night?

MR. PEWTERSCHMIDT: Sorry, honey. I'd rather be stuck in an elevator with Nathan Lane, Gilbert Gottfried, Carrot Top, uhhhhh . . . Sean Hayes, well, you get the picture.

Peter Meets Bill Gates

MR. PEWTERSCHMIDT: Uh, Bill, Peter's an antitrust lawyer with the Justice Department. *(Bill Gates punches Peter in the face. Mr. Pewterschmidt laughs.)*

MR. PEWTERSCHMIDT: Nah, just kidding. He's a fisherman or some stupid thing.

Who Invited Him?

PETER: Okay, guys, we're playin' Texas Hold 'Em.

TED TURNER: Are aces high or low?

PETER: They go both ways.

BILL GATES: Huh, he said, "They go both ways." *(They all laugh.)*

TED TURNER: *(laughing)* Like a bisexual.

MICHAEL EISNER: Thank you, Ted, that was the joke.

> Which of the following two phrases best describes Brian Griffin: Problem drinker or African–American haberdasher?

Scene Stealers
CARTER'S LAWYER

SPECIALTY
Digging up dirt, incredibly leading questions, entrapment

HIS ACE IN THE HOLE
Using the rental of Pauly Shore movies against a witness

HOW CARTER PAYS HIM
In gold bars

A View from
Behind the Scenes

"We changed our mind at the last minute, of course, but we had considered not doing an act break where one of our characters is having sex with a dog. Not due to matters of taste, but just because I was pretty sure they'd already done that on Suddenly Susan."

—SETH MACFARLANE, CREATOR AND EXECUTIVE PRODUCER

STUFF THAT MIGHT HAVE SLIPPED BY

■ Peter's "poker face" is actually a totally blank face, entirely free of all facial features.

■ When Peter and Lois walk in on Brian in the bathroom, he is reading a magazine called *Kinky Canine Coeds*.

■ Brian turns on the TV to get his mind off his primal urges just as World's Sluttiest Dogs is airing on Fox.

■ Bill Gates summons a helicopter by simply shining a light of the Windows logo into the sky.

■ The sign in front of the motel that Brian and Sea Breeze stay at reads, "Ed's Motel: As seen on *America's Most Wanted*."

■ After the police find Brian and Sea Breeze, the newspaper headline reads "Race Dog Found." The smaller head-line, in reference to Tom Tucker's ren-dezvous at the same motel, reads "Sleazy Prostitute Given Important Position at Local News Station."

■ The sign in front of the Quahog Animal Clinic reads "Euthanasia, 2 for 1 with coupon."

Early Night

MR. PEWTERSCHMIDT: Well, I'm gonna turn in.

MICHAEL EISNER: Yeah, me too. I gotta be at Disneyland before it opens. We're ethnically cleansing the "Small World" ride.

Out of Touch

PETER: Aw, man, there's a tollbooth. Hey, anybody got a quarter?

BILL GATES: What's a quarter?

Brian and Sea Breeze Are Shown to Their Room

MOTEL CLERK: And this is the bathroom. But watch out, we got some bad roaches here.

(Two human-sized Cockroaches, with goatees and do-rags, lamely jab switchblades at Brian and the Motel Clerk.)

COCKROACH #1: Eh, you're on our turf, man.

COCKROACH #2: Eh, man, I-I cut you, I cut you up so bad you, y-you gonna, you gonna wish I no cut you up so bad.

(The Motel Clerk shuts the door.)

BRIAN: Those are bad roaches.

MOTEL CLERK: I blame the schools.

Yes, That Explains It . . .

LOIS: Daddy, please, stop this. Brian has every right to see his puppies when they're born.

MR. PEWTERSCHMIDT: Sorry, pumpkin.

LOIS: I had no idea you could be so cruel. I'll never forgive you for this.

MR. PEWTERSCHMIDT: Ah, you'll be fine. You're just having your period.

Very Cross Examination

LAWYER: Mr. Griffin, which of the following two phrases best describes Brian Griffin: Problem drinker or African-American haberdasher?

PETER: Uh, do I-I guess, problem drinker, but that's uh—

LAWYER: Thank you. Now: Sexual deviant or magic picture that if you stare at it long enough, you see something?

PETER: Well, sexual deviant, but that other one's not even, eh—

LAWYER: Thank you.

There's Gotta Be a Story There

PETER: Your Honor, Brian'll be a great dad. Hell, if I was half the parent Brian is, I'd know that Chris's favorite ice cream is . . .

BRIAN: Chocolate chip.

PETER: . . . and Stewie's favorite bedtime story is . . .

BRIAN: *Good Night Moon*.

PETER: . . . and Meg's real father's name is . . .

BRIAN: Stan Thompson.

Episode
PETER GRIFFIN: HUSBAND, FATHER... BROTHER?

SUMMARY

Chris begins to adopt Black mannerisms and speech habits after serving as the towel boy for the school basketball team. Peter, concerned about the change in Chris, asks Cleveland for advice. Cleveland suggests that perhaps Chris has adopted another culture because he doesn't know enough about his own. So, Peter takes Chris to the Irish Heritage Museum and the library to learn about their roots. In the process, Peter is surprised to discover that one of his early ancestors was actually Black. Meanwhile, Stewie becomes intrigued by the power cheerleaders have to get an entire group of people to obey them. Eager to discover their secret, he vows to infiltrate their coven and study their methods.

NATE GRIFFIN

Peter isn't sure what to make of his newfound ancestry until Cleveland encourages him to embrace Black culture. Peter's first few attempts to do so misfire, but ultimately he gains the acceptance of the local Black community. When he and his posse return home, they find Lois's parents, Babs and Carter, there for a visit. In light of Peter's recent discovery, Babs and Carter feel it is important for the kids to learn more about the Pewterschmidt side of the family as well. The only thing is, in doing so, it comes out that the Pewterschmidt family once owned Peter's Black ancestor as a slave. Meanwhile, Stewie has fully immersed himself in the cheerleaders' clique—even going so far as to dabble in bulimia to fit in. Peter is appalled and plays victim, demanding reparations from Carter. When Carter actually does cough up $20,000, Peter is astonished and quickly wastes it on frivolous things. Lois, Cleveland, and ultimately the entire local Black community become upset with Peter for not sharing some of his reparations with his brothers. After Peter has had a heartfelt talk with the ghost of his long-deceased Black relative, he decides to give the money back, but chooses to do so by tossing piles of cash to the crowd at the school basketball game. Finally, Stewie takes the place of the head cheerleader at the basketball game in the hope of getting the crowd to follow his evil commands, but his best efforts are thwarted once more.

A View from Behind the Scenes

"This episode aired around the time that we all pretty much figured we were cancelled for good. We'd written the five scripts that had been requested, but there weren't any further requests for scripts forthcoming . . . so that was definitely a clue. Well, that, and the fact that a big Russian guy from the network came to haul away my computer. At least I think he was from the network . . ."

—SETH MACFARLANE, CREATOR AND EXECUTIVE PRODUCER

EPISODE NUMBER: 3ACX06

ORIGINAL AIRDATE: 12/6/01

WRITERS: Mike Barker & Matt Weitzman

DIRECTOR: Scott Wood

EXECUTIVE PRODUCERS: Seth MacFarlane, Daniel Palladino

MEMORABLE MOMENTS

Fatherly Pride

PETER: *(to Tom Tucker and his son, Jake)* Hey, uh, that's my son out there. I taught him how to wipe.

JAKE: Why won't you teach me how to wipe, Dad?

TOM: Because you don't have a bottom, son.

JAKE: Aw!

Scene Stealers
NATE GRIFFIN

OCCUPATION
Nineteenth-century horse groomer and slave of the Pewterschmidt family

COMMONALITIES WITH PETER
His appearance, his same dopey laugh, work ethic

MOST NOTABLE DIARY ENTRY
"May 7th, 1836. I was brushing down Lucy, the new colt, when she let out a fart right near my face. So I took her head and stuck it by my butt and blew a huge fart right back at her!"

LITTLE-KNOWN FACT ABOUT HIM
He slept with not one, but two, of Peter's relatives

Oh, don't worry about me. If it makes you feel any better, I peed in my owners' cereal every morning.

Stewie Discovers the Power of the Cheerleaders

STEWIE: My God, what, what just happened to me? It's those sirens! They had us all completely under their spell. Like that hypnotist at the airport Hilton.
(Flashback to a Hotel Convention Room, where a large crowd laughs as they watch Brian and Stewie make out on stage. A Hypnotist looks on.)
HYPNOTIST: And . . . three.
(Brian and Stewie break away from each other and look around confused.)
BRIAN: Oh, wow, were-were we just hypnotized?
STEWIE: Well, that's incredible. I don't remember a thing. *(then)* Why do I taste crotch?

Give Him Credit for Trying to Be Supportive

PETER: Hey, nice job out there tonight, Chris. You wiped the floor with that towel.

Parental Panic

CHRIS: Yo, did y'all check me when that hottie was all up in my Kool-Aid? Yeah, I was lookin' to break off a little somethin' somethin', but my crew gave me the four-one-one on that skank and she's all about the bling-bling.
(Peter slams on the brakes and pulls the car over.)
LOIS: Peter, what's wrong?!
PETER: He's speaking in tongues, Lois. Our son is possessed.
(Peter opens the glove box and pulls out a Bible and a small vial. He tosses the Bible to Meg.)
PETER: Meg, start at Psalm Forty-One and don't stop reading 'til I tell you.
(Peter begins sprinkling Chris with liquid from the vial.)
PETER: The power of Christ compels you! The power of Christ compels you!
CHRIS: Aaaa! Aaaa! Aaaa! Aaaa! Aaaa! Aaaa!

Peter Seeks Counsel

(Peter and Cleveland are at the bar drinking beers.)
PETER: And-and-and then Chris starts in with all this "yo-yo-yo" stuff and I-I don't know what the hell he's talking about. So I started beating him with a hose, then my arm got tired so I came here.

Technically True, I Suppose . . .

CHRIS: What's a library, Dad?
PETER: Oh, it's just a place where homeless people come to shave and go B.M. Let's go inside.

Peter and Chris Explore Their Roots

PETER: Hey, look, here's a picture of your great-great-granddad, Osias Griffin. He owned one of the first dozen telephones.

(Flashback to an old-fashioned parlor where Osias Griffin answers his ringing telephone.)

OSIAS GRIFFIN: Hello?

MAN'S VOICE: Hello, Jonathan?

OSIAS GRIFFIN: No. What number are you calling?

MAN'S VOICE: Seven.

OSIAS GRIFFIN: Well, this is three.

MAN'S VOICE: Oh, sorry.

(Osias hangs up.)

The Family Reacts to the News of Peter's Black Ancestor

CHRIS: Cool! I get to be Black and Irish!

MEG: Yeah, and now I can wear clothes that actually show off my big butt!

LOIS: Oh, I gotta tell Bonnie I'm sleeping with a Black man!

So, It's Stewie's Fault

STEWIE: I know something about bad ideas.

(Flashback to a bar, where a drunk Stewie is having cocktails with O. J. Simpson.)

STEWIE: I'm-I'm telling you, Juice, she's screwing around behind your back. And-and if I were in your Bruno Magli's, I wouldn't stand for it.

(Stewie turns to look for the waitress.)

STEWIE: Another mai tai. Thanks. *(he turns back)* So, listen—

(He realizes O. J. has bolted.)

There's Probably More to It Than That

PETER: Yeah, but see, the problem is I got no idea how to be Black. You know, except for not smiling when I get my picture taken.

Stewie Is Becoming a Cheerleader

STEWIE: Uch, look at how fat you are. You disgust me. Oink, oink, fatty. Oh, yes, yes, you'll take butter on that English muffin, won't you, because you're the cheerleading squad's token blimp! You don't deserve to eat!

(Stewie sticks his finger down his throat and retches into the toilet.)

Cleveland Makes an Announcement

CLEVELAND: Yesterday I received reparations from the family that enslaved my ancestors.

(Everyone applauds and cheers.)

CLEVELAND: Now, the family has become poor white trash since then, so they only gave what they could: This tray of scrumptious Rice Krispies Treats. I share them with all of you in the hopes that one day your wounds may be healed as well.

A Visit from Grandma and Grandpa

CARTER: Now, Chris, this one's for you: What's the secret to happiness?

CHRIS: Money!

CARTER: Very good. Babs, give him a caramel.

STUFF THAT MIGHT HAVE SLIPPED BY

■ The Buddy Cianci Middle School basketball team is called the Dust Mites.

■ Peter being mesmerized by the turkey legs coming out of the cheerleader's sweater is a parody of a famous scene in *American Beauty*.

■ There is a Leprechaun on display at the Irish Heritage Museum.

■ When Peter wins over the Quahog African-American League, he is cheered on by the kids from *Fat Albert*.

■ The book of Pewterschmidt ancestry shows what Carter describes as "Silas Pewterschmidt, bartering with some local Indians," but the photo actually shows Silas, holding an Indian child hostage with a knife to his neck, across from a frightened father and mother Indian, who offer forth a bushel of corn.

■ In a cheerleader's locker, Stewie finds a pamphlet titled "Your Body and You."

■ **After Peter realizes he has a Black ancestor he renounces his "slave name" of Peter and dubs himself Kichwa-Tembo.**

Carter and Babs Show Their True Colors

BABS: Peter, we hear you're a negro now.
PETER: Yep. I even got my own posse.
(Three young Black men enter.)
PETER: Hey, ah, Big Dawg, T-bone, Shades. Uh, you guys go make yourselves some sandwiches, we'll hook up later.
(The posse walks through the living room and into the kitchen.)
CARTER: *(to the posse)* My jacket's in the kitchen. Please don't write on it.

An Embarrassing Revelation

PETER: Lois, your family owned my family!
LOIS: Daddy, is that true?
CARTER: Well, it appears so. Boy, this is pretty embarrassing.
PETER: Yes, it is! And don't call me "boy"!

Stewie Inadvertently Sees the Cheerleaders Disrobe

STEWIE: Oh, I mustn't watch. It's not the proper thing to— Whoa! I say, nice ones, Janine! And look at Lisa in all her curvaceous glory! *(he looks down)* Heavens, it appears that my wee-wee has been stricken with rigor mortis.

Peter Learns the Downside of Being Black

(A Cop has pulled Peter over.)
COP: Hey, you're that Black guy I saw on the news conference, ain't ya?
PETER: Uh, yeah, that's me.
COP: *(into his radio)* This is car fifteen, I'm gonna need backup. I've got a stolen vehicle here.
PETER: But this is my car—
COP: *(into radio)* Suspect's getting belligerent.
PETER: What?
COP: *(into radio)* Officer down.
(The cop falls to the ground. Three other cop cars screech up to them.)

Nice Try

CLEVELAND: Peter, we know about your selfish squandering of your reparation money. I shared mine. You, however, have given nothing back to the community.
PETER: *(grasping)* Wha . . . that's not true. I've brought you the greatest gift of all: a child's laughter.
(Peter giggles in a high-pitched voice.)

Peter Talks to His Ancestor, Nate

PETER: Wait, wait, wait. Ah, b-before you go. What's Heaven like?
NATE: Oh, it's fine. There's a shortage of chairs.
PETER: Oh.
NATE: Yeah.

Episode
READY, WILLING, AND DISABLED

SUMMARY

All the neighbors on Spooner Street come together to hold a charity car wash to help one of Chris's classmates who is in an iron lung. When a thief steals all the money they've raised, Joe tries to chase the guy down, but loses him. Joe becomes very upset since this is the first time he's ever let a suspect get away and the first time he's ever truly felt handicapped. Peter, in an effort to cheer up Joe, encourages him to compete in the Special People's Games. He even offers to be Joe's coach. Meanwhile, Stewie, Meg, and Chris find $26 on the street and are informed that they must keep the money for two weeks and search for its owner before they can claim it as their own.

Peter helps Joe get into shape for the Special People's Games. When the competition rolls around, Joe excels at first, but then suffers a crisis of confidence, prompting Peter to secretly give Joe steroids so he'll win. At the same time, Stewie, Meg, and Chris squabble over the $26, causing Brian to act as a neutral party by taking possession of the money for the remainder of the two weeks.

After Joe's win at the Special People's Games, he is approached by a slimy sports agent who quickly secures various commercial endorsements and a biographical TV movie for Joe. Peter, who feels forgotten by his star athlete, tries to gain similar acclaim by pretending to be handicapped himself. But when that fails, he spitefully reveals to the town that Joe only won at the Special People's Games because of the steroids Peter gave him. Joe feels horrible about this, but rebounds when he tracks the thief who stole the money from the car wash in the first place. And, finally, Stewie, Chris, and Meg continue to struggle over the $26, only to have it taken from them at the last minute by its rightful owner.

EPISODE NUMBER: 3ACX07

ORIGINAL AIRDATE: 12/20/01

WRITERS: Alex Barnow & Marc Firek

DIRECTOR: Andi Klein

EXECUTIVE PRODUCERS: Seth MacFarlane, Daniel Palladino

GUEST VOICES: Tony Danza as himself, Valerie Bertinelli as herself

MEMORABLE MOMENTS

Stewie's Car Wash

STEWIE: *(to Kid on a Big Wheel)* Okay, so you want the full wash, and, uh, oh, you got a nick there, I can probably get that out for you. Now, if you want to go with a scent, I've got P-B-and-J, sugar cereal, and new toy.

Looking for Ways to Spend Found Money

STEWIE: I say we buy twenty-six-dollars worth of ice cream and just pig out. Oh, we can dish, talk about who's getting fat. Oh, we'll just be great big bitches.

Where to Store the Money

MEG: So, um, the twenty-six dollars would probably be safe in my room.

STEWIE: Yeah, right. It'd probably get lost among the pinups of Justin Timberlake and Tom Cruise and, and uh . . .oh blast, who do the teenage girls like? Uh, uh . . . Morgan Freeman.

A Violent Conscience

LOIS: Peter, Bonnie says Joe's been really depressed about that robbery. Why don't you go talk to him?

PETER: Well, I don't know. There's a game on.
(A miniature Angel Peter appears on Peter's shoulder.)

ANGEL PETER: Shame on you. You march right over there and cheer your old friend up.
(A miniature Devil Peter appears on Peter's other shoulder.)

DEVIL PETER: Don't listen to that sissy. Grab a beer and watch the game.

PETER: Yeah, that sounds good.
(Angel Peter pulls out a gun and shoots Devil Peter, who goes flying against the wall, bleeding.)

PETER: Oh, my God!
(Angel Peter then cocks the gun and holds it to Peter's head.)

ANGEL PETER: Now, get your fat ass over to Joe's!

You've Got to Think about Your Audience

PETER: Oh, come on, Joe, cheer up, huh? Hey, hey, what do you say you and me go rollerska— Bike ri— Jump ro— Go lie on the grass?

Way to Work Those Thighs

PETER: Trust me, Joe. I know physical fitness. I was in *Richard Simmons's Sweatin' to Books on Tape.*
(Flashback to a fitness studio, where Richard Simmons leads a group, including Peter, through strenuous aerobic exercises. A somber voice plays in the background.)

SOMBER VOICE: The Red Sox were in town, but I didn't care. Because it was Tuesday, and I was on my way to see Morrie. He couldn't go to the bathroom by himself anymore, but his indomitable spirit—

Bottom-Notch Medical Care

PETER: So, how's he check out, doc? Is my boy ready to compete?

DOCTOR: Um, I don't quite know how to tell you this, Mr. Swanson. *(solemnly)* You're paralyzed from the waist down.

JOE: I know.

DOCTOR: Oh, thank God. Oh, God, I was standing out there for, like, ten minutes. Whew! Boy, is that a load off.

Stewie Searches Meg's Purse

STEWIE: Let's see . . . makeup . . . chewing gum . . . a picture of Meg in a two-piece swimsuit. Ugh! God, I pray this is not my first memory.

The Play-by-Play

TOM: Hello, and welcome to the Quahog Special People's Games. I'm Tom Tucker.

DIANE: And I'm Diane Simmons. It's a great day to be alive, Tom, able-bodied or not.

TOM: It sure is, Diane. Today, we'll see some of Quahog's finest athletes struggle valiantly against God's twisted designs. You'll cheer, you'll cry, you might even get a cheap laugh or two.

DIANE: I know I will, Tom. In fact, there's the distinct possibility that by the end of the day we'll all be going to hell.

TOM: I'll see you there, Diane.

Just Trying to Make a Point

JOE: Well, if I couldn't catch a two-bit criminal, how am I supposed to win a race?

PETER: Hey-hey-hey, what kind of talk is that? It's un-American! Did-did George W. Bush quit even after losing the popular vote? No. Did he quit after losing millions of dollars of his father's friends' money in failed oil companies? No. Did he quit after knocking that girl up? No. Did he quit after he got that D.U.I.? No. Did he quit after gettin' arrested for drunk and disorderly conduct at a football game? No. Did he quit—

JOE: I get the message, Peter.

A View from Behind the Scenes

"We worried about the potential tastelessness of this episode, but then we realized, 'What are we talking about? We're constantly tasteless.'"

—SETH MACFARLANE, CREATOR AND EXECUTIVE PRODUCER

Not His Cup of Tea

JOE: Uh, gee, Peter, this water tastes kind of funny . . .

PETER: Uh, uh, uh, uh, you mean like, ha-ha, Jerry Seinfeld funny, or Elaine Boosler, God-bless-her-she's-trying funny?

Hard Sell

AGENT: *(to Joe)* He-ey, Greased Lightnin'!

    (The Agent hops out of his car and stands next to Joe.)

JOE: Do I know you?

AGENT: Jim Kaplan, sports agent. You like this car?

JOE: Yeah . . .

AGENT: It's yours! You like my pants?

JOE: Uh, sure.

    (The Agent rips off his pants.)

AGENT: They're yours! You know what a merkin is?

JOE: No.

AGENT: Pubic wig. I got one. You want it?

JOE: No.

AGENT: Course you don't. You're a classy guy. You wanna be rich?

JOE: Yes.

AGENT: Sign here.

    (The Agent thrusts a contract toward Joe.)

Plugging Joe's TV Movie

ANNOUNCER: *Rolling Courage: The Joe Swanson Story*, Friday on ABC, followed by *Dharma & Greg. (whispers)* But you don't have to watch that.

You Know What They Say About Cleanliness

PETER: Just don't forget our deal, Lois. I sit through this, and later tonight I get anal. You hear me? No matter how neat I want the house, you have to clean it.

And Now for the Neat and Tidy Wrap-up . . .

PETER: Say, uh, what happened to the car wash thief?

JOE: Ironically, I severed his spine when I landed on him.

PETER: Eh, looks like you got more competition at next year's games, huh?

JOE: Nope, he's dead.

Episode

A VERY SPECIAL *FAMILY GUY* FREAKIN' CHRISTMAS

SUMMARY

It's Christmas time in Quahog and Peter is more than ready to enjoy a little rest, relaxation, and quality time with his favorite holiday TV specials. The only problem is that Lois keeps dragging him to Christmas-related activities. She gets so into the spirit she even makes Peter bring Joe along with Cleveland and Quagmire on their annual drunken caroling expedition. The next morning Peter finally feels like he's earned the right to relax until he realizes he accidentally gave all the family's presents away to a charity. Meanwhile, Stewie learns about Santa Claus and is confounded by how he's able to keep tabs on all children everywhere.

When Peter's attempts to get the family's gifts back fail, the Griffins have to brave the mall to replace them. At the mall, Peter not only misses his favorite Christmas TV special, *KISS Saves Santa*, but he also finds himself in a tussle with a terrorizing old woman over the last pair of barrettes. When they finally arrive home, the family discovers that there's been a huge fire in their house. But just when it seems that Peter is going to lose his cool, it's actually Lois who loses it, accusing the family of not appreciating all she does to pull off Christmas for them every year. Lois then dashes maniacally off into the night. Meanwhile, Stewie's run-in with Santa at the mall results in him promising to be a "nice boy" so that Santa will bring him the plutonium he's asked for.

Lois goes on an angry rampage through Quahog until the rest of the family catches up to her at the town Christmas pageant. There, Stewie plays baby Jesus (still bent on proving to Santa that he can be nice), giving a performance that calms Lois down. Nevertheless, the police shoot Lois with a tranquilizer dart to get her out of the town Christmas tree. The family returns home, where everyone opens their gifts, all happy with what they received, including Peter who gets his very own copy of *KISS Saves Santa*.

EPISODE NUMBER: 2ACX03

ORIGINAL AIRDATE: 12/21/01

WRITER: Danny Smith

DIRECTOR: Brian Hogan

EXECUTIVE PRODUCERS:
Seth MacFarlane,
David Zuckerman

GUEST VOICES: Peter Criss, Ace Frehley, Gene Simmons, and Paul Stanley as themselves
(a.k.a. KISS)

MEMORABLE MOMENTS

Show Some Holiday Cheer

LOIS: Brian, you're not wearing the sweater I made you.

BRIAN: Aw, well, it's a little warm in here, you know—

LOIS: Don we now our gay apparel.

(Brian sighs and puts on a red doggy sweater that reads "Ho! Ho! Ho!" He smiles a phony smile.)

BRIAN: Doesn't get much gayer than this.

You Gotta Have All Your Paperwork in Order

BRIAN: Oh, sorry, the VCR hasn't worked since you tried to tape *Monday Night Football.*

> *(Flashback to the Griffins' living room, where* Monday Night Football *plays on the TV. Peter presses the record button on the VCR. Suddenly, a group of flak-jacketed FBI Agents bursts in.)*

FBI AGENT: Do you have the express written consent of ABC Sports and the National Football League?

> *(Peter slowly holds up a contract.)*

PETER: Just ABC.

> *(Peter dives for cover as the agents riddle the VCR with bullets.)*

There's a Certain Logic to That . . .

MEG: Hey, Mom, I got something to add to my Christmas list. A pair of those jewelled bug barrettes. Not costume. Real.

CHRIS: I just want peace on earth. That's better than being selfish like Meg, right? So I should get more than her.

Brainfart

LOIS: Hey, why don't you take Joe along?

PETER: Yeah, Lois, that'll be about as much fun as a lecture on ontological empiricism.

LOIS: What?

PETER: What?

Losing the Christmas Spirit

CLEVELAND: Sounds like somebody's got a humbug up his butt.

> *(The guys laugh at Peter.)*

QUAGMIRE: Maybe we should set him up with another lemon Sno-Kone, huh?

PETER: No thanks. The last one you gave me didn't taste like lemon at all. It tasted like— *(realizing)* Oh, you guys are asses.

Santa Antagonizes Stewie in His Dream

STEWIE: Huh, it's just a dream. I needn't fear this Santa. If he were truly omnipotent, he'd have the testicular fortitude to show himself! See? I'm just barking in the dark. No one here but me.

> *(Stewie smiles and sings to himself happily. Then, paranoid, he tears his crib mattress apart. Feathers fly everywhere.)*

STEWIE: All right, where is it? Where's the wire? Show yourself, Claus!

> *(Stewie tears apart his teddy bear and pillows.)*

LOIS: *(from outside the room)* Stewie, go to sleep.

STEWIE: This doesn't involve you, Lois.

LOIS: I don't want to have to come in there.

STEWIE: I don't want to have to come in there.

Scene Stealers
MALL SANTA

OCCUPATION
Pretending to listen to
the requests of snot-nosed
brats all day

NON-CHRISTMASTIME OCCUPATION
Cashing fraudulently
earned disability checks

LARGEST NUMBER OF
TIMES HE'S BEEN PEED ON
IN A SINGLE DAY
11

WHAT HE'S DOING AFTER WORK
A couple of lap dances,
followed by reruns of
Unsolved Mysteries

Okay, wrap it
up, kid . . .

It's Better to Indian-Give Than Indian-Receive

PETER: No, no, no, it's true, that remote-control car was for my son, and, and those barrettes were for my daughter, and— Hey, where's my VCR?

MA: What's a vee-see-ar?

(Two teenage boys, Buck and Skeeter, with their pants around their ankles, fight over a VCR.)

SKEETER: Dang it, Buck, it's my turn to use the sex box!

BUCK: It's my sex box! And her name is Sony!

Already Getting a 'Tude

LOIS: We'll shop, come home, eat, and then it's off to the pageant to see our little Stewie play Baby Jesus.

STEWIE: Oh, yes, yes. By all means, turn me into a child star. Perhaps I can move to Californ-i-ay and wrangle me a three-way with the Olsen Twins.

An Easy Target

LOIS: Kids, why don't you take Stewie to see Santa!

STEWIE: Santa?

(He turns to see a long line leading up to a Mall Santa.)

STEWIE: Oh, it's not possible. Sitting alone in this public setting? No bullet-proof glass? Claus, you make it too easy. *(to Meg)* Change me. I've leaked through my ski pants and I won't face him wet.

Take a Look at the Calendar

PETER: Hey, I was watchin' that!

SALESMAN: It'll be on next Christmas.

PETER: Well, who the hell knows when that's gonna be?

The Problem as Old as Time

LOIS: We're almost home, honey. Oh, look, there's the star on the town Christmas tree. We're following it home, just like the three wisemen.

(Flashback to the desert, where a bright star shines in the east as Three Wisemen ride their camels.)

WISEMAN #1: So what did you get him?

WISEMAN #2: Gold.

WISEMAN #3: Gold?! I thought we agreed on a five-dollar limit.

WISEMAN #1: Yeah, I just got him a crappy little bottle of myrrh.

WISEMAN #3: Hello? *(he holds up a little bottle)* Frankincense. *(to #2)* You always do this!

WISEMAN #1: Okay, okay, okay, look, we'll put everything together and put all our names on it.

WISEMAN #2: No!

That's Commitment

PETER: My couch! My TV! *(to Brian)* What the hell did you do?!

BRIAN: Me? Who the hell buys a novelty fire extinguisher?

PETER: I'll tell ya who. Someone who cares enough about physical comedy to put his whole family at serious risk!

Giving Up Easy

CHRIS: Dad, what happened to Mom? What if she never comes back?

PETER: I think the bigger question is, if this is the way she's gonna act at Christmas, do we even want her back?

Bad Planning

CHRIS: Where do you think she is?

PETER: Well, luckily Chris, years ago I planted a homing device in your mother's skull for just such an occasion.

(Peter pulls down a map of Rhode Island with flashing red lights all over it.)

PETER: Oh, I forgot. I also put them in a bunch of squirrels. This isn't gonna do us any good. May as well see if she's at the pageant.

Off Topic

PETER: Wa-wa-wait! Hang on! Look, Lois is only up there because we sucked the Christmas spirit right out of her. Maybe if she sees the pageant it'll bring her around. Give her a chance, huh?

BRIAN: Trust him, Joe. This man has seen every Christmas special ever made.

JOE: Are you wearing a girl's sweater?

BRIAN: Does that really matter right now?

Better Check Your Facts

(A spotlight hits Peter, who stands on the stage.)

PETER: As we all know, Christmas is that mystical time of year when the ghost of Jesus rises from the grave to feed on the flesh of the living. So, we all sing Christmas carols to lull him back to sleep.

(Two guys in the audience react.)

GUY #1: Outrageous! How dare he say such blasphemy. I've gotta do something!

GUY #2: Bob, there's nothing you can do.

GUY #1: Well, I guess I'll just have to develop a sense of humor.

(Guy #2 pats his shoulder, sympathetically.)

STUFF THAT MIGHT HAVE SLIPPED BY

■ Members of the Senior Center, who decorated the town Christmas tree, strung lights on the tree reading "Young People Suck."

■ When Lois asks Peter to get the family a Christmas tree, he runs outside during a commercial break to cut one down from the Griffins' front yard.

■ The TV in the mall where Peter watches a few seconds of *KISS Saves Santa* is located inside a shop called "Bill's Ham Radio Hut," which has a sign reading "We Have Other Stuff, Too."

■ Some of the other shops in the mall include "Clothes Minded" and "The Age of Aquariums."

■ When Peter is chasing the old woman through the mall, he stops to look at the mall directory, which contains an arrow reading "You Are Here" as well as another arrow reading "She Is There."

Oh, our savior has arrived.

Episode

BRIAN WALLOWS AND PETER'S SWALLOWS

SUMMARY

After another unsuccessful date, Brian is depressed about his romantic prospects. Lois encourages Peter to take Brian with him and the guys to the laser rock show, but when Brian notices that nearly everyone at the show has a mate but him, he just gets more depressed and drinks. On their way home, Brian is pulled over by Joe, who arrests him for driving under the influence. Meanwhile, Peter decides to grow a beard.

Brian is ordered by the court to do community service, which in his case means assisting a shut-in. The old woman, Pearl, proves to be an ill-tempered shrew who makes Brian's life hell. She becomes so intolerable that he quits, only to discover that the source of her bitterness was an inability as a young woman to make the transition from acclaimed commercial jingle performer to serious opera singer. Brian, realizing their common ground, rushes to be with Pearl and finds her on the brink of hanging herself. Meanwhile, Peter's beard becomes a nesting place for an endangered bird species. While he is annoyed by his new "tenants" at first, he soon develops a paternal fondness for them.

Brian lovingly (and in song!) shares with Pearl all that she's missed these past decades holed up in her house, wallowing in her own bitterness. Brian wins Pearl over and she joyfully exits her house for the first time in many years . . . where she is immediately mowed down by a truck. At the hospital, Brian enjoys one last moment with Pearl just as Peter faces the difficult task of parting with the birds for whom he has come to have such affection.

EPISODE NUMBER: 3ACX03

ORIGINAL AIRDATE: 1/17/02

WRITER: Allison Adler

DIRECTOR: Dan Povenmire

EXECUTIVE PRODUCERS:
Seth MacFarlane,
Daniel Palladino

GUEST VOICE: AJ Benza as himself

MEMORABLE MOMENTS

Peter Decides to Grow a Beard

PETER: No, no, Lois, it's time I joined the ranks of great men with beards. Why, why do you think Jesus Christ was so popular? Huh? Cuz, cuz, 'cause of all them magic tricks?

Peter Cheers Up the Ramseys

PETER: Mr. and Mrs. Ramsey, JonBenet's untimely death is a tragedy. And I will not rest until I find her killer. Or killers.

MRS. RAMSEY: *(nervously)* Oh, really don't bother. Nothing's going to bring our baby back.

PETER: No, no, I insist. I will make it my life's work—

MR. RAMSEY: We're fine! Just drop it!

At the Planetarium

(An Old Man stands next to a very plain-looking lamp, clicking it on and off. The spectators watch blankly.)

OLD MAN: What, you don't think this is amazing? When I saw this at the 1904 World's Fair, I nearly crapped my pants!

Contemplating the Big Questions

CLEVELAND: Okay, Johnny Depp or Richard Grieco?

QUAGMIRE: Oh, that's gross.

PETER: Let's not do this.

CLEVELAND: Come on, if you're secure in your masculinity, you can answer a simple hypothetical.

QUAGMIRE: All right, Johnny Depp, 'cause he kinda looks like a chick, I guess.

CLEVELAND: What about you, Peter?

PETER: Oh, man. Well, Richard Grieco'd probably appreciate you more. Y'know, not take you for granted. I mean, with Johnny Depp, it's like he wouldn't really need you, y'know? He'd probably sneak out after you fell asleep. Of course with Johnny, you'd get the financial security. I'd, I'd go with Johnny.

A Simple Courthouse Ceremony

(Mayor West enters the courtroom wearing a full tux. He puts a bridal veil over his right hand.)

JUDGE: Dearly beloved, we are gathered here to join these two in holy matrimony. If anyone objects to this union, speak now or forever hold your peace.

(Mayor West's left hand shoots up.)

MAYOR WEST: Quiet down! You had your chance!

Let the Punishment Fit the Crime

BRIAN: I got assigned to the Outreach to the Elderly Program. I've gotta take care of some old woman who hasn't been out of her house in thirty years.

CHRIS: When I got caught at school with my hand down my pants, I had to keep it there for a whole week. Ha— What a week.

Brian Arrives for His Court-Ordered Community Service

(As Brian enters Pearl's house, she immediately douses him with a white powder.)

BRIAN: Ah! What the hell is this?

PEARL: Delousing powder. Everyone on the outside is filthy.

BRIAN: Well, you could've given me some warning.

PEARL: Here's your warning. It's gonna burn like hell in thirty seconds. Now, I like my tea at four and my dinner at six. And I take my bath

Scene Stealers
PEARL BURTON

OCCUPATION
Old-time commercial jingle singer and wanna-be opera singer

HIGHEST-PAYING GIG
Warbling about the virtues of Gold Bond Medicated Powder

PASTIMES
Listening to Paul Harvey, delousing things, putting her caretakers through hell

WHAT MOST PEOPLE DON'T KNOW ABOUT HER
Back in the day, she was a major hottie

What is this, diarrhea soup?

STUFF THAT MIGHT HAVE SLIPPED BY

■ The judge in this episode is the same judge from the pilot episode.

■ The Griffins are eating at a restaurant called The Chicken Coop.

■ Of Brian's imagined kids with Pearl, half are children and half are puppies.

A View from Behind the Scenes

"The musical number in this show won an Emmy for Best Song. Seth told me that he felt guilty that I didn't get a statue because he thought the visuals played a huge part in the win. That's a nice sentiment and all, but did he offer to give me his? No! And it's not like he doesn't already have two of his own just sitting in his house!"

—DAN POVENMIRE, DIRECTOR OF THE EPISODE

at seven sharp so I can listen to Paul Harvey. You will warm up my bath water with quick bursts from the faucet during commercials only. It's gonna take you a while to get the rhythm; Paul Harvey moves seamlessly into commercials. By the way, it's been thirty seconds.

BRIAN: AAAAAAHHH!

Fun for the Whole Family

(Peter scratches his beard.)
LOIS: Peter, stop scratching that thing.
PETER: I can't, it's itching like crazy.
CHRIS: Dad, can I scratch your beard?
PETER: Have you finished your homework?
CHRIS: Yes.
PETER: Okay then.

No Love for the Working Class

(A waiter dressed as a Big Chicken deposits their orders.)
BIG CHICKEN: Here you go. Enjoy your food.
(The Big Chicken places a plate in front of Stewie.)
STEWIE: Enjoy your studio apartment.

That's Some Inflation

AJ BENZA: At her peak, Pearl Burton earned twenty-six grand a year, which by today's standards would be just under forty-nine billion dollars.

Brian Goes to Pearl in the Hospital

DOCTOR: She's right in here, sir. Just tell the disorderly when you're ready to leave.
BRIAN: Don't you mean the orderly?
DOCTOR: No, I mean the disorderly. That's a little doctor joke we like to make around here. We also like Kevin Pollak.

Episode
FROM METHOD TO MADNESS

SUMMARY

Inspired by the dreadful one-man show of an old friend, Brian decides to audition for a local performing arts program. When he shows up for the audition, Stewie has come along to cheer him on, having realized that if Brian gets into the program Stewie will have the house to himself more often. But, when Brian is rejected, Stewie gives an impassioned speech on Brian's behalf, prompting the school to offer Stewie a spot in their "Rising Stars" program instead. Of course, Stewie happily accepts. Meanwhile, Peter rescues a swimmer from the sea and is invited over for dinner as a show of thanks. When the Griffins arrive, they realize (to their horror) that their new neighbors, the Campbells, are a family of nudists.

Stewie's dreams of being the class standout are cut short when he meets Olivia, the precocious toddler diva of the program. He butts heads with her for a while until he overhears that both of them are in danger of being expelled from school. Stewie proposes that Olivia and he join forces to create a duet that will make them both look good. Stewie's plan succeeds as they both earn A's in the class and win the respect of their instructor, Simon. Meanwhile, Meg develops a liking for Jeff Campbell, the young nudist up the street, but Peter and Lois are not very excited about Meg seeing him. Meg gets upset with Peter and Lois because, although he's a nudist, Jeff is the first boy in a long time to even remember Meg's name.

Simon wants Stewie and Olivia to take their act on the road, which they do with some degree of success. However, the backstage infighting gets the best of them, causing the pair to ultimately go their separate ways. When Stewie's solo act proves to be nowhere near as popular as his and Olivia's act was, Stewie begins to descend into a downward spiral of depression and ultimately a touch of madness, from which Brian finally has to rescue him. Meanwhile, Peter and Lois extend an olive branch to Jeff by inviting him over to the house, where he and Meg find Lois and Peter naked. They really want Jeff to feel at home and not judged. While grossed out, Meg appreciates what her parents did for her.

EPISODE NUMBER: 3ACX11

ORIGINAL AIRDATE: 1/24/02

WRITERS: Mike Barker & Matt Weitzman

DIRECTOR: Bert Ring

EXECUTIVE PRODUCERS: Seth MacFarlane, Daniel Palladino

GUEST VOICE: Fred Willard as Dave Campbell

MEMORABLE MOMENTS

Lying His Ass Off

BRIAN: Okay, ready for the best acting you've seen all night?
(Brian turns to Mark.)
BRIAN: Mark! Wow, what a journey. Thank you so much! I-I, those three and a half hours just flew by!

Not the Best Sounding Board

BRIAN: Uh, say, Peter, um, my audition's coming up. W-w-would you mind listening to my monologue?
PETER: Sure, buddy, let's hear it.
(Brian takes a deep breath, shakes out his paws, and closes his eyes. He stands still for a beat, then calmly opens his eyes.)
BRIAN: "Julie, there's something I gotta tell you—"
PETER: Ha! That's awesome! Go on.
BRIAN: " ...Um, uh, tell you. I-I saw Doctor Phillips—"
PETER: Wow! WOW! Yes! Yes! I love it!
BRIAN: " ...uh, Doctor Phillips today. I ...might not make it to Christmas."

Scene Stealers
OLIVIA

OCCUPATION
Precocious toddler diva

STRENGTHS
Singing, ballet, tap

WEAKNESSES
Not being a bitch

This table is reserved for people with talent.

A View from Behind the Scenes

"It was terrific having Fred Willard perform the voice of Dave Campbell, the Griffins' nudist neigbor. Only problem was the guy's such a method actor that in the recording booth he insisted on wearing no pants."

—SETH MACFARLANE, CREATOR AND EXECUTIVE PRODUCER

PETER: Oh, yeah, drop the bomb! Drop it! There's not a dry eye in the house. Keep goin'!

BRIAN: No, no, y-you-you know what, I'm gonna stop. Um, may-maybe we'll work on it later.

PETER: Well, just so you know: It was good, but I was also being pretty generous.

Meeting the Campbells

LOIS: You're, uh . . . you're completely . . .

DOTTY CAMPBELL: Nude? Yes, we're nudists.

CHRIS: Permission to freak out!

Prized Trophy

(Jeff Campbell, their naked teenage son, enters holding a large trophy over his groin.)

JEFF CAMPBELL: I got first place, Dad.

DAVE CAMPBELL: Way to go, champ. *(then)* Jeff plays varsity tennis for St. Genevieve High.

MEG: Oh, cool.

JEFF CAMPBELL: Is this the biggest thing you've ever seen?

DAVE CAMPBELL: Hey, don't get too cocky. I had a big one like that when I was your age.

DOTTY CAMPBELL: Oh, you were a show-off yourself, Dave. *(to the Griffins)* He brought it out on our first date.

PETER: Lois, I'm scared.

Don't Diss Stewie

SIMON: Any comments?

(Olivia raises her hand.)

OLIVIA: You are the weakest link. Good-bye.

(The students giggle.)

STEWIE: Oh, gosh, that's funny, that's really fu— Do, do you write your own material? Do you? Because that is so fresh. "You are the Weakest Link. Good-bye." You know I've never heard anyone make that joke before. Hm, you're the first. I've never heard anyone reference, reference that outside the program before. Because that's what she says on the show, right? Isn't it? "You are the Weakest Link. Good-bye." And, and yet you've taken that and used it out of context to insult me in this everyday situation. God, what a clever, smart girl you must be to come up with a joke like that all by yourself. Hm, that's so fresh, too. Any, any *Titanic* jokes you want to throw at me as long as we're hitting these phenomena at the height of their popularity? Hm? 'Cause I'm-I'm here. God, you're funny.

Stewie's Olive Branch Swatted Down

STEWIE: So, Olivia . . . beautiful day.

OLIVIA: You're not gonna fart again, are you?

(Lois drives up and toots the horn. Stewie hops up and heads toward the car.)

STEWIE: Well, I'd love to stay and chat, but you're a total bitch.

STUFF THAT MIGHT HAVE SLIPPED BY

■ The one-man show Lois and Brian sit through is called "Nobody Said It'd Be Easy," and it stars Mark Hentemann, who is named after a *Family Guy* writer.

■ The sign outside the auditions for the Quahog School of the Performing Arts reads "Today: Auditions! Tomorrow: Principles of Catering."

■ When Meg and Jeff meet at the mall, Meg's face blushes and all of Jeff's body blushes.

■ The marquee outside one of Stewie and Olivia's performances reads "Garfunkel, Oates & Nash" above where it reads "Olivia and Stewie in 'You Do!'"

■ Stewie's one-man show is called "It's Funny Because It's True."

Now, That's Just Pathetic

(Meg and Jeff are at the counter making sandwiches.)
MEG: Do you like yours with crust or without?
JEFF: How do you like yours?
MEG: Okay, let's both answer at the same time. One, two, three.
JEFF: Without.
MEG: *(waits a split second)* Without!
JEFF: Holy moley, that's eight things we have in common!

Jot That Down, People

(A Boy is on stage dressed in black, miming being in a box.)
SIMON: Okay, nice effort, Brad, but, uh, let's remember our performance hierarchy. Legitimate theater, musical theater, stand-up, ventriloquism, magic, mime.

Someone's Got Stage Mom-itis

SIMON: Okay, no secrets— I wanna share Stewie and Olivia with the world. We'll start with a barnstorming tour of the local circuit. Anyway, it's gonna be a long road, it's gonna be a tough road, but it's gonna be a yellow brick road leading right to Broadway.
LOIS: Well, they're awfully young. Is this really a good idea?
OLIVIA'S MOM: It's a great idea. I've always dreamed of becoming an actress. But that's not why I'm pushing Olivia to do it. Is it suspicious that I brought that up unprovoked?

Parental Reflection

LOIS: Peter, do you think maybe it was unfair of us to tell Meg she couldn't see that boy?
PETER: Oh, completely. We totally reamed her. Did-did you see that look in her eyes? She *hates* you.

Backstage Turmoil

STEWIE: Wait a minute . . . you're wearing ruby lipstick. You're painted up like some attention-grabbing jezebel!
OLIVIA: Well, you're one to talk! You've been stuffing your diaper since day one!
STEWIE: It's where I keep my peppermint Mentos! Just because your breath reeks of rotten Lunchables, doesn't mean mine has to.

And That's Just *Really* Pathetic

STEWIE: But, hey, um . . . You know, if you're not busy, um, what say you and I get the old team back together?
OLIVIA: Well, actually, I-I can't. I'm on my way to Hollywood. Uh, I got this part in a movie, and . . .
STEWIE: Oh, oh, oh, oh, oh, oh, oh, what am I thinking, I-I'd love to, but I-I-I just, I'm booked solid. I-I'm doing a three-episode guest shot on the *Gilmore Girls*, I-I play, uh, uh, Rory's motorcycle-driving boyfriend, he's a bad boy at heart you know, but, but, there's, there's some good in there, Olivia, and it comes through, absolutely.

Episode
STUCK TOGETHER, TORN APART

SUMMARY

Lois runs into an old boyfriend, Ross Fishman, who invites her to have coffee with him, but she's reluctant to accept the invitation due to Peter's history of jealousy. When Lois ultimately decides to take her friend up on his offer, she never counts on Peter spotting them together. Meanwhile, Stewie's hand and Brian's paw become accidentally attached with industrial strength adhesive and they have to wait two weeks for the arrival of the solvent that will get them unstuck.

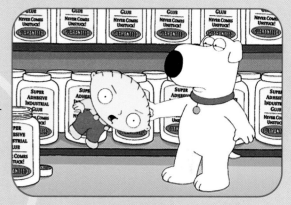

Peter becomes upset when he realizes that Lois saw an old boyfriend behind his back, so he chooses to retaliate by looking up various old girlfriends (but with very unsatisfying results). Peter then hires a hooker to come to the house to pose as an old girlfriend. Lois gets angry when she realizes how Peter is reacting to her simply having coffee with an old friend. Lois suggests that she and Peter seek marriage counseling. But after a week of observing the family's behavior, the marriage counselor recommends a trial separation where Lois and Peter live apart from each other and date other people.

Because Peter and Lois miss each other at first, they are reluctant to see anyone else. Ultimately, though, Lois accepts a date with Quagmire and Peter allows himself to be set up with the Goldmans' niece (who happens to be Jennifer Love Hewitt). Peter is a complete pig on the date, but this actually turns Jennifer on. Lois, who happens to be at the same restaurant with Quagmire, sees Peter and Jennifer kissing and loses her cool. She beats up Jennifer Love Hewitt and tells Peter she now understands what he must have felt when he saw her with Ross Fishman. Meanwhile, Stewie and Brian, still struggling with being attached to each other, finally get the solvent they need to become unattached. During their last moments of being attached, though, they are able to use their combined arm span to reach down into a well to save a trapped child.

EPISODE NUMBER: 3ACX10

ORIGINAL AIRDATE: 1/31/02

WRITER: Mark Hentemann

DIRECTOR:
Michael Dante DiMartino

EXECUTIVE PRODUCERS:
Seth MacFarlane,
Daniel Palladino

GUEST VOICE: Jennifer Love
Hewitt as herself

MEMORABLE MOMENTS

You Ask a Dumb Question . . .
PETER: God, some of this stuff, you wonder who would ever need it in bulk. I mean, like watermelons . . .
(Peter points to a twenty-four-pack bag of watermelons. Gallagher approaches with a cart and adds a bag of the watermelons to it.)
PETER: Touché, Costmart.

Jealously Gets the Best of Us
(The Griffins gaze up at a movie screen, which shows Hugh Grant.)
HUGH GRANT: Uh, I, oh, oh, oh, this is terribly awkward. I-I-I-I wanted to, um, tell you something, but, but I-I seem to be charmingly befuddled.
(Lois sighs.)

LOIS: Oh, that Hugh Grant is so handsome!
PETER: Oh, is that how it is?
> *(Peter gets up and storms toward the screen.)*
PETER: *(to the screen)* C'mere, you home-wrecking bastard!
> *(Peter attacks the movie screen.)*
CHRIS: Don't do it, Dad! He's bigger than you!

Lois Passes the Buck, So to Speak

> *(Lois changes Stewie's diaper.)*
LOIS: Would you mind finishing up?
BRIAN: Uh, sure. *(Lois exits. Brian takes over.)*
STEWIE: Do you like cleaning my doodie, Brian? Say it. Say, "I like cleaning your doodie, Stewie." Ha! And don't forget the 'taint.

Throwing Themselves into the Part

PETER: Hey, Lois, could you grab me a beer? Lois?
CHRIS: Dad, I think she went out.
PETER: All right, then you be Lois.
CHRIS: Okay.
PETER: Lois, could you grab me a . . . *(looks at Chris)* . . .oh, my God, you've really let yourself go!
CHRIS: Well, maybe if you bought me some nice clothes once in a while!

Pulling Your Leg

JOE: It's the new police surveillance van. We're going on a beer run. Wanna join us?
PETER: Nah, I quit drinkin'. I think I might be an alcoholic.
JOE/CLEVELAND/QUAGMIRE: Oh, my God!/ What?/ Aw, man!
PETER: Hehehehe, fooled ya! C'mon, let's go drink 'til we can't feel feelings anymore.

Almost Too True to Reality

JOE: This van has the latest in law-enforcement technology. Watch.
> *(Joe escorts Peter into a circle and flips a switch.)*
COMPUTER: Suspect! Suspect!
> *(Two mechanical arms lower and restrain Peter.)*
COMPUTER: You have the right to remain silent . . .
> *(Peter, Quagmire, and Cleveland are impressed. The arms release Peter and he steps away.)*
PETER: Hehehe . . . Sweet!
> *(Cleveland steps into the circle.)*
CLEVELAND: Hey, let me try.
JOE: Cleveland, don't—
COMPUTER: Minority suspect! Minority suspect!
> *(The mechanical arms start administering a severe beating.)*
COMPUTER: Danger! He's got a gun!
> *(Another mechanical arm lowers and drops a gun at Cleveland's feet as the machine continues to beat him.)*

Self-Centered

CLEVELAND: Hey, Peter, isn't that Lois over there in that diner?

PETER: Nah. What would Lois be doing at a diner? I already ate.

Take Two

PETER: What the hell is Lois doing with another man?

QUAGMIRE: Is it possible she's a whore? You know, just on the weekends to help pay for her mom's dialysis . . . as in my fantasy? You know what? Let's start over. Hi, I'm Quagmire.

Welcome to Brian's Routine

STEWIE: What the hell do you think you're doing?

BRIAN: I'm cleaning myself.

(Brian goes back to washing himself. Stewie rolls back over and lies down.)

STEWIE: Ugh, you were clean fifteen minutes ago. Now you're just on vacation.

Peter's Search for Past Flames

(Peter knocks on the door. It opens, revealing a hideous, 400-pound Woman wearing an eye patch. She has Babies suckling on each of her breasts and smokes out of a hole in her throat.)

PETER: Brenda?

BRENDA: Peter? Oh, my God. It's been twenty-five years.

PETER: Yeah. So, uh, I guess you're married now.

BRENDA: Yeah.

(Brenda inhales her cigarette deeply as there is a thud. She looks down at her feet and there is the wail of a brand-new baby. She calls to her husband.)

BRENDA: Hey, Ricky, you were right. I was pregnant.

Talking Behind Their Backs

(Brian drives with one hand, his other stuck to Stewie's.)

STEWIE: . . . yes, Chris is a little bit of a lummox, but he's got a good heart.

BRIAN: Heart of gold.

STEWIE: Now, the other one . . .

BRIAN: Meg?

STEWIE: Meg. Yes. It's just so difficult to watch her defeat herself. She's her own worst enemy.

A View from Behind the Scenes

"The name of Lois's old boyfriend, Ross Fishman, is derived from the name of an old boyfriend of one of our writer's wives. I'm not going to say who, but they know who they are."

—SETH MACFARLANE, CREATOR AND EXECUTIVE PRODUCER

Not Helping

POLICE OFFICER: You were going sixty-five, fella. That's ten miles over the— Why are you holding that infant's hand?

STEWIE: Oh, we met on the Internet.

BRIAN: Shut up.

STEWIE: Yes, he lured me down to the park with promises of candy and funny stories.

Even Stewie Loses His Nerve

(Stewie and Brian eye the hooker.)

STEWIE: Should I say it?

BRIAN: Yeah, yeah, say it.

STEWIE: I can't—

BRIAN: Just, just say it.

STEWIE: *(holding out a banana)* How far can you get this banana down . . . I can't say it, she's looking right at me.

Kinda True

DR. FRANKLIN: I'd like to put video cameras in every room of your house so that I can observe your uncensored behavior.

PETER: Wow, just like that show *Big Brother*, except somebody will be watching.

What the Camera Captured

(Peter, Lois, Chris, and the still-attached Brian and Stewie sit around Meg's room. Lois reads from a small book labeled "Meg's Diary.")

LOIS: "Dear Diary, Kevin is so hot. Today he was out in the yard, raking leaves. God, I wish he'd throw me into that pile of leaves . . ."

(Lois wipes a tear from her eye as they all howl with laughter. Meg bursts in.)

MEG: Hey, what's everybody— Oh, my God, my diary! I hate you all!

(Meg runs out crying. A pause as everyone takes that in.)

PETER: Keep going.

(He cracks open a beer.)

Splitting Up Is Hard to Do

PETER: I don't know, Lois. Splitting up didn't work too well for Pac-Man and his wife.

(Cutaway to Pac-Man's House, where a depressed Pac-Man sits in his chair, smoking. He's surrounded by three of the Colored Monsters from the game.)

RED MONSTER: C'mon, buddy, forget about her.

GREEN MONSTER: Yeah, you're too good for her anyway.

(Pac-Man is inconsolable.)

YELLOW MONSTER: Cheer up, man.

RED MONSTER: Hey, you wanna eat us?

GREEN MONSTER: Uhp, look, look, we're turning blue!
   (They all turn blue as they flash.)
MONSTERS: Oh, my God! / He's gonna get us! / Nowhere to run!
   (They turn back to their regular colors.)
RED MONSTER: Ah, he's not budging. C'mon, let's go to Q∗Bert's.
   (They float out the door.)

Was That Called For?
BRIAN: All right, it says it takes an hour for this solvent to take effect.
STEWIE: Well, let's see. What takes an hour? We could watch Rita Rudner do five minutes of stand-up.
BRIAN: Ba-zing.

Can't Quite Place Her
JENNIFER LOVE HEWITT: *I Know What You Did Last Summer*?
PETER: Nah, never heard of it.
JENNIFER LOVE HEWITT: *The Devil and Daniel Webster*?
PETER: Nope.
JENNIFER LOVE HEWITT: *Party of Five*?
PETER: Was that a porno?
   (Jennifer shakes her head and sighs, insulted.)
PETER: Hey, don't worry about it. Sometimes you gotta do a lot of crap before they put you in anything decent.

Lois Takes Back the Compliment
JENNIFER LOVE HEWITT: What's your problem, Grandma?
LOIS: You are! And I only saw *Heartbreakers* on a plane.
   (Lois shoves Jennifer offscreen with a crash.)
LOIS: And the flight was delayed, so the headsets were free!

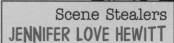

You ordered a pie for an appetizer?

Scene Stealers
JENNIFER LOVE HEWITT

OCCUPATION
Famous actress and Mort and Muriel Goldman's niece

POSITIVES OF BEING ON A DATE WITH PETER
A free meal

NEGATIVES OF BEING ON A DATE WITH PETER
Just about everything else (including getting your ass kicked by his wife)

STUFF THAT MIGHT HAVE SLIPPED BY

■ In the scene where the Griffins are at the movies, the marquee out front reads "Hugh Grant in *What's My Appeal*?"

■ As Quagmire offers to give his jacket to Lois, he has tucked one of the sleeves into his fly.

Episode
ROAD TO EUROPE

SUMMARY

Stewie becomes obsessed with *Jolly Farm Revue*, a British television show for preschoolers. Imagining *Jolly Farm* to be an idyllic place where he can become the person he wants to be, Stewie decides to run away, not realizing that Jolly Farm is a made-up place. So, while Brian is babysitting Stewie for Peter and Lois (who have gone to see a five-day-long KISS concert known as KISS-Stock), Stewie stows away on a British Airlines flight. Brian chases after him, but before they can deplane, the flight takes off for its destination.

Brian and Stewie discover that rather than arriving in England, they've actually ended up in an Arabian village. Having very little money, Brian and Stewie use only their wits and charm to get themselves out of the country, and as far as Vatican City. There, Brian declares that they're heading home, but Stewie insists that he won't be swayed from reaching Jolly Farm. Brian, realizing that Stewie believes Jolly Farm to be a real place, agrees to take him there, knowing that it will only burst Stewie's bubble. Meanwhile, Peter and Lois are soaking up all that KISS-Stock has to offer, until Lois humiliates herself and Peter by not knowing the lyrics to one of KISS's biggest hits.

Stewie and Brian finally make their way to Britain and the BBC, where Brian drops Stewie off at Jolly Farm. Stewie's illusions about the place are immediately shattered when he comes face to face with the cheesy set, phony props, and foul-mouthed cast. Disenchanted, he decides to return home with Brian. Meanwhile, Peter's disappointment with Lois continues until they run into KISS at a Denny's and Peter learns that Lois once slept with Gene Simmons before he was famous. Peter's attitude changes instantaneously—he's now unbelievably proud to be married to the woman who slept with one of his idols.

EPISODE NUMBER: 3ACX13

ORIGINAL AIRDATE: 2/7/02

WRITER: Daniel Palladino

DIRECTOR: Dan Povenmire

EXECUTIVE PRODUCERS:
Seth MacFarlane,
Daniel Palladino

GUEST VOICES: Lauren Graham as Mother Maggie, Michael McKean as Pengrove Pig, Gene Simmons as himself, Andy Dick as himself

MEMORABLE MOMENTS

That's Why They Call It the Boob Tube

BRIAN: How can you stand watching this?
  (Stewie ignores him, his eyes glued to the screen.)
BRIAN: It's dreck, and you know it. *(then)* Oh, don't have the guts to respond, huh? No intelligent defense of this unmitigated crap?
STEWIE: Commercial!
  (Stewie hurries over to Brian and, without warning, kicks him violently in the groin. Brian groans and falls heavily.)
STEWIE: I'm gonna get some graham crackers.
  (He exits to the kitchen.)

Getting Ready

PETER: *(yelling)* Hey, yo, Lois!

LOIS: What?!

PETER: I'm packin' for KISS-Stock, and I can't find my favorite underwear.

LOIS: You mean the pair with the rip in the right butt cheek from when you stepped on 'em pulling 'em up in that airplane bathroom from when you had the trots?

PETER: No, no, the pair with the hole in the left butt cheek from when I held it in for two hours because it was that extra long Palm Sunday church sermon and I thought blowin' gas would offend Jesus so I let go in the vestibule after Mass and it sounded like Louis Armstrong.

LOIS: Oh, bottom drawer.

A Man of Many Words

BRIAN: Hey, Stewie, what do you want for lunch?

(He sees a note attached to the TV screen. He grabs it. As Brian reads the note, we hear Stewie's voice.)

STEWIE: Dear stupid dog: I've gone to live with the children on Jolly Farm. Good-bye forever. Stewie. P.S. I never got a chance to return that sweater Lois gave me for Christmas. I-I left the receipt on top of my bureau. I'm probably over the thirty-day return limit, but I'm sure if you make a fuss, they'll at least give you a store credit. It's actually not a horrible sweater, it's just I can't imagine when I would ever wear it. Oh, I also left a button on the bureau. I'm not sure what it goes to, but I-I can't bring myself to throw a button away. I know as soon as I do, I'll find the garment it goes to and— Wait a minute, could it have been from the sweater? Did that sweater have buttons? Mm, well I should wrap this up before I start to ramble. Again, good-bye forever. P.P.S. You know what, it might be a little chilly in London, I'm actually gonna take the sweater.

You're the One Who Asked

BRIAN: Great. I'm stuck on a trans-Atlantic flight with a petulant runaway. How could this get any worse?

(Andy Rooney leans over from the seat next to Brian.)

ANDY ROONEY: You know what I hate about flying? The peanuts. First of all, you can't get 'em open. Who are they trying to keep out of these things?

(Brian turns away from him. Jerry Seinfeld pops up from the row behind him.)

JERRY SEINFELD: And what's the deal with the razor blade slot in the bathroom? Are people actually shaving in there?

(Brian turns away from him. Andy Dick approaches their aisle with a carry-on bag.)

ANDY DICK: Hi, Andy Dick, here. Excuse me I've gotta get my bag in the overhead bin here.

Piss off, ya grotty little wanker.

Scene Stealers
MOTHER MAGGIE

OCCUPATION
Beautiful hostess of
Jolly Farm Revue

HOW STEWIE SEES HER
As having the voice of an
angel . . . not to mention
a balcony you could do
Shakespeare from

WHAT SHE'S REALLY LIKE
Chain-smoking harpy seeking
an easy paycheck

(He opens the overhead bin. Stuff starts to fall out and he crazily tries to deal with it.)
ANDY DICK: Oh, whoooaaaa! No, no! (laughs) Wow, that's wacky!
(Brian sighs.)

Different Country, Same Pitch
STEWIE: Where are we going?
BRIAN: I don't know. I'm not exactly familiar with this particular Arabian village.
(They make their way down a long row of merchants' stands.)
BAZAAR SALESMAN #1: Stuff for sale! Bad, cheaply made stuff for sale!
BAZAAR SALESMAN #2: Hey, Americans, you like movies? I've got *Dude, My Car Is Not Where I Parked It, but Praise Allah We Are Not Hurt.*
BAZAAR SALESMAN #3: Camels for sale! This one owned by a little old man who only drove it to mosque on Sundays. Just had its knees replaced!

You Gotta Do What You Gotta Do
BRIAN: We have to slice open our camel's stomach and shelter ourselves in its entrails.
STEWIE: Eviscerate Chuckie? I won't do it!
BRIAN: We're gonna die if we don't.
STEWIE: All right.
(Brian draws his sword along the dead camel's stomach.)
STEWIE: Oh, God!!! It's like Orson Welles's autopsy.

Not Known for Their Cuisine
BRIAN: How in the hell are we gonna get outta here?
STEWIE: Are you going to finish your red paste?
BRIAN: No.
STEWIE: What about your sweet, crusty thing?

Don't Piss Off the Pope
(The Pope runs up to Brian and Stewie.)
POPE: You make-a the Pope look like a fool. God will make you pay!
(The Pope looks heavenward.)
POPE: Smite them! *(long pause, then to Brian and Stewie)* He's a-cookin' a-somethin' up.

A View from Behind the Scenes

"It was a pleasure having Gene Simmons back on the show. Nice guy. And a tongue that stretches all the way to next week! You know what? I'm gonna say it. It's actually a little freaky."

—SETH MACFARLANE, CREATOR AND EXECUTIVE PRODUCER

You Never Know

STEWIE: I say, Brian, look, three rows down.

BRIAN: What?

STEWIE: Is that Tom Bosley?

BRIAN: What would Tom Bosley be doing on a train in Switzerland?

STEWIE: I'm-I'm almost certain. *(yells)* Tom!
  (Stewie quickly lowers his head in his magazine.)

STEWIE: Did he look?

BRIAN: I don't know.

STEWIE: Well, if I yell, you have to watch. *(yells)* Tom Bosley!
  (He quickly lowers his head again.)

BRIAN: No, it's not him.

STEWIE: Huh.

The Truth Hurts

LOIS: I wanted to share in all aspects of your life, Peter. But, I just was never that big a KISS fan.

PETER: Yeah, I shoulda guessed that when you were willing to dress up as Peter Criss. No one wants to be Peter Criss, Lois. Not even Peter Criss.

And Hurts Some More

LOIS: Peter, are you ever gonna forgive me?

PETER: Lois, I am obligated to keep loving you, so I will take my rage out on my own body. Let's go to Denny's.

No Need to Be Starstruck

GENE SIMMONS: You look great, Lois. Anyone nailin' ya now?

LOIS: Yes, my husband nails me. This is him, Peter.

Consider the Bubble Burst

STEWIE: Oh, my, the Magic Tome!
  (Stewie opens the book, but it's a hollow prop that opens to one fake page.)

STEWIE: Well, it's-it's cardboard. And there are no words, there are just . . . What is it you've drawn here?

PENGROVE PIG: Oh, that's Oswald Owl slammin' Mother Maggie in one of them Chinese baskets.

A View from Behind the Scenes

"This show was huge fun because I got to spend two weeks drawing a KISS concert. I remember back in high school when I was drawing pictures of KISS on my notebook, one of my teachers told me in a stern voice that I couldn't make a living drawing pictures of KISS. Well, IN YOUR FACE MR. BOYD!! YEAH!! HOW DO YOU LIKE THAT?!! NOT SO SMART NOW, ARE YOU, BIG MAN?!!!"

—DAN POVENMIRE, DIRECTOR OF THE EPISODE

STUFF THAT MIGHT HAVE SLIPPED BY

■ During his song with Stewie, Brian does a brief imitation of Triumph the Insult Comic Dog.

■ The Pope's laundry hamper has a cross on it.

Episode
FAMILY GUY VIEWER MAIL #1

EPISODE NUMBER: 3ACX12

ORIGINAL AIRDATE: 2/14/02

WRITERS: Gene Laufenberg (Part 1), Seth MacFarlane (Part 2), and Michael Shipley & Jim Bernstein (Part 3)

DIRECTORS: Pete Michels (Part 1), Scott Wood (Part 2), and Michael Dante DiMartino (Part 3)

EXECUTIVE PRODUCERS: Seth MacFarlane, Daniel Palladino

GUEST VOICES: Regis Philbin as himself, Kelly Ripa as herself, Adam Carolla as Death

SUMMARY

In the first of three stories inspired by viewer mail, "Peter's Three Wishes" tells the story of Peter's encounter with a magic genie. Peter bumbles through his first two wishes until, in a moment of panic, he uses up his third wish by asking to have no bones. Immediately, Peter is transformed into a gelatinous blob—nothing more than a burden to his family.

Depressed about his condition, Peter leaves to find work in Hollywood as a human stunt bag. There, he meets a doctor who tries an experimental procedure in which he reinserts donated bones into Peter's body. In the end, Peter realizes it was his family who donated the bones and the group of Griffin misfits happily heads home together.

In "The SuperGriffins," a truck full of toxic waste crashes in front of the Griffins' house and ends up giving the family a variety of superpowers. Stewie gains telekinetic powers, Chris can make fire, Brian gains super speed, Peter can morph into any object, Lois becomes super strong, and Meg can grow her fingernails a little bit faster than usual. Despite their agreement to only use their newfound skills for good, the family soon is corrupted by their powers, so much so that the town bands together to try to stop them. It isn't until Mayor West contracts lymphoma in an ill-advised attempt to stop the Griffins that they all realize how out of control they've become and vow to change their ways.

In "Li'l Griffins," each member of the gang from Quahog is depicted as a young child in the style of *Our Gang*. Peter and Quagmire vie for the affection of the new student, Lois, by proving at Lois's request that they are each brave enough to spend the night in a local haunted house. In the

end, neither of them is able to do it. But when they go to Lois to confess their lack of bravery, she informs them that she has changed her mind: she's not looking for a brave boy after all, but rather one who has smarts. Peter and Quagmire realize they were right to want to swear off girls in the first place.

STUFF THAT MIGHT HAVE SLIPPED BY

■ When Chris lights his classmate on fire, the kid runs screaming down the hallway under a banner reading "Fire Safety Month," which catches on fire.

■ As Tom and Diane report on how the Griffins are terrorizing the town with their superpowers, the graphics behind them show Stewie levitating an ice cream truck upside down, shaking ice cream bars out; Peter, morphed into a gigantic wave, terrifying Beachgoers; and Meg popping a Kid's balloon with her long fingernails.

■ Li'l Death's T-shirt reads "Smoke Cigarettes."

MEMORABLE MOMENTS

Careful What You Wish For

PETER: Oh, my God! A genie!

GENIE: I am here to grant you three wishes.

LOIS: Peter, three wishes! Oh, this is so exciting!

MEG: I want a new hat!

CHRIS: I want a new hat!

STEWIE: I want them to have new hats.

Making the Best of a Bad Situation

CHRIS: Dad's just like Silly Putty. Look what I can do to Mary Worth's smug sense of self-satisfaction.

(Chris stretches the imprint, expanding Mary Worth's body.)

PETER: Hehehe. That's right, son. Take her down a peg.

Buck Up, Kids

LOIS: Kids, we just have to learn to accept this. Like one of those stories on *Dateline*, where a family member suffers a horrible accident, and becomes a burden on everybody. Sure, they pretend to be happy, but they're dead inside. They're dead.

You Never Know Where New Material Will Come From

DIRECTOR: Great job, Peter. Are you comin' to the wrap party tonight?

PETER: Ah, gee, I don't know. I got a stand-up comedy class I'm taking at the Learning Annex. Actually, I won't be a stand-up comic, I'll be an amorphous blob comic. Oh, I gotta write that one down.

That's Just Being Resourceful

PETER: Y-you mean . . . it's your bones that are inside me?

STEWIE: Well, mostly. We picked up a drifter to fill in the torso.

Just Being Curious

PETER: Hey, is the Count a vampire?

BRIAN: What's that?

PETER: Well, he's-he's got those big fangs. Have-have they ever shown him doin' somebody in and feedin' on 'em?

BRIAN: You're-you're asking if they've ever done a *Sesame Street* in which the Count kills somebody and then sucks their blood for sustenance?

PETER: Yeah.

BRIAN: No, they've never done that.

Sounds Like Peter Logic

PETER: Well, we promised Lois we'd use our powers responsibly, but I suppose doing the exact opposite couldn't hurt.

Not So Undercover

(A flash of light surrounds Peter as he morphs into Britney Spears. He approaches the guard.)

A View from Behind the Scenes

"This episode contains one of several shots that we take at Dharma & Greg. Why? No particular reason. It's just fun."

—SETH MACFARLANE, CREATOR AND EXECUTIVE PRODUCER

> If nuclear refuse gave them super-powers, it can do the same for me! Citizens, I'm off to the toxic waste dump!

Scene Stealers
MAYOR WEST

OCCUPATION
Mayor of Quahog

WHY HE'S NOT SUCH A GREAT MAYOR FOR QUAHOG
He's rather eccentric and more than a little bit paranoid

WHY HE'S THE PERFECT MAYOR FOR QUAHOG
He's rather eccentric and more than a little bit paranoid

PETER: Hi, there, Britney Spears. You mind if I go in?
SECURITY GUARD: Oh, uh, uh, not at all, Miss Spears!
PETER: Oh, call me Peter.

What's the Opposite of Scary?

CHRIS: We demand obedience!
MEG: Or else!
(As Meg says this, she grows her fingernails. A Townsperson seated near her watches.)
TOWNSPERSON: Is that all you can do?
(Meg turns and scratches the guy on the arm with one of her nails.)
TOWNSPERSON: Ow! That kind of hurt. Aw, is that bleeding? No, I guess it's all right. Ouch, though.

Probably Harsher Than He Intended

PETER: Look, why don't you make like Siamese twins and split. And- and then one of you die!

Too Smart for His Own Good

MORT: You can't stay in that house. Old Man Selberg's ghost still haunts it. Not to mention the myriad of bacteria and allergens from years of substandard housekeeping. It does not augur well for you.
PETER: Ah, zip it, egghead. You, you with your big words and your, and your small, difficult words.

Fighting with Each Other Even Way Back Then

TOM: Huh, get used to this sight, Diane. Guys running away from you.
DIANE: Tom, you're so deep in the closet, you're finding Christmas presents.

Peter and Quagmire Swear Off Women

PETER: I say, Quagmire, it seems to me we've each made another five hundred million dollars.
QUAGMIRE: Good thing we swore off women so we wouldn't be distracted and unable to accumulate this vast amount of wealth.
PETER: Yes, hey, you watch the ticker, I'm gonna go microwave a bagel and have sex with it.
QUAGMIRE: Butter's in the fridge!

A View from Behind the Scenes

"The writing hours were long, and games became pathologically important. Two of the most popular were Slappywag and Slam Pong. Slappywag, named after a joke in 'E Peterbus Unum,' was an intense and eventually very high-stakes form of Penny Pitching we'd play on the terrace outside the writers' room. Slam Pong was a bloodthirsty form of Ping-Pong with two players per side—a Setter and a Slammer. Ricochets off anything were allowed and the ball stayed in play until it touched the floor or one team hit it more than two times without getting it over the net. Lives were lost."

—MICHAEL SHIPLEY, ONE OF THE WRITERS FOR PART 3 OF THE EPISODE

Episode

WHEN YOU WISH UPON A WEINSTEIN

EPISODE NUMBER: 2ACX05

ORIGINAL AIRDATE: 8/6/03 (Cartoon Network), 12/10/04 (Fox)

WRITER: Ricky Blitt

DIRECTOR: Dan Povenmire

EXECUTIVE PRODUCERS: Seth MacFarlane, David Zuckerman

GUEST VOICES: Ben Stein as Rabbi Goldberg, Mark Hamill as Luke Skywalker, and Ed McMahon as himself

SUMMARY

Peter is persuaded by a door-to-door salesman to use Lois's "rainy day fund" to buy volcano insurance just about the time Meg needs a new pair of glasses. Lois chastises Peter for not being very good with money. When Quagmire and Cleveland happen to mention that their stockbroker and their accountant did well by them financially, Peter listens no further than the surnames of those involved and concludes that the answer to his fiscal woes is to get himself a Jew. So, when a Jewish man's car happens to break down in front of the Griffins' house, Peter assumes the man must have been sent to him by some divine force.

The man whose car has broken down, Max Weinstein, agrees to help Peter try to get his money back from the insurance salesman. After Peter gets the money back, Max stays for dinner at the Griffins' house and then takes the Griffins' with him to temple, where they get a glimpse of Jewish life. When it finally becomes time for Max to leave, he realizes he never had time to help Chris with his homework like he'd promised, but he assures the Griffins' that Chris seems very capable. As Max leaves, Peter gets the idea that the way to insure Chris's future success is to convert him to Judaism. Of course, Lois will hear nothing of it, so Peter and Chris sneak off to "turn Chris Jewish."

When Peter's first attempt to convert Chris fails, he decides to drive them both to Las Vegas for a "quickie bar mitzvah." When Lois gets word of this, she borrows Quagmire's car and rushes to Vegas herself, arriving just in time to stop the bar mitzvah (in a scene reminiscent of *The Graduate*). When Peter explains why he wanted so badly to insure Chris's future success, Lois explains to Peter that a person's religion is no predictor of future fortune, and the three of them all head home together.

A View from Behind the Scenes

"As most people know by now, this was the episode Fox refused to air initially. What they don't know is the real reason why it was banned: Fox felt the 'Meg needs new glasses' storyline was a little too edgy for network TV. True story."

—SETH MACFARLANE, CREATOR AND EXECUTIVE PRODUCER

MEMORABLE MOMENTS

Not-So-Tough Customer

SALESMAN: Hello, sir.
PETER: Enough with the foreplay, sailor. What are you selling?
SALESMAN: Well, I was gonna try to sell you some handsome cream, but I can see you already bought out the store.
PETER: Go on.

Not a Test You Want to Fail

LOIS: Oh, don't worry, honey. We'll get you a new pair tomorrow.
(Lois hugs Meg.)

STEWIE: Yes, and in the meantime, here's a little vision test.
(From Meg's point of view, she's sees a blurry Stewie.)
STEWIE: What is this, a poopie or a Toblerone?

You Can Never Be Too Careful

LOIS: Volcano insurance? That's ridiculous.
PETER: Oh, that's the same thing you said when you talked me out of getting that cloud insurance.
(Peter looks out of the window, up to the sky.)
PETER: Look at them up there, just plotting, picking their moment.
(In the sky, one Cloud speaks to another Cloud.)
CLOUD #1: So, Bill. We attack tomorrow.
CLOUD #2: Yes. Tomorrow.
CLOUD #1: I mean it this time.
CLOUD #2: I do, too.

Good Comeback

PETER: You better watch who you're callin' a child, Lois, because if I'm a child, you know what that makes you? A pedophile. And I'll be damned if I'm gonna stand here and be lectured to by a pervert.

Everyone's a Critic

CLEVELAND: Let me buy the drinks, Quagmire. My accountant, Larry Rosenblatt, just got me a huge tax refund. And tickets to *Bring in Da Noise, Bring in Da Funk*. The noise was good, but I thought they phoned in a lot of the funk.

Peter Flies Off the Handle

CLEVELAND: Peter, not every Jewish person is good with money.
PETER: Well, yeah, I guess not the retarded ones, but why would you even say that? For shock value? Geez, Cleveland, there's edgy and there's offensive. Good day, sir.

That's the One You Pick?

PETER: I prayed for you, Max Weinstein. And here you are.
MAX: Okay. Listen, thanks for letting me use your phone.
PETER: Thanks for *Spaceballs*.

Let's Call a Spade a Spade

MAX: Look, I'll do what I can, but I don't know why you think I can get your money back—
PETER: Max, let's not deny our heritages. You're Jewish, you're good with money. I'm Irish, I drink, and I ban homosexuals from marching in my parade. Now, help me get my money back.

Scene Stealers
MAX WEINSTEIN

OCCUPATION
Accountant (as Peter would say, "Hello? 'Max Weinstein'?")

UNINTENDED OCCUPATION
Enlightening Peter about Judaism

FELLOW JEWS
Bill Nye, the Science Guy, half of Lenny Kravitz, and Optimus Prime

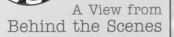

Peter, play with this while I talk to the nice man.

A View from Behind the Scenes

"I honestly don't know what the big fuss was about this show. If you watch it, it's MUCH more offensive to Catholics, salesmen, transformers, cartoon villains, and the non-Jewish half of Lenny Kravitz than it is to Jewish people."

—DAN POVENMIRE, DIRECTOR OF THE EPISODE

In Search of an Excuse

MAX: Lois, I appreciate the marshmallow and fish casserole, but I'm sorry, I-I can't eat this.

LOIS: Oh, because it's not kosher.

MAX: Yeah, let's go with that.

You Might Want to Have That Looked At

LOIS: You'll have to excuse Peter, he can be a little tactless sometimes.

BRIAN: Yes—like the time he soiled himself at that dinner party.

(Flashback to a Dining Room, where Peter and Lois are at an elegant dinner party with Other Couples.)

LOIS: I was so sorry to hear that your father passed away.

WOMAN: Yes, it spread through his body so fast. But he's at peace now. And the whole thing—

(Peter's eyes widen.)

PETER: UH-OH!

Let's Call a Spade a Spade, Part 2

PETER: I don't know, Max. The kid's not exactly an honor roll student. Watch.

(Peter smacks Chris in the back of the head.)

CHRIS: Hey!

(Peter points to a lamp.)

PETER: He did it.

(Chris tackles the lamp and flails away at it.)

PETER: See.

If You Didn't Want an Honest Answer . . .

MEG: So? How do I look in my new glasses?

STEWIE: Hm, how shall I put this? In an attic somewhere there's a portrait of you getting prettier.

Ohhh, That Kind . . .

(Lois pounds urgently on Quagmire's door. Quagmire, in a robe, opens it.)

QUAGMIRE: Well, hellllois. Forgive me for pointing.

Peter Comes Clean

PETER: I'm sorry, Lois. I just wanted our son to be Jewish so he'd be smarter. Then maybe his wife wouldn't be sorry she didn't marry the chimp next door.

LOIS: Oh, Peter, just because Stephen makes more money than you doesn't mean he's any smarter. And I think Chris'll do just fine.

STUFF THAT MIGHT HAVE SLIPPED BY

■ The guy who works at the gas station talking to Chris is wearing a hat that reads "Pump This."

■ The temple Max Weinstein takes the Griffins to is called Temple Beth Thupporting Actor.

■ After the nuns learn that Peter has entered a temple, they break a glass case of rulers that is labeled "In Case of Heresy Break Glass."

■ Some of the signs Peter and Chris pass on the Las Vegas strip include "Weddings While-U-Wait"; "99 cent Communion—All-U-Can-Eat!!!"; and one with a neon slot machine, the tumblers of which land on "Bar" . . . "Bar" . . . "Bar," then the machine flashes "Mitzvah!"

■ Peter leaves a note for Lois before he takes off with Chris. The note reads "Dear Lois: Chris and I went to the library to read lots of books." This has been crossed out and replaced with "Have gone clothes shopping with you." This, too, is crossed out and replaced with "Are invisible but right here anyway." This, too, has been replaced with "Have gone fishin'." It's signed, "Peter."

■ The quickie bar mitzvah place Peter and Chris go to has a sign on the wall reading "Featuring the Amazing Rabbi Copperfield."

TV SHOW PARODIES BY EPISODE

1ACX01 ("Death Has a Shadow")
The Brady Bunch
TV's Bloopers and Practical Jokes

1ACX02 ("I Never Met the Dead Man")
Star Trek
ChiPs
Fast Animals, Slow Children
NYPD Blue
Scooby-Doo
Klondike Bar commercial

1ACX03 ("Mind over Murder")
"Mintos" commercial
Homocide: Life on Sesame Street

1ACX05 ("A Hero Sits Next Door")
Teletubbies
Wheel of Fortune

1ACX06 ("The Son Also Draws")
Happy Days
One Day at a Time

1ACX07 ("Brian: Portrait of a Dog")
Eight is Enough
douche commercial
Murder, She Wrote

1ACX08 ("Peter, Peter, Caviar Eater")
Frasier
The Cosby Show

1ACX11 ("Holy Crap")
"Got Milk?" commercial
The Dick Van Dyke Show

2ACX01 ("Brian in Love")
The Jetsons
The Price Is Right

1ACX14 ("Death Is a Bitch")
60 Minutes

2ACX02 ("I Am Peter, Hear Me Roar")
Pawtuket Patriot Beer commercial

1ACX12 ("If I'm Dyin', I'm Lyin'")
Gumbel 2 Gumbel: Beach Justice
Good Times

2ACX08 ("Fifteen Minutes of Shame")
The Joy of Painting (with
Bob Ross)

2ACX04 ("Let's Go to the Hop")
Doublefresh Gum commercial

1ACX10 ("There's Something about Paulie")
Dharma & Greg
Entertainment Tonight

2ACX14 ("The Story on Page One")
Sherry and the Anus

2ACX16 ("Fore, Father")
Little House on the Prairie

2ACX17 ("The Thin White Line")
Behind the Music

2ACX20 ("Brian Does Hollywood")
Kids Say the Darndest Things

2ACX22 ("And the Weiner Is . . .")
Rudolph, the Red-Nosed Reindeer

3ACX04 ("Mr. Saturday Knight")
Match Game

3ACX05 ("A Fish out of Water")
The Tom Green Show

3ACX01 ("Emission Impossible")
The Smurfs

3ACX09 ("To Love and Die in Dixie")
E! True Hollywood Story: Alf

3ACX08 ("Screwed the Pooch")
Survivor

3ACX06 ("Peter Griffin: Husband, Father . . . Brother?")
Dennis Miller Live

3ACX07 ("Ready, Willing, and Disabled")
Touched by an Angel

2ACX03 ("A Very Special *Family Guy* Freakin' Christmas")
Rudolph, the Red-Nosed Reindeer
Bob Hope Christmas Special
"KISS Saves Santa"

3ACX03 ("Brian Wallows and Peter's Swallows")
The Life and Times of Grizzly Adams

3ACX10 ("Stuck Together, Torn Apart")
Magnum, P.I.

3ACX13 ("Road to Europe")
Snuff Island

3ACX12 ("*Family Guy* Viewer Mail #1")
The Newlywed Game

2ACX05 ("When You Wish upon a Weinstein")
Girlfriends (on Lifetime)
Seinfeld

214

LYRICS TO ORIGINAL SONGS

1ACX08 ("Peter, Peter, Caviar Eater")
We Only Live to Kiss Your Ass
< a.k.a. This House Is Freakin' Sweet >

SERVANTS: WE ONLY LIVE TO KISS YOUR ASS.

SEBASTIAN: Kiss it? Hell, we'll even wipe it for you.

SERVANTS: FROM HERE ON IN, IT'S EASY STREET.

PETER: Any bars on that street?

SEBASTIAN: Twenty-four happy hours a day!

PETER: Oh, boy!

GUARDS: WE'LL STOP JEHOVAHS AT THE GATE.

GUARD #1: *(to Jehovah's Witness)* Can I see that pamphlet, sir?

> *(The Guard takes the pamphlet and whacks the Jehovah's Witness.)*

PETER: MY GOD, THIS HOUSE IS FREAKIN' SWEET.

BRONSON: I MAKE BRUNCH / CLIVE COOKS LUNCH.

BRONSON & CLIVE: EACH AND EVERY DAY.

BLAKE: CHOCOLATE CAKE / A LA BLAKE.

PETER: HUNDRED BUCKS BLAKE IS GAY.

SERVANTS: WE'LL DO THE BEST WE CAN WITH MEG.

MEG: Are you saying I'm ugly?

LUCILLE: It doesn't matter, dear. You're rich now!

SERVANTS: *(to Lois)* WE'LL DO YOUR NAILS AND RUB YOUR FEET.

LOIS: Oh, that's not necessa— *(as they rub)* Oh, my.

SERVANTS: *(to Chris)* WE'LL DO YOUR HOME-WORK EVERY NIGHT.

CHRIS: It's really hard.

SEBASTIAN: That's why we've got that Stephen Hawking guy.

> *(Stephen Hawking sits in his chair tapping one foot.)*

PETER: MY GOD, THIS HOUSE IS FREAKIN' SWEET. USED TO PASS / LOTS OF GAS / LOIS RAN AWAY. /
NOW WE'VE GOT / THIRTY ROOMS. HELLO, BEANS. / GOOD-BYE SPRAY!

SERVANTS: WE'D TAKE A BULLET JUST FOR YOU.

STEWIE: Oh, what a coincidence! I've got one!

LOIS: Stewie!

SERVANTS: PREPARE TO SUCK THAT GOLDEN TEAT. NOW THAT YOU'RE STINKIN' RICH / WE'LL GLADLY BE YOUR BITCH.

PETER: MY GOD THIS HOUSE IS . . .

PETER & SERVANTS: . . . FREAKIN' SWEET.

SERVANTS: WELCOME!

2ACX06 ("Da Boom")
Randy Newman Riffs

RANDY NEWMAN: FAT MAN WITH HIS KIDS AND DOG / DROVE IN THROUGH THE MORNING FOG / HEY, THERE, ROVER / COME ON OVER . . .

LOIS: Well, it's nice to have music while we eat.

> *(Lois starts to pick an apple.)*

RANDY NEWMAN: RED-HEADED LADY / REACHIN' FOR AN APPLE / GONNA TAKE A BITE / UHP, NOPE, NOPE, SHE'S GONNA BREATHE ON IT FIRST / WIPING IT ON HER BLOUSE . . .

> *(Lois just looks at him. He stops singing. Then she takes a bite.)*

RANDY NEWMAN: SHE TAKES A BITE / CHEWS

IT ONCE / TWICE / THREE TIMES / FOUR TIMES / STOPS, SALIVA WORKIN', TAKES A LONG HARD LOOK AT RANDY . . .
> (*Lois glares at him. Then starts to eat.*)

RANDY NEWMAN: FIVE TIMES.
> (*Peter walks over to Lois.*)

RANDY NEWMAN: FAT OL' HUSBAND WALKIN' OVER.

LOIS: Let's get the hell out of here.
> (*The Griffins head down the highway on foot.*)

RANDY NEWMAN: HEY THEY'RE WALKIN' DOWN THE ROAD / LEFT FOOT / RIGHT FOOT / LEFT FOOT / RIGHT FOOT / LEFT—
> (*A half-eaten apple pelts Randy in the head.*)

1ACX15 ("The King Is Dead")
From Peter's Version of "The King and I"

CHORUS: ANNA RULES!

PETER: 'CAUSE I KICKED ALL THE BAD GUYS IN THEIR JEWELS!

CHORUS: ANNA WON!

PETER: THANKS TO MY GAMMA RAY ATOMIC GUN!

CHORUS: DANCE AND SHOUT! / HE'S THE WORLD'S GREATEST NINJA, THERE'S NO DOUBT!

PETER: THOUGH THEY TRIED TO DEFEAT ME / THEY CAN ALL JUST FREAKIN' EAT ME.
> (*Brian sits up from being "dead."*)

BRIAN: 'CAUSE HE BLEW ALL OF US AWAY!

PETER: IN THE PLANET OF SIAM / THERE'S NO ONE AS TOUGH AS I AM.

CHORUS: JUST AS SURELY AS PAUL LYNDE WAS GAY!

1ACX12 ("If I'm Dyin', I'm Lyin'")
Dying Boy of Quahog

CANDLELIGHT VIGIL SINGERS: OH, DYING BOY OF QUAHOG / CHRIS GRIFFIN YOU'RE SO BRAVE / THERE'S A SMILE ON YOUR FACE AND A BOUNCE IN YOUR STEP / AS THEY

DIG YOUR GRAVE. (*clap, clap*) AS THEY DIG YOUR GRAVE!

1ACX09 ("Running Mates")
Vagina Junction

FEMALE BLUES SINGERS: VAGINA JUNCTION, WHAT'S YOUR FUNCTION?

JACK SHELDON VOICE: TAKIN' IN SPERM AND SPITTIN' OUT BABIES!

2ACX04 ("Let's Go to the Hop")
Give Up the Toad

PETER: You're gonna do toad?

DOUG: What's the big deal?
> (*Peter takes his gum out, then grinds it out with his shoe like it's a cigarette.*)

PETER: Let me tell you about it, stud.

PETER: YOU'LL GET CHILLS / ALL THROUGH YOUR BODY / AND YOU'LL LOSE ALL CONTROL / OF YOUR BLADDER AND YOUR SPHINCTER / THAT'S YOUR BUTTHOLE! / 'CAUSE IF YOU USE TOAD / THEN I'M TELLING YOU / YOU CAN KISS YOUR LIFE GOOD-BYE / YEAH, WHEN YOU USE TOAD / IT'LL MESS YOU UP / IT'LL MAKE YOUR MAMA CRY / THAT'S NO LIE / YOU'LL

CHOKE ON YOUR TONGUE AND DIE. / GOTTA GIVE IT UP!

Doug: GIVE UP THE TOAD NOW?

Peter: IT'S NO JOKE, BUDDY! / GIVE IT UP!

Chuck and John: GIVE UP THE TOAD NOW!

Peter: OR YOU'LL CROAK, BUDDY / GIVE IT UP!

Kids: GIVE UP THE TOAD NOW!

Peter: AND DON'T SMOKE / OR YOU'LL SEE / IT HURTS TO PEE! / THERE'LL BE BLOOD GUSHIN' FROM YA / EVERY TIME THAT YOU COUGH / AND FORGET GETTING LUCKY / IT FALLS OFF / YEAH, YOU BETTER WISE UP/ 'CAUSE I'M TELLIN' YOU / TOAD'S WHAT LANDO FORBIDS / GOTTA GIVE IT ALL UP / OR YOU'RE GONNA SEE / YOU'RE THE ONE WHO'LL HIT THE SKIDS / AND OUR KIDS WILL BE BORN WITHOUT EYELIDS.

Peter and the Kids: GONNA GIVE IT UP / GIVE UP THE TOAD NOW / THANKS TO YOU, LANDO! / GIVE IT ALL UP!

(In the Griffins' Living Room, Brian lowers his newspaper.)

Brian: GIVE UP THE TOAD NOW!

Peter and the Kids: THANKS TO YOU, LANDO / GIVE IT UP! / GIVE UP THE TOAD NOW / DATE RAPE, TOO, LANDO / I'M NO FOOL / LANDO'S COOL . . . YEAH!

2ACX07 ("A Picture's Worth a Thousand Bucks")
Peter Finds a New Plan to Have a Legacy

Peter: I HAVE A DREAM / IT'S ALL ABOUT YOU, MEG GRIFFIN / NOT MUCH YOU CAN DO, MEG GRIFFIN / YOU CAN'T DANCE / YOU CAN'T SING / NO YOU PRETTY MUCH CAN'T DO A THING / NEVER FEAR / DADDY'S HERE / HONEY, YOU'RE GONNA MAKE OUR NAME FAMOUS! / YOU'LL BE LARGE— / —ER THAN LIFE / I'LL BE PROUD YOU FELL OUT OF MY WIFE / YOU'LL BE KNOWN / FAR AND WIDE / LIKE THAT PRINCESS WHO DIED / I'M GONNA MAKE YOU FAMOUS, WAIT AND SEE / HONEY, I'M GONNA DO THIS FOR YOU / BUT IT'S REALLY FOR MEEEEEEE!

2ACX12 ("Road to Rhode Island")
Road to Rhode Island

Brian/Stewie: WE'RE OFF ON THE ROAD TO RHODE ISLAND / WE'RE HAVING THE TIME OF OUR LIVES.

Stewie: Take it, dog.

Brian: WE'RE QUITE A PAIR OF PARTNERS / JUST LIKE THELMA AND LOUISE / 'CEPT YOU'RE NOT SIX FEET TALL.

Stewie: YES, AND YOUR BREASTS DON'T REACH YOUR KNEES.

Brian: Give it time.

Brian/Stewie: WE'RE OFF ON THE ROAD TO RHODE ISLAND / WE'RE CERTAINLY GOING IN STYLE.

Brian: I'M WITH AN INTELLECTUAL WHO CRAPS INSIDE HIS PANTS.

Stewie: How dare you. *(singing)* AT LEAST I DON'T LEAVE URINE STAINS ON ALL THE HOUSEHOLD PLANTS.

Brian: Oh, pee jokes.

Brian/Stewie: WE'VE TRAVELED A BIT AND WE'VE FO-OU-OUND / LIKE A MASOCHIST IN NEWPORT WE'RE RHODE ISLAND BOUND.

Brian: Crazy travel conditions, huh?

Stewie: *(indicates himself)* First class and *(indicates Brian)* no class.

Brian: Whoa. Careful with that joke, it's an antique.

BRIAN/STEWIE: WE'RE OFF ON THE ROAD TO RHODE ISLAND/ WE'RE NOT GONNA STOP 'TIL WE'RE THERE.

BRIAN: Maybe for a beer.

BRIAN: WHATEVER DANGERS WE MAY FACE / WE'LL NEVER FEAR OR CRY.

STEWIE: That's right. *(singing)* UNTIL WE'RE SYNDICATED FOX WILL NEVER LET US DIE. *(spoken)* Please.

BRIAN/STEWIE: WE'RE OFF ON THE ROAD TO RHODE ISLAND / THE HOME OF THAT OLD CAMPUS SWING

BRIAN: WE MAY PICK UP SOME COLLEGE GIRLS / AND PICNIC ON THE GRASS.

STEWIE: *(speaking)* Hmm-mmm. *(singing)* WE'D TELL YOU MORE / BUT WE WOULD HAVE THE CENSORS ON OUR ASS.

BRIAN: Yikes!

BRIAN/STEWIE: WE CERTAINLY DO GET AROUND / *(spoken quickly)* Like a bunch of renegade pilgrims who were thrown out of Plymouth Colony. *(sung)* WE'RE RHODE ISLAND BOUND!

BRIAN/STEWIE: *(spoken)* Or like a group of college freshmen who were rejected by Harvard and forced to go to Brown. *(singing)* WE'RE RHODE ISLAND BOUND!

2ACX13 ("E Peterbus Unum")
Can't Touch Me

PETER: CAN'T TOUCH ME. / CAN'T TOUCH ME . . . JU- JU- JU- JUST LIKE THE BAD GUY / FROM "LETHAL WEAPON 2" / I'VE GOT DIPLOMATIC IMMUNITY.
    (Peter turns to Hammer and a group of Dancers behind him.)

PETER: SO HAMMER, YOU CAN'T SUE . . . / I CAN WRITE GRAFFITI / EVEN JAYWALK IN THE STREET.
    (Peter strolls into the street, causing a five-car pileup.)

PETER: I CAN RIOT, LOOT, NOT GIVE A HOOT . . .
    (Peter kicks over a garbage can, spilling trash all over the place. In the background, an angry Woodsy the Owl has to be restrained by the gathering Crowd of Onlookers.)

PETER: AND TOUCH YOUR SISTER'S TEAT . . . CAN'T TOUCH ME / CAN'T TOUCH ME.

MAYOR WEST: What in God's name is he doing?

PETER: CAN'T TOUCH ME.
    (Peter starts break-dancing.)

CLEVELAND: I believe that's "the worm."

PETER: STOP! / PETER TIME! / I'M A BIG SHOT / THERE'S NO DOUBT / LIGHT A FIRE . . .
    (Peter lights a tree on fire.)

PETER: THEN PEE IT OUT . . .
    (Peter urinates on the tree.)

PETER: DON'T LIKE IT? / KISS MY RUMP / JUST FOR A MINUTE / LET'S ALL DO "THE BUMP." / CAN'T TOUCH ME. *(spoken)* Yeah, do the Peter Griffin bump. *(singing)* CAN'T TOUCH ME . . . I'M PRESIDENTIAL PETER / INTERNS THINK I'M HOT / DON'T CARE IF YOU'RE / HANDICAPPED / I'LL STILL PARK IN YOUR SPOT.
    (Peter grabs Joe's wheelchair and attaches it to a passing truck.)

PETER: I'VE BEEN AROUND THE WORLD / FROM HARTFORD TO BACK BAY / IT'S PETER / GO PETER / M.C. PETER / YO PETER / LET'S SEE REGIS RAP THIS WAY . . . / CAN'T TOUCH ME!
    (Peter turns to a Beautiful Woman in the now-angry crowd.)

PETER: Except for you. You can touch me.

2ACX15 ("Wasted Talent")
Chumba Wumba Song

CHUMBA WUMBAS: CHUMBA WUMBA GOBBLEDY GOO / LIFE ISN'T FAIR IT'S SAD BUT IT'S TRUE / CHUMBA WUMBA GOBBLEDY GEE / WHEN YOUR POOR LEGS ARE STIFF AS A TREE / WHAT DO YOU DO WHEN YOU'RE STUCK IN A CHAIR? / FINDING IT HARD TO GO UP AND DOWN STAIRS? / WHAT DO YOU THINK OF THE ONE YOU CALL GOD? / ISN'T HIS ABSENCE SLIGHTLY ODD? / MAYBE-HE'S-FORGOTTEN-YOU / CHUMBA WUMBA GOBBLEDY GORSE / COUNT YOURSELF LUCKY YOU'RE NOT A HORSE / THEY WOULD TURN YOU INTO DOG FOOD / OR TO CHUMBA WUMBA GOBBLEDY GLUE!

Pawtucket Pat's Intro to the Beer Room

PAWTUCKET PAT: TAKE A DRINK / AND YOU'LL SINK / TO A STATE OF PURE INEBRIATION / YOU'LL BE TANKED LIKE THE WHOLE IRISH NATION / WHEN YOU DRINK ENOUGH OF MY BEER / YOU WILL FIND THIS MAGIC BREW'LL / MAKE YOUR EVERY JOKE A JEWEL / YOU'LL DRIVE DRUNKER THAN / OKSANA BAIUL . . . GO ON, BUDS / DRINK MY SUDS / 'TIL YOU'VE REACHED / THAT PURE INEBRIATION / THOUGH THE BEER MAY BE FREE / YOU'RE JUST RENTING IT FROM ME.

2ACX16 ("Fore, Father")
Hic-a-doo-la

BOYS AND GIRLS: I'M GONNA GRAB MY GIRL AND HEAD TO THE BEACH / HIC-A-DOO-LA! / WE'RE GONNA ALL HANG TEN AND MAYBE THEN / HIC-A-DOO-LA!
BOYS: 'CAUSE I'M A HIC-A-DOO-LA BOY
GIRLS: AND I'M A HIC-A-DOO-LA GIRL
BOYS AND GIRLS: AND TOGETHER IT IS A HIC-A-DOO-LA WORLD / HIC-A-DOO-LA!

2ACX17 ("The Thin White Line")
Stewie's Dream of a Life at Sea

(Stewie is standing before his CREW, wearing a very flashy, nineteenth-century Captain's outfit.)
STEWIE: I AM THE GREATEST CAPTAIN OF THE QUEEN'S NAVY . . .
CREW: AND YOUR RECORD WILL STAND AS PROOF.
STEWIE: BE IT GALLEON OR A FREIGHTER / I'M AN EXPERT NAVIGATOR . . . .
CREW: AND YOU'RE ALSO A WORLD-CLASS POOF!
STEWIE: MY MANNER, QUITE EFFETE / IS MIS-TAKEN ON THE STREET / FOR A SAILOR WHO CAN PIROUETTE ON CUE / WELL, DESPITE YOUR POINT OF VIEW / I CAN THRILL A GIRL OR TWO . . . /
(Stewie winks at the crew.)
STEWIE: BUT I'D RATHER GET IT ON WITH YOU.

Peter's Tie *(Sung by Brian as Paul Shaffer)*

BRIAN: PETER'S TIE, PETER'S TIE / THAT'S BECAUSE PETER'S THE GUY.

Coked Up *(To the tune of "La Cucaracha")*

LOIS: . . . HE WAS ALL COKED UP / AND WE WERE CHOKED UP / BUT NOW WE'RE HAPPY BRIAN'S HOME / CHA-CHA-CHA!

2ACX19 ("One if by Clam, Two if by Sea")
The Life of the Wife

STEWIE: *(spoken)* I think she's got it! *(to Rupert)* I think she's got it!

ELIZA: THE LIFE OF THE WIFE IS ENDED BY THE KNIFE!

STEWIE: By George, she's got it! By George, she's got it! *(sings)* NOW WHAT ENDS HER WRETCHED LIFE?

ELIZA: THE KNIFE! THE KNIFE!

STEWIE: AND WHERE'S THAT BLOODY KNIFE?

ELIZA: IN THE WIFE! IN THE WIFE!

STEWIE AND ELIZA: THE LIFE OF THE WIFE IS ENDED BY THE KNIFE!

STEWIE: *(spoken)* Bravo, Eliza!

STEWIE AND ELIZA: THE LIFE OF THE WIFE IS ENDED BY THE KNIFE!

(Stewie grabs Eliza and they begin to polka across the yard.)

2ACX21 ("Death Lives")
A Song About Mopping

SAILORS: WE'RE MOPPING THE DECK / WHICH IS NAVY FOR FLOOR / AND WHEN WE'RE DONE MOPPING / WE'LL MOP IT SOME MORE, OH!

(Young Quagmire dances over to Young Peter. In the background the Sailors form a semicircle and one Sailor takes center stage and tap dances to the following.)

SAILORS: SWAB / MEANS MOP / DECK / MEANS FLOOR.

3ACX03 (Brian Wallows and Peter's Swallows)
You've Got a Lot to See

BRIAN: *(spoken)* Come on, Pearl. There's so much you've missed in the last thirty years. In fact . . . allow me to fill you in:
THE SIXTIES BROUGHT / THE HIPPIE BREED / AND DECADES LATER THINGS

HAVE CHANGED, INDEED. / WE LOST THE VALUES BUT WE KEPT THE WEED / YOU'VE GOT A LOT TO SEE. / THE REAGAN YEARS / HAVE LAID THE FRAME / FOR MOVIE STARS TO PLAY THE WHITE HOUSE GAME. / WE'RE NOT TOO FAR FROM VOTING FELDMAN / HAIM / YOU'VE GOT A LOT TO SEE. *(Brian indicates a poster reading "Corey Feldman for President.")*

BRIAN: THE TOWN OF VEGAS / HAS GOT A DIFFERENT FACE / 'CAUSE IT'S A FAMILY PLACE / WITH LOTS TO DO. / WHERE IN THE FIFTIES / A MAN COULD MINGLE WITH SCORES OF ALL THE SEEDIEST WHORES / WELL, NOW HIS CHILDREN CAN TOO! / YOU HEARD IT FROM / THE CANINE'S MOUTH / THE COUNTRY'S CHANGED / THAT IS, EXCEPT THE SOUTH. / AND YOU'LL AGREE / NO ONE REALLY KNOWS, MY DEAR LADY FRIEND / JUST QUITE HOW IT ALL WILL END. / SO HURRY / 'CAUSE YOU'VE GOT A LOT TO SEE. / THE BALDNESS GENE / WAS CAUSE FOR DREAD / BUT THAT'S A FEAR THAT YOU CAN PUT TO BED. / THEY'LL SHAVE YOUR ASS AND GLUE IT ON YOUR HEAD / YOU'VE GOT A LOT TO SEE. / THE PC AGE / HAS MOVED THE BAR. / A WORD LIKE REDNECK IS A STEP TOO FAR. / THE PROPER TERM IS COUNTRY MUSIC STAR. / YOU'VE GOT A LOT TO SEE. / OUR FLASHY CELL PHONES / MAKE PEOPLE MUMBLE, "GEE WHIZ. / LOOK HOW IMPORTANT HE

IS. / HIS LIFE MUST RULE." / HE'LL GET A TUMOR / BUT ON YOUR SURGERY DAY / THE DOCTOR WILL SEE IT AND SAY / "YOU MUST REALLY BE COOL."

TOM TUCKER: *(spoken)* There's lots a things you may have missed.

MAYOR WEST: *(spoken)* Like Pee-Wee and his famous wrist.

CLEVELAND: *(spoken)* Or Sandy Duncan's creepy phony eye.

NEIL GOLDMAN: *(spoken)* That awesome *Thundercats* cartoon.

DIANE: *(spoken)* Neil Armstrong landing on the moon.

MEG: *(spoken)* Neil Armstrong—wait, was he the trumpet guy?

BRIAN: *(sung)* SO LET'S GO SEE / THE USA. / THEY'LL TREAT YOU RIGHT / UNLESS YOU'RE BLACK OR GAY / OR CHEROKEE. BUT YOU CAN FORGIVE THE WORLD AND ITS FLAWS / AND FOLLOW ME THERE BECAUSE YOU'VE STILL GOT A HELLUVA LOT TO SEE. / YOU'VE GOT A LOT TO SEE!

3ACX09 ("To Love and Die in Dixie")
"Stewie and the Cowtones" Have a Jam Session on the Porch

STEWIE: Warm out today. Warm yesterday. Even warmer today.

(One by one, the guys start playing a song.)

STEWIE: MET HER ON MY CB / SAID HER NAME WAS MIMI / SOUNDED LIKE AN ANGEL COME TO EARTH / BUT WHEN I WENT TO MEET HER / MAN, YOU SHOULDA SEEN HER / TWICE AS TALL AS ME, THREE TIMES THE GIRTH / OH, MY FAT BABY LOVES TO EAT / A BIG OL' BUDDHA BELLY / AND HER BREASTS SWING PAST HER FEET / MY FAT BABY LOVES TO EAT / MY BIG OL' FAT ASS BABY LOVES TO EAT.

(The band continues on as Stewie takes a solo.)

STEWIE: I got blisters on me fingers!

3ACX06 ("Peter Griffin: Husband, Father . . . Brother?")
Peter's Playhouse Song

COME ON GET UP / KNOCK OFF YOUR NAP-PING / IT'S A CRAZY MESSED UP PLACE WHERE ANYTHING CAN HAPPEN / THERE'S A CHAIR THAT FREAKIN' TALKS / HEY, LOOK! / THERE'S SOME FISH THAT GIVE ADVICE / HOLY CRAP! / IT'S SCREWY IN PETER'S PLAYHOUSE!

3ACX11 ("From Method to Madness")
Stewie and Olivia's Routine

STEWIE: WHO'S GOT THE GREATEST GAL AROUND?

OLIVIA: YOU DO! / WHO'S GOT THE SWEETEST MAN IN TOWN?

STEWIE: YOU DO!

OLIVIA: WHO'S GOT A GUY WHO MAKES HER SMILE ALL DAY?

STEWIE: BY THE WAY, I'M NOT SO BAD TO LOOK AT, EITHER.

OLIVIA: WHO'S GOT A GUY WITH LOTS OF BRAINS?

STEWIE: YOU DO! / WHO'S GOT A GIRL WHO LOVES CHOW MEIN?

OLIVIA: YOU DO!

STEWIE: WHO'S GOT THE GREATEST LOVE IN THE WORLD?

OLIVIA: YOU DO!

STEWIE: AND YOU DO!

OLIVIA/STEWIE: THANK GOODNESS I'VE GOT YOU!

OLIVIA: WHO'S GOT A GUY TO TELL HER JOKES?

STEWIE: YOU DO! / WHO'S GOT A GIRL TO SHOW THE FOLKS?

OLIVIA: YOU DO!

STEWIE: WHO'S GOT A GIRL HE'D LIKE TO ONE DAY UNDRESS?

OLIVIA: GIVE IT A REST. I TOLD YOU NOT UNTIL WE'RE MARRIED.

STEWIE: WHO'S GOT THE GAL WITH ALL THE SNAZZ?

OLIVIA: YOU DO! / WHO'S GOT THE FELLA WITH PIZZAZZ?

STEWIE: YOU DO! / WHO'S GOT THE GREATEST LOVE IN THE WORLD?

OLIVIA: YOU DO!

STEWIE: AND YOU DO!

STEWIE/OLIVIA: THANK GOODNESS . . . I'VE . . . GOT . . . YOU!

    Stewie Tries to Go It Alone:

STEWIE: I GOT MY TOP HAT AND CANE / AND A POCKET FULL OF MIRACLES / POCKET FULL OF MIRACLES / POCKET FULL OF—

3ACX12 ("*Family Guy* Viewer Mail #1")
Peter Sings to His Own Theme Song

PETER: Oh, c'mon, pal, that's classic traveling music. Eh, try to enjoy it. *(singing)* RIDING ON THE BUS. / RIDING ON THE BUS. /

SITTING NEXT TO BUMS. / THERE'S AN OPEN SEAT. / HOPE THAT ISN'T PEE.

3ACX12 ("Road to Europe")
Brian and Stewie Create a Distraction

BRIAN/STEWIE: YOU AND I ARE SO AWFULLY DIFFERENT / TOO AWFULLY DIFFERENT TO EVER BE PALS./

STEWIE: *(spoken)* Do you want to go first?

BRIAN: *(spoken)* Yeah, I'll go.

BRIAN: *(sung)* YOU'RE FAVORITE HERO IS THE MARQUIS DE SADE./

STEWIE: *(spoken)* Oh, you're one to talk. *(sung)* YOU GET A STIFFY FROM PHYLICIA RASHAD./

BRIAN: *(spoken)* Oh, one time!

STEWIE: *(sung)* I'VE A STYLE FLAIR, JUST LOOK AT MY HIP HAIR.

BRIAN: *(spoken)* Oh, yeah, th-that's quite a nice do there.

STEWIE: *(spoken)* Oh, thanks.

BRIAN: *(spoken)* For me to poop on.

STEWIE: *(spoken)* What?

BRIAN: *(spoken)* Oh, come on, you look like Charlie Brown.

STEWIE: *(spoken)* Oh, bite me Snoopy.

BRIAN/STEWIE: *(sung)* THERE'S NOT A WHOLE LOT THAT WE'VE GOT TO AGREE ON./

BRIAN: *(sung)* 'CAUSE I LOVE THE STRINGS OF A CLASSICAL SCORE./

STEWIE: *(sung)* AND I LIKE THAT SINGER WHO LOOKS LIKE A WHORE./

BRIAN: *(spoken)* Ricky Martin?

STEWIE: *(spoken)* Love him.

BRIAN/STEWIE: *(sung)* WE'RE TOO DIFFERENT TO EVER BE PALS. / YOU AND I ARE SO AWFULLY DIFFERENT / TOO AWFULLY DIF-FERENT / TO EVER BE PALS./

BRIAN: *(sung)* YOUR HEAD'S AS MASSIVE AS A METEORITE./

STEWIE: *(spoken)* Oh, very funny. *(sung)* YOU HAVE A HAVE A WEENIE LIKE A CHRISTMAS TREE LIGHT./

BRIAN: *(sung)* I'D BET MONEY/YOU'LL MARRY A HONEY / WHO'S PRETTY AND FUNNY / AND HER NAME WILL BE TED./

STEWIE: (spoken) Oh, a gay joke.

BRIAN: (spoken) I just work with what you give me.

BRIAN/STEWIE: (sung) YOU MIGHT THINK WE'RE IN SYNC / BUT WE STINK AS A DUO./

BRIAN: (sung) 'CAUSE YOU GET A KICK OUT OF CARNAGE AND GUTS./

STEWIE: (sung) AND YOU GET A KICK OUT OF STROKING YOUR—

BRIAN: (spoken) Whoa, whoa, whoa, you can't say that on TV.

STEWIE: (spoken) What, ego?

BRIAN: (spoken) Never mind.

BRIAN/STEWIE: (sung) WE'RE TOO DIFFERENT TO EVER BE PALS./

2ACX05 ("When You Wish upon a Weinstein")

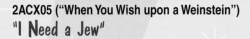
"I Need a Jew"

PETER: I gotta get a Greenstein or a Rosenblatt of my very own. NOTHING ELSE HAS WORKED SO FAR / SO I'LL WISH UPON A STAR. / WONDROUS DANCING SPECK OF LIGHT / I NEED A JEW. / LOIS MAKES ME TAKE THE RAP / 'CAUSE OUR CHECKBOOK LOOKS LIKE CRAP. / SINCE I CAN'T GIVE HER A SLAP / I NEED A JEW. WHERE TO FIND / A BAUM OR STEEN OR STYNE, / TO TEACH ME HOW TO WHINE / AND DO MY TAXES. / THOUGH BY MANY, THEY'RE ABHORRED / HEBREW PEOPLE, I'VE ADORED / EVEN THOUGH THEY KILLED MY LORD . . . I NEED A JEW.

Later . . .

MAX: Hi, my name's Max Weinstein. My car just broke down . . . May I use your phone? *(Peter looks Heavenward.)*

PETER: NOW MY TROUBLES ARE ALL THROUGH / I HAVE A JEW!

Acknowledgments

First and foremost, this book owes its very existence to the brilliance and wit of the immensely talented writers and artists who crafted the first fifty classic episodes of *Family Guy* (and whose names can be found throughout these pages). Also invaluable was the thoughtful guidance of Debbie Olshan, the tireless work and endless creativity of Hope Innelli, and the always cheerful assistance of Matt Fleckenstein and Joanna Fuller. In addition, I am also indebted to Beth and Quinn for their support and understanding during the sometimes trying writing process. And, of course, none of this would be possible at all without the genius of Seth MacFarlane, who has been both a professional inspiration and a marvelous friend.